T0158852

Repo Blood

Repo Blood

A Century of Auto Repossession History

Kevin W Armstrong

Archway Publishing books may be ordered through booksellers or by contacting:

Archway Publishing
1663 Liberty Drive
Bloomington, IN 47403
www.archwaypublishing.com
844-669-3957

ISBN: 978-1-6657-1821-9 (sc)
ISBN: 978-1-6657-1822-6 (e)

Library of Congress Control Number: 2022901508

Print information available on the last page.

Archway Publishing rev. date: 02/17/2022

This book is dedicated to the fallen, wounded and forgotten of the repossession industry. It is as well for their Families and the generations of men and women who have labored over the decades to scratch out a living in it. I also dedicate it to the two people I love most in this world, my love, Alda and son Robert.

Introduction

"That's so cool! What did you get paid for that?" asked the paramedic picking glass out of my face in the back of the ambulance. *"I really don't want to say."* I replied with some embarrassment as I held the cold compress against my forearm swelling from defensive wounds acquired by the same pipe that smashed the driver side window into my head. *"$75."* I admitted after some coaxing as the Oakland police released my attackers from their handcuffs. *"That's just stupid. You're an idiot."* he replied shaking his head as I considered the same.

This wasn't the first, or even last time that I contemplated the lunacy of my profession, or addiction as I would later come to recognize it. I was just another "Adjuster", just another "Repo Man" in the long line of men and women who'd fallen into the business before me. My injuries were nothing big and nothing new in this line of work. You sucked it up and moved on thankful that you didn't pay the ultimate price as countless others have.

That was me in 1993 and after 7 years in the business, I got out, or so I thought. A haircut, a shave and a suit weren't enough to get it out of my blood. I was an adrenaline junkie. I could leave the field, but I couldn't quite get it out of me. That's what this business does to some people.

The repossession industry is and always has been loaded with people like me. Many are born into it, sometimes three or four generations deep. Most, like myself, stumble into it and it fits, for awhile at least. It is a world and society of its own and historically, one that keeps to itself.

It is a shadowy industry where keeping secrets is deeply ingrained into its fabric. Historically this comes from the need to keep tactics hidden so as to not alert the public and make their jobs more difficult. This also comes from long held attempts to paint a rosier picture of the industry than it really is to keep the clients (lenders) happy. Before the internet and half-a-dozen stupid reality shows, it was easy to stay hidden, but not anymore.

It's kept to itself so much, that most in the industry know very little of its beginnings. Even to myself, whose been involved and written about it for over ten years, have at times had some difficulty getting people in it to open up about themselves, their families or experiences. Fortunately, some have, and I've had the honor of having access to some of the industries most respected veterans who shared their knowledge, insight and tales that provided much of this previously unwritten history.

Years of obsessive-compulsive skip tracing learned in this industry led me to the Library of Congress and other newspaper archives, where I've discovered long forgotten articles and stories that helped to reassemble much of its lost past. Yes, there is a lot of crime and violence, but that's just the nature of business. As I wrote this, I often wondered how the industry ever made it this far, but this is a uniquely American business with uniquely American experiences.

To the outside world, it's all about stealing cars, or something like those stupid tv shows with actors wrestling around in the front yard on camera. Those perceptions couldn't be more wrong. It is a business and a damn serious one at that. It is an essential part of the automotive and financial sector of the economy and one that without, access to credit and auto sales would plummet.

This hundred-year history of cat and mouse is played out on the streets, rural roads, and driveways of America every single day. It is a history of conflict, injury and death by murder or misadventure woven around people and small businesses adapting to a growing auto industry and the ever-changing world. It is a history of the men and women who lived and died providing for their families and those trying to make it a better one for all. It is at times like a car crash that you know you shouldn't look at but can't help and stare anyway.

I find it of little surprise that no one has attempted to make a historical record of this odd and addictive industry before. Getting a grip on its history and the people in it is like trying to nail Jell-O to a wall. No one in this industry expects the world to feel good about them and I suppose neither do I, but that's not really the point. Through this decade-by-decade hundred-year history I hope to illuminate its evolution and share its past for those in it, those who've left it and those who want to know the truth.

Contents

Curtis Steamer - Public domain

CHAPTER 1 – AUTO GENESIS

Car – (noun) - An abbreviation of the root Latin word *carrum*, *carrus* (plural *carra*), which was applied to carts, chariots, and carriages.

The very first known auto repossession occurred just two years after the Civil War in 1867. While the name of the debtor and exact date of the first repossessed automobile is unknown, Francis Curtis of Newburyport, Massachusetts, holds the dubious distinction of being the first known "repo man." Given the fact that Curtis was also the man who built, sold, and financed the steam carriage, it should come as no surprise that this incident is also the first recorded auto loan default and repossession.

According to *The Standard Catalog of American Cars, 1805-1942*, Curtis's horseless carriage had an eighty-pound coal capacity, a twenty-gallon water tank, forty-to-forty-five-pound vertical boiler steam system and a five hp engine capable of breakneck speeds of up to twenty-five miles per hour with a maximum range of thirty miles. Impressive for its time, unfortunately, with a simple leaf spring carriage suspension, on unpaved roads, any speed over ten miles per hour was likely to cause enough vibration and jolting to fracture a tooth.

As things turned out, the first recorded auto loan borrower also became the first auto loan default and Francis Curtis took it upon himself to conduct the first auto repossession. While no details of the time of day or exact circumstances exist, the process must have been loud and lengthy, as the steam powered carriage required time to bring the water to a boil before making his getaway. One can only imagine that the scene was loud and disruptive to the entire neighborhood, because an arrest warrant was sworn against Curtis by one of his debtor's neighbors.

According to the *Standard Catalog*, "When the sheriff arrived, Francis Curtis left, in his car, with the lawman in hot pursuit on foot." This may have been the first automotive getaway in American history. The fact that the neighbor, without a telephone, had time to complain to the police and the officer had time to walk to the scene, illustrates that Curtis spent a very long time in that driveway waiting for the car to warm up. Not sure this really counts as a repo, but either his borrower was a really heavy sleeper, or this was a voluntary repossession in broad daylight.

1918 Ford dealership – (photo courtesy of the National Archives)

These slow, awkward Steam powered carriages dominated the latter part of the nineteenth[th] century, but internal combustion vehicles were beginning to make their mark. According to *Cars: Early and vintage, 1886-1930*, by 1902, 485 of the 909 new vehicle registrations were for steam powered "cars." Just a year later, only forty-three of the known eighty-four steam carriage manufacturers were in existence. By 1910, only six of these companies remained.

The Gas Age

By 1910, like their predecessors the steam carriage, there were wide varieties of internal combustion automobiles, sometimes referred to as "machines", manufactured all around the world. But it wasn't until Henry Ford rolled out the first Model T in 1908, that the automobile began finding its way into mainstream America. By 1910, it was all over for the steam carriage and there were already an estimated five hundred thousand autos and trucks on the mostly unpaved roads of America.

With an average price of $850, the 2021 equivalent of $24,085, most auto purchases were made with cash. Regardless, as early as 1910, banks began making auto loans with 35 percent down payment requirements and payment schedules of $10-$20 per month. Repossessions at this time were conducted primarily by bank officers and were usually voluntarily surrendered.

William Crapo Durant, GM CEO –
(photo courtesy of the National Archives)

Appalled to find out that teens and others were having sex in the backseat of his Model T, Henry Ford ordered its length reduced to 38 inches. Ford also held the ultra-conservative view that lending was usurious and immoral, as did many Americans of the era. Aside from cash purchases, he only offered layaway plans with weekly payment schedules for his morally contraceptive "Tin Lizzies". His nemesis and main competition, William Crapo Durant and General Motors held differing views and soon capitalized on the growing American appetite for better and more expensive vehicles, with of course, bigger backseats!

Just as the industry was taking off, on April 2, 1917, under President Woodrow Wilson, the United States declared war on Germany. By World War I's end in 1918, over 2 million men had been deployed to Europe and 117,000 were dead. No sooner had the boys returned from the horrors of the war than the world was hit with the Spanish Flu pandemic.

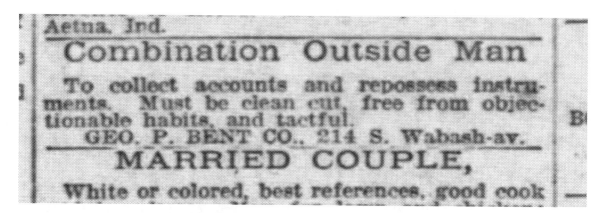

Repossessor want ad – March 20, 1918, Chicago Tribune

An estimated 500,00 to one million Americans died before this disaster came to an end in 1919. Despite these massive disruptions and war era resource rationing, an estimated 3.5 million automobiles were manufactured. Over this decade, auto production exploded from 130,000 to 1.4 million per year. Nothing could stop the automobile and America's transformation was well underway.

The Adjustment Bureaus

In the pre-telephone era, lenders performed collections activities in person or by mail. Most of these were home or farm-based equipment or materials ranging from pianos to sewing machines, which Singer actually began making loans on in 1850. In person collections became impractical when debtors resided long distances away from their offices. As the availability to credit expanded, there became the need for third party collectors.

Historically, "Adjustment Bureaus" were created as a means to mitigate losses and resolve disputes. These "Adjusters" were problem solvers who applied their skills to everything from insurance to freight claims since at least as far back as 1896 and for the purposes of this history, we will focus on the financial adjustment bureaus. These bureaus were in the practice of collecting and repossessing chattel, both terms of common industry use well into the 1990's.

A National Association of Credit Men lapel pin "ORGANIZED VIGILANTIA 1896" on center blue disc – (courtesy of The Smithsonian National Air and Space Museum Collection - Donated by Miss Katherine M. Smart).

Of curious origin was the first national association that created these adjustment bureaus partially for collections and repossessions, "The National Association of Credit Men" (NACM), established in 1896. While being merchants, they were also in the practice of collecting on defaulting commercial and consumer credit. Their first president, William H. Preston, railed against the state of lending, saying that *"Credit is cheap, too easily obtained"* which he stated in his manual, "Credits, Collections and their Management" in 1897.

Their initial primary goal was stated by Preston in a June 6,1896 New York Times article as; *"The better protection of our credits, the reduction of losses through bad debts, the prevention of fraud and injustice to creditors, the prosecution and punishment of fraud, the reformation and improvement of our collection laws, the improvement of our commercial reporting systems, the improvement of collection methods, and the improvement of present methods of handling bankrupt estates, & etc."*

According to the 1906 bulletin of the National Association of Credit Men the purpose of the "Adjustment Bureaus" was, *"to handle cases first hand, to keep them out of the courts and to make settlements at the minimum amount of expense and the maximum percentage of dividends."* As an arm extended to their members, they created "Adjustment Bureaus" to enforce these goals. If this sounds a lot like the collections and self-help repossession industries, that is because it was the probably the earliest known root of it.

All across the nation credit mens associations" were created at both the state and sometimes city levels. Of no big surprise, "the National Association of Credit Men" eventually changed their name to "The National Association of Credit Management" in 2011, and still exists to this day.

Somewhere along the way lost to time, adjustment bureaus became private businesses charging fees on a sliding scale or a flat fee depending on the amount assigned for collection or repossession. Payment of these fees was contingent to the successful resolution of the assignment. In other words, they had to collect or initiate a consumer payment or recover the chattel, if it was secured credit. This payment scenario existed clear into the 1980's. With Adjustment Bureaus, sometimes referred to as "Finance Adjusters" also providing auction services, their fees could include a wide variety of surcharges depending upon the lender's needs.

- Just a snippet of the collections section of the 1911 Lakeside annual directory of the city of Chicago. Collections and adjustment companies were already in abundant quantity.

In this era, most creditors had in house collectors and repossessors and as stated earlier, these services tended to only be used when it was impractical or too difficult to do so on their own. Along with these professional bureaus, there were always loose-knit crews of men to do these jobs on a flat fee, often saving the lenders a great deal of money. Of course, the professional caliber and tactics of these men were often questionable, and as the following historical accounting will show, dangerous and often deadly.

It is unknown how many, if any of these adjustment bureaus specialized in automotive repossession, but it was likely few.

From the Bemidji Daily Pioneer. (Bemidji, Minnesota), October 10, 1913 – (Library of Congress, Public Domain)

chat·tel - noun

(in general use) a personal possession.

LAW - an item of property other than real estate.

noun: chattel personal; plural noun: chattels personal; noun: chattel real; plural noun: chattels real

Brooklyn Daily Eagle Article - December 1925 – Public domain

CHAPTER 2 – THE 1920'S – THE BIG BANG

"The one aim of these financiers is world control by the creation of inextinguishable debt."
- Henry Ford

Woodrow Wilson was President to a US population of about 106 million people earning an average of $2,160 per year thanks to a rapidly growing American economy. The average low-end price of an automobile was $525. And while the worst of times may have seemed behind America, the god of calamity said, "Hold my beer." While he could still have one that is.

America Goes Dry

Sometimes you just can't suffer enough and having endured a World War and an international pandemic, it only made sense that in January of 1920, the United States ushered in the new decade with "The Prohibition." Otherwise known as the "Volstead Act" or the "Dry Act", the production and consumption of alcoholic beverages became illegal. This was to the delight of teetotaling buzzkill, Henry Ford who celebrated the reduction in lost factory man hours from Saturday night drinking.

Despite the puritanical fervor sweeping the nation and forced onto the mostly unwilling populace, the new freedoms of auto travel were spreading like wildfire.

The Auto Explosion

In a world where most people lived within walking distance of work, the need for an automobile was initially limited. The Ford Model T, priced at $900, was more than the average person making $2,160 a year could afford. As the result, most autos were purchased by the wealthy and for business purposes. Even when Ford's assembly lines driving the price down to $395, it was still more than the average consumer could afford.

While Ford held a commanding lead in auto sales and manufacturing, their "layaway" option was basically a flop. Durant and GM had the solution. Established in 1919, General Motors Acceptance Corporation (GMAC) had grown to five offices nationwide and, one in Great Britain. With a 35 percent down payment and monthly installment payments ranging from $30 to $75 to fit their numerous auto models, their sales boomed.

1925 GMAC ad – (Public Domain)

Still maintaining a commanding sales lead, the stubborn Ford refused to budge from his usurious view of lending. In the meanwhile, GM's sales continued to eat away at his market share as additional auto finance companies began to enter this new market. By 1923, Ford relented and launched their first auto lending program with a more conservative weekly payment plan. By 1928, Ford was all in and established the Universal Credit Company, the first of many financing plans until establishing the Ford Credit in 1959.

The explosion in auto financing spurred sales and massive economic growth nationwide. Federal highway programs began to transform the nations largely unpaved roads, smoothing and speeding up the connection between cities to farms. Cities began adapting to the proliferation of these "machines" and soon, carriages (cars) took over the roads. No longer a novelty, the automobile took America by storm, but of course, there were a lot of details to work out and some stiff resistance to change.

If not for the competitive drive of Henry Ford and William Durant, there would not have likely been a repossession industry as we know it. But that took a lot of growing into, as time will show.

The New Wild West

Defaulting loans were initially dealt with by the lenders themselves. The average American, being honest, would simply surrender the vehicle upon demand. However, the natural sense of resentment to lenders often led to resistance, a trend that only grew with time. Lenders, not having the time nor means to pursue these debtors began employing others to do their dirty work.

Filling that void were adjustment bureaus, private investigators, mechanics and a broad range of assertive natured individuals that contributed with the act of repossession being rife with conflict and trouble. Criminal acts of trespassing and violence, on both debtors and Repossessors, became common. It took little time for public condemnation of self-help repossession and the men who performed it to follow. The negative image of the repossession industry was born and resonates to this day.

In the early days, auto theft was a huge problem and the line between a repossession and a crime was a thin one. Repossessors, lenders and car dealers not communicating the nature of their actions often found themselves on the wrong side of the law.

A Thin Line

Sheriff Steps in As Dealers Seize Auto Special Dispatch to The Call.

AUBURN, CA, July 10.- The efforts of Malcolm & Bird, Sacramento automobile dealers, to repossess an automobile they had sold Clarence Fenton or Jenkee Jim's, caused much excitement here yesterday. Fenton, the dealers claimed, had become delinquent in his payments. The Sacramento men saw the car in front of a barber shop and grabbed it, starting for Sacramento. The barber notified the sheriff, who directed the deputy at Newcastle to block the road and went in pursuit. The dealers were overhauled by the sheriff before they struck the barricade, however. A settlement with Fenton finally ended the matter. - The San Francisco Call (San Francisco, California) - July 10, 1920

Auburn, California was a small town at this time, and I am pretty sure that everyone knew everyone. It is interesting that the story ended with "a settlement" being reached with the borrower. It does not take a lot of imagination to see that the "good old boy" local sheriff probably had a heavy hand in that.

The Pursuit of Happiness

In 1920, perhaps at the urging of the powerful Henry Ford, the Federal Reserve attempted to put a stop to auto lending all together by issuing a memorandum to all banks: "do not offer financing for automobiles used for pleasure." Such concern was based primarily on a fear that this was just a growing fad and that when it passed, the banks would be put at risk from massive losses. This conservative viewpoint was met with skepticism and opposition in that it created challenges to lenders in determining the difference between a loan applicant using an automobile for business or for pleasure. It even went as far as becoming a constitutional question posed, that the right to automobile ownership was clearly stated in the Declaration of Independence:

"The "pursuit of happiness' is one of the inalienable right that was woven into the Declaration of Independence and even tho it may appear to some of us that a man engage in this pursuit foolishly, yet so long as he remains within the law, pays his debts, and harms no one, his conduct should be free from the restricted action of the Federal Board and all other Governmental agencies. This is Democracy." - The Willmar Tribune - July 28, 1920

The inalienable right to purchase an automobile never rose to the level of Supreme Court intervention, and the Federal Reserve's guidance was dismissed. With affordable vehicles in production and easier access to credit, the American auto culture was born. With this relaxing cultural shift in the perception of lending, The Federal Reserve's fears came partially true as the inevitable defaults increase, and with them, repossessions.

Sheriff Purple and a Shotgun

For any of you that believe that repossessions should only be conducted by court order and enforced by law enforcement (replevin), I offer you this old tale.

Bearing a resemblance to actor Sam Elliot, Will S. Purple was the first elected Sheriff of Emmet County, Michigan in 1912. Served a writ of execution from a local bank to collect on a defaulted loan cosigned by a thirty-five-year-old World War I veteran and farmer named Francis Joseph Grosskopf, Purple's first attempt to collect ended with the farmer stating his intention to defend his property. Knowing there might be trouble, Purple brough a local attorney, Charles Pailthorp, son of the bank's attorney as a witness should anything occur on the afternoon of Wednesday, September 5, 1923, when he returned intent on serving the execution of the writ. Under Michigan law, the Sheriff was permitted to reposses any property of equal or lesser value to the amount of the writ.

Having spotted a pair of worthy horse on his first visit, he was initially resolved to repossess them, but upon arrival, he found an automobile in front and chose to repossess it instead. Grosskopf and his wife emerged with a fresh bill of sale for the vehicle showing it was owned by Mrs. Purple, which both Purple and the attorney, Pailthorp, suspected was a fake. Purple advised Grosskopf that he

Repo Blood

was taking the car prompting Grosskopf to march into the house leaving Purple and Pailthorp on the front steps. "Joe's gone for his gun. You'd better get out of the line of fire." suggested Mrs. Grosskopf.

Undettered, Sheriff Purple stood his ground while the lawyer ran for his life. Differing versions of murder and self-defense were later told, but at the end of the conflict, Sheriff Will S. Purple died from a shotgun blast to the abdomen and another to the base of the skull. Grosskopf was struck by six rounds and hospitalized with murder charges pressed against him. – Charlevoix Courier (Emmet County, MI) – September 12, 1923

While a badge may hold all of the authority of the law, when used to execute civil contracts, the borrower's response can be volatile. Just imagine the scene if a sheriff's deputy arrived with a tow truck to repossess a vehicle in most neighborhoods. The results would often involve copious amounts of mace, taser shots and possible gunfire. This scene has played itself out many times over the following hundred years proving that the legal process is just as, if not more dangerous than the self-help repossession process.

Is it Kidnapping?

Father of Girl Taken by Auto Repossessing Agents to Ask Judge About It

On a sunny California afternoon, Frank Parker of Glendale was visiting a friend's house in Burbank while his teen daughter waited in the passenger seat of his Chevrolet sedan. Looking out the window, he noticed two men pull up behind his car. In a flash, one of the men jumped into his car and sped away, seventeen-year-old daughter and all. Rushing out the front door, he shouted out "*Kidnappers*!" as they disappeared from sight.

With only 35 percent, or so, of houses having a phone, Parker ran as fast as he could to a nearby Burbank police station, where breathless and panicked, he reported the abduction. In an instant, every motor cop in the Burbank police was on the hunt. All afternoon, officers scrambled across the L.A. suburbs with no luck finding the car, the driver, or his pretty, blond daughter Helen. Roused from a relaxing weekend at home, Deputy Sheriff Allen arrived on the scene to investigate.

"*Ever have any trouble with the company that financed your car?*" he asked. "*Now that you speak of it, there is an argument over what I think is an overcharge of $5 on the last payment.*" Parker replied, still unable to connect the dots. Rolling his eyes and picking up the phone, Deputy Allen called the finance company.

11

"Yeh, we got the car." advised a finance company representative who had been involved in the repossession. *"The girl? We took her home."* The Parker residence, in the new Glendale addition of Verdugo, like the entire neighborhood, did not have phone service. Having no way to reach her father, Helen just waited. Helen later said that she simply did not have time to get out of the car.

Mr. Parker advised police and reporters that he was going to seek a judicial definition for the men who took his car and daughter, repossessor or kidnappers? - The Los Angeles Times – December 1, 1926

A Job for Veterans

America was loaded with World War I veterans. Many out of work or scratching out a living with manual labor. To aid these men, congress overrode President Coolidge's veto and enacted The World War Adjusted Compensation Act of 1924. Each veteran was to receive a dollar for each day of domestic service spent overseas as compensation for reduced incomes while serving.

However, these payments, up to a maximum of $500, were not payable until 1945. Many of this population of underemployed veterans, eager to earn a living, leaned into their acquired strengths. Armed with the guts to charge across an open field into machinegun fire and endure horrific conditions, many took side jobs repossessing cars and other forms of chattel. A job that often took a special kind of blood to perform these unpleasant and risky tasks.

Auto Insecurity

During this era, auto theft by "auto snatchers" was rampant. While Bosch had invented the keyed ignition in 1911, they were not in common use. With little more than a pair of switches to engage the common ignition switch, auto theft deterrence was primarily limited to a padlock and a chain. At this time, a pair of bolt cutters, if anything at all, was practically all that was needed to affect a repossession.

As closed canopy model vehicles grew in popularity, the addition of door locks became common in 1920. While picking locks was an option for entry, bendable wire was usually quicker and more practical for entry.

First Knowns

It will probably never be known who the first repossession agency was, since Detective agencies and Adjustment Bureaus were also conducting them, but we do know who some of the oldest and still operating agencies are. According to current owner Gary Deese, Conrad "Connie" Wembish founded the "Home Detective Agency" in Greensboro, North Carolina In 1922. Deese, who first worked for him, bought the agency in 1966. Deese credits much of everything he knows about skip-tracing from the agencies in-house skip tracer, HK Williams, who he referred to as the greatest skip tracer in the world.

In 1925, William "Frank" Greenwood of "Greenwoods Garage" at 1150 E. North Ave., Baltimore, Maryland earned the distinction of being the first known repossession service company. "Greenwoods Garage" later transformed into a staple of the Baltimore area. "Greenwood Towing" and "Greenwood Recovery" which are still in operation, are in the hands of his grandson, Burton "Buzz" Greenwood.

"Auto Snatching" 1925 – An Early Adjusters Account

Brooklyn Daily Eagle article - December 1925 (Public domain)

The earliest written account of life as a repossession agent, referred to as an "Auto-Snatcher" can be found in a December 10, 1925, story in the Brooklyn Daily Eagle. According to the article, the agent states that the profession did not exist as recent as ten years ago and attributed it as an outgrowth of the installment loan plan. He describes the majority of borrowers being honest and prompt paying but describes the need for his services when "*a certain class of thieves and deadbeats attempt to beat the finance companies. That's where I come in, when a man has fallen down on his installments and we are satisfied that he is trying to gyp us, I go out and repossess the car.*"

Odd enough, he refers to his profession in the "Auto-Snatching" term which had been a term long used for auto thieves and also often refers to the cars as "machines." Throughout the lengthy article, he describes repossessing cars chained to trees, placed on elevators, disabled, and hidden between floors or on upper floors of buildings. His experiences resonate with a big city feel, while not naming one, as he discusses having been in numerous fights and having been shot four times. As has become a custom of such articles, he boasts of his immediate return to work from injury without losing a step.

This was the "Roaring Twenties" and the mob and prohibition were in full swing. It comes of little surprise that he would share the tale of his encounter with a "*Notorious Gang*" of seven brothers "*three of whom have gone to the chair*" who "*have stolen millions of dollars of goods and are still feared by police and civilians alike.*" His story goes on to reveal his successful repossession of a vehicle that he had to hide in the city as the gang watched out for it at every exit from the city.

GEORGE D. WRIGHT OF DETROIT. ORIGINATOR OF THE PROFESSION OF "CAR SNATCHING." HE KNOWS ALL THE TRICKS OF DEADBEATS WHO BUY MOTOR CARS ON TIME

George D. Wright - The First Professional Auto Repossessor - The Kansas City Times (Kansas City, Missouri) - 24 December 24, 1925

Finally attempting to get it out of town, he reports that the gang "*ran their vehicle directly into the front of the sedan, overturning it. The gang sped away leaving me unconscious beneath the wreckage. I was three months in the hospital and two months convalescing at home.*" An entertaining story, but odd they didn't get out and just kill him, if you ask me.

While speaking lightly of recovery tactics, he mentions using a "tow machine" or "tow wagon" as he refers to it, but never speaks of hot-wiring, breaking in or picking locks. Blocking in and disabling vehicles appear to be primary methods of recovery employed by this agent at least. Interesting enough though, he does discuss the use of law enforcement under conversion laws of the time. Regardless, he does caveat this stating that "*this is not often done, though the courts have confirmed this right.*"

In closing the article, he claims that "*A good investigator, or a repossessor is known as a very valuable asset to a finance company. I know of one finance company that keeps a force from ten to fifteen men busy at all times.*"

His perspective on borrowers is interesting in that he seems to draw an extremely hard line between two types. "*Honest people never lose their automobiles through defaulting payments. They can always make arrangements to keep their cars. It is the crooks and deadbeats who are my prey. Nine times out of ten, it is the man who attempts to cheat the finance company that has beaten the eyes out of the butcher, the baker and the candlestick maker.*"

He doesn't speak of commissions or being part of any detective agency or adjustment bureau and appears to be a "lone wolf" repossessor, which was likely common in this era. Articles like these, which have been a constant in the industry, feed the presses morbid curiosity and can be difficult to judge for credibility. Regardless, they do offer an intriguing glimpses into the repossession industries past during different eras.

Weeks later, on December 24, 1925, in a different article titled "Car Snatching" a New Art, Detroit News writer E.J. Beck interviewed a man with an identical story. The man interviewed was George D. Wright of Detroit. This places Detroit as the cradle of professional repossessions and Detroit would go on to play a prominanet role in its history. By virtue of this article, George D. Wright can reasonably be credited as being the first professional auto repossessor, his motto was; *"Don't fight-em, fool 'em."*

The Shylocks

By 1926, the first known documented public outcry against the repossession process was editorialized. On November 13, 1926, "The Evening Independent" of Massillon, Ohio, reported that three men were held in custody by the local magistrates for being "Loan Sharks" and charged with demanding usurious interest rates. In these hearings, the first known testimony from an unnamed repossessor, states that he was being paid $25 per vehicle for repossessions. That equates to $365.36 at the time of this writing in 2021 (Kind of funny how anyone would accept less than that now.)

An editorial published on the same day, stated; *"And my opinion is that the taking of a car on the public streets is not a peaceable repossession. Bloodshed, criminal prosecution, hatred, malice, and increased litigation flow from the exercise of force and violence in the clandestine taking from a buyer the car in his possession. To allow the auto dealer to take cars in this manner is to sanction furniture dealers in going into private homes and taking furniture held by the buyer, upon the installment plan.*

Repo Inventory - November 5, 1925 -
Passaic Daily Herald (Passaic, New Jersey)

"Contrary to Policy"

The exercise of the right to repossess under any strategy or by force and violence is contrary to public policy; is exposing the seller to actions sounding in tort; for trespass, and in many cases laying himself liable in other ways."

"*Fifty percent interest*" testified New York cab driver Abraham Schwartz when asked about the loan terms charged him by the Mosee Credit Company of New York. This was an opening statement testimony during a federal hearing on the practices of "Loan Sharks" before United States Commissioner Garret W. Cotter. These hearings were reported on by the "Brooklyn Daily Eagle" on March 22, 1928, in an article titled "*Says Loan Sharks Broke Up Home.*" Included in the testimony was that of a Joseph Rogers, a self-confessed repossessor for several unnamed lenders, but the article shed no light on his tactics or pay.

Schwartz's testimony goes on to state that the car he purchased immediately needed to be repainted, for which the financier charged him $120 ($1,889 in 2021) plus $40 interest. The car soon broke down and they offered to repair it. Of course, the catch was, they charged him $347 ($5,462 in 2021) for the repairs and another $80 interest. Keep in mind, a Ford Model T cost about $395 new and the average American earned $2,160 a year. Under financial pressure from the "loan sharks", Schwartz claimed that he had to send his wife away to stay with her mother for safety. – The Brooklyn Daily Eagle (New York, New York) – March 22, 1928

Neither article provides names or details of the actual tactics employed, but it is worthy to remember that this was during the Prohibition.

Organized crime was spreading across large swaths of America. With organized criminal enterprises flourishing, loan sharks and their nefarious collections tactics were rampant. To the wary public, the repossession process was likewise suspect, and for good reason.

At the same time, legitimate bank and finance company repossession activity was still primarily performed by the lenders themselves. When locating the borrower became a problem or the vehicle was too far to travel, private investigators or hired locals with no specific industry affiliation were employed. This recovery process was often maintained clear into the 1990's with some lenders who still maintained the decentralized branch lending structure.

Pistol Whipped

Sirens screaming, Ventura County Sheriff's deputies sped across county for what they thought was a murder call. Upon arriving at the remote country general store in Triunfo Pass, they found that is was only an altercation between the storekeeper Irving Stollmack and an unknown repossessor for an unnamed Los Angeles finance company who had already fled.

Pride injured, as well as his head, Stollmack reported that he had witnessed the repossessor enter his vehicle and was getting ready to drive it away when he ran out to stop him. According to Stollmack and witnesses, the repossessor drew a gun and struck him on the head. Deputies marked it up as a civil action and did not file charges on the unnamed man and left it to Stollmack to file civil charges at a later date. - The Ventura County Star and the Ventura Daily Post and Weekly Democrat - (Ventura, California) June 9, 1927

The willingness of law enforcement to reign in such blatant breaches of peace were erratic during this era. Opting to either intervene on the borrower's favor or simply leave it for civil recourse, a state of ambiguity persisted for decades in law enforcements dealing with matters of this nature.

The Blockade Runner

In September of 1926, Berry Furman, was a repossessor for the South Carolina based Franklin Greenville Finance Company. Arriving at the home of debtor and lawyer, Harry Watkins he made a direct attempt to collect delinquent payments or repossess his car. Watkins did not have funds for payment but claimed that he would surrender the car at a later date if still unable to make payments. Furman left empty handed, but this would not be their last encounter.

Several weeks later, while on a leisurely drive through the country, Watkins was flagged down from the side of the road by a seemingly friendly Furman. Advised that the tire on Watkins' car was running flat, Furman suggested that Watkins drive into the alley behind a nearby Payne Oil station and have it fixed. Thanking him for the advice, Watkins naively fell into the trap. After having the tire fixed, Watkins found himself trapped in to the dead-end alley with a locked and parked car blocking his escape.

An angry Watkins demanded Furman move the blocking car to no avail and called the police. Furman tried to get the responding police to remove Watkins from the vehicle, which they refused and the ordeal carried on with Sheriff's deputies arriving and conferring with District Attorney before advising that they would take no action as it was a civil matter. A crowd of fifty had gathered to watch the conflict play out, and Watkins did not disappoint them.

Fair warnings given, Watkins pulled the car as far forward as he could before putting it in reverse and stomping on the accelerator. A roar of applause and cheering erupted as he smashed past the blocking car and made his getaway. Aside from the damage to the vehicle, Watkins claimed a sprained wrist, ruined clothes as damages done by Furman and another repossessor. Adding to the list of physical damages, humiliation and impairment of reputation were added claims to his lawsuit filed later in June of 1927. - The Greenville News - (Greenville, South Carolina) - June 12, 1927

Depression era soup line – (photo courtesy of the National Archives)

Skips and Forwarding

Brimming with the confidence of a robust peacetime economy, auto lending had expanded to almost every economic class of America, when on October 24, 1929, it all came to a screeching halt. Over the next four days, stocks lost over 22 percent of their value in what became known as the "Stock Market Crash" of 1929. The banking industry went into a panic and over one-third of them closed their doors for good. Auto lending ground to a near halt and "The Great Depression" soon followed.

With 25 percent of the population unemployed and 50 percent of the population owning at least one automobile, loan defaults soon followed. Without the public safety nets of welfare, unemployment, or social security, a swell of farm and home foreclosures soon followed, and homelessness exploded across the nation. Without jobs or homes, whole families were uprooted in a mass exodus to find jobs, and of course, they brought their cars with them.

With this tsunami of transiency and loan delinquency, the still fledgling repossession industry boomed. Lenders, flooded with more delinquent loans than they could manage themselves became reliant on their loose networks of private investigators and repossession agents to manage the overflow and time-consuming distant recoveries. When these agents found leads to the debtors outside of their travel range, they would "forward" the repossession assignments to another agent in the new area for a small fee to the lender. This informal practice persisted well into the latter part of the twentieth century as lenders began developing deeper long-term relationships with their repossession agents.

In natural response to rising losses, loan underwriting guidelines tightened, interest rates skyrocketed, and the auto industry slowed to a crawl. As the auto loan volume plummeted, the defaults spiked, and collateral became increasingly more difficult to repossess. During this era, only 41 percent of American households owned a telephone and deteriorating financial circumstances led to rising disconnected phone numbers.

Unable to reach borrowers by phone, collectors, mostly bank officers, were forced to make field calls. Burdened by heavy caseloads, visiting debtors after banking hours and travelling all the extra miles became unmanageable. Recognizing the inefficiency of these tactics, lenders became increasingly more reliant upon their networks of adjusters, private investigators and repossessors.

Bring on The Bullets

On a chilly February night, Edward Bishop, an attaché on a Naval Air Station, was moonlighting part time as a repossessor for an un-named motor finance company. Arriving at the residence of James A. Tatum on the 200 block of Massachusetts St. in Washington DC, Bishop spotted his vehicle on the side of the house. Leaving the warmth of his car, he creeped up to it, gained entry, put it in neutral and was quietly "drifting" it down the driveway when all hell broke loose. Tatum had tied some pots, pans and bottles to it as an improvised alarm.

Bishop's heart leapt through his chest in surprise as the clang and rattle of debris broke the still of the crisp night air. Then the house lights burst to life and a second-floor window slid open. Gun in hand, Tatum opened fire and struck Bishop in the hip with two rounds. Tatum was charged with assault with a dangerous weapon, and police turned the vehicle over to the lender.

The next month, Judge Isaac R. Hitt dismissed the charges against Tatum and demanded the lender return the truck to him. The judge claimed that Bishop had no legal right to be on the property at the time of the recovery and that Tatum had a legal right to defend his property. – The Afro American - February 14, 1929 (same day as the infamous Chicago St. Valentine's Day Massacre)

This legal sentiment and borrower response had already become the unfortunate industry standard. Incidents like this and the legal apathy to them would be repeated with frequency over the next ninety years with often deadly results.

Depression desperation – (photo courtesy of the National Archives)

Off to a Rough Start

Streets, long open and for common use by pedestrians and horse alike, had been overtaken by cars. Stop lights and crosswalks were rare and for the most ignored and in 1920, at least 15,000 pedestrians were killed by cars. Speed limits were almost non-existent and in 1930, only twenty-four states required a license to drive with only fifteen states requiring a driver's exam. The fact that America was also wrestling with the issue of self-help auto repossession was par for the course of America's automotive evolution.

Ray and Lorna Lou Barnes - September 18, 1949, Washington Evening Star Article

CHAPTER 3 – THE 1930'S –
THE BIRTH OF AN INDUSTRY

With the Great Depression ushering in the new decade, global gross domestic product (GDP) had dropped by 15 percent. In relation to the modern era, it only dropped 1 percent during the Great Recession of 2008-2009. International trade had dropped by 50 percent and unemployment in the United States of America lingered at a stubborn 23 percent. Under these desperate conditions, the dream of car ownership was fading, as mainstream America struggled just to keep their families fed.

Auto sales had fallen by seventy-five percent and the auto manufacturing industry showed combined losses of $191 million in 1932, that is $2.9 billion in current value. Amazingly, General Motors showed a profit in every year of this decade and Chrysler only showed one year with a loss. Regardless, the banking and lending industries suffered. Over 744 banks had failed during the first ten months of the decade and another 9,000 would follow suit over the next ten years.

By now, almost 50 percent of American families owned at least one automobile and it had become an essential part of daily life. The average annual income had taken a huge hit and was now a mere

$1,368 per year, almost 30 percent less than a mere decade earlier. For this population of now 123 million, led by Republican President Herbert Hoover (1929-1933), the mood of the nation was bleak.

More Kidnapping

Car Taker Hunted as Boy Kidnaper Because He Forgot to Take a Small Boy out of it When He Repossessed a Car

Mrs. N. D. Rosenberger, of Buena Park had parked on the curb of Anaheim Street and had stepped inside the drug store for a quick errand. Returning to her car, she found it missing and worse, her six-year-old son Calvin who she'd left inside it. Police were called and the panicked hunt for the boy and the car commenced.

O. K. McWha, was employed by a used car dealer in Long Beach, California. Spotting the vehicle in front of the drug store, he rushed into it and was likely startled by the presence of the boy, that is, if in his excited state he'd noticed at all. Whether or not he tried to induce the child to get out is unknown, but McWha took the car with the child inside. McWha then drove cross town and dropped the Rosenberger's home before returning the car to the used car lot of his employer.

How much time had passed before anyone knew the child was safe at home is unknown, but in an era when less than forty percent of people owned a phone, it was probably an agonizing hour or two at least. For his misplaced efforts, McWha was rewarded with a kidnapping complaint filed by Mrs. Rosenberger. - The Los Angeles Daily News (Los Angeles, California) - December 8, 1930

The more things change, the more they stay the same. Not a year goes by without someone, somewhere, repossessing a vehicle with a child in it.

The Skips

With lenders trying to trace the whereabouts of the many transient American borrowers who'd "skipped" town with their collateral, private investigators were in high demand. This was the birth of the term "skip tracer." Their tactics usually involved simple interviews with family and neighbors, but bribery

1930's transient camp – (photo by National Archives)

and third-party disclosure were common practices as was the offering of rewards in in newspaper classified ad sections.

Long before the Fair Debt Collections Practices Act (FDCPA) and laws against use of false identities, they would often result to false pretext to coax information. Claiming themselves to be everything from law enforcement, possible employers or even claims to be lawyers searching for heirs to inheritances, there was little they would not do. Clear into the 1960's, newspaper ads were posted offering rewards for information on the whereabouts of skipped borrowers.

Who Do You Trust?

All across the nation, banks, floundered and failed. Auto loan delinquency soared and lenders struggled to survive while facing new challenges. Amongst those challenges was where to find credible and qualified repossessors?

For lenders, their loose networks of known local agents was sufficient enough in their own areas, but once their debtors left the range of these networks, they had to rely on out-of-town lenders for agent references. Knee deep in the Great Depression, it was the era of Bonnie and Clyde, and John Dillinger, banks and lenders were vilified. Times were hard for most everyone and for some agents, the lure of pocketing collected payments or stealing a repossessed car or its parts was seen as justifiable and more than they could resist.

Unlike their bonded insurance company brethren, the repossession industry was still in its infancy. Operating on both sides of the law, the industry at times employed tactics both professional and, at other times, extortionary. Unlicensed, unregulated, and uninsured, assigning repossessions out of town was always a gamble. This lack of regulation and the risk posed to lenders carried on well into the mid-1930's.

Karma Hates a Snitch

In early 1920's Detroit, the Wysocki gang ran amuck committing armed robberies, assaults, theft and shooting at least one police officer in a crime spree across Michigan, Ohio and Illinois. The gang was led by brothers Frank and Walter Wysocki, and even included Frank's new wife Theresa Kaul. Things began to fall apart after police killed one gang member and captured the brothers in June of 1921. Frank, his brother and other gang members were sentenced to serve terms of fifteen to twenty years in Michigan's Jackson Prison, but they had other plans.

Just days after his wife filed for divorce from him from her jail cell, on January 16, 1922, Frank, Walter and another man broke out. Frank was identified as the hold-up man of a soda shop the very same night and went on a long crime spree. Following the recapture of his brother and the other man, as well as the arrest of a third brother, Frank dropped off the face of the earth, that is until 1931.

SAY PAIR ADMIT MANY HOLDUPS

Police, Prosecutor Announce Confessions by Members of 'Wysocki Gang.'

In statements made to Assistant Prosecuting Attorney Robert Speed two members of the Frank Wysocki gang, so called by the police, including the leader, are reported to have admitted their part in numerous recent holdups in Detroit. The statements were made Saturday night, police announced Sunday.

Wysocki, whom police say has been the leader of the gang since all the members were attending school, and Joseph Burecki, both of whom are charged with robbery while armed, were the only men who would make any admissions to the detectives who questioned them and to the assistant prosecuting attorney. Wysocki told Mr. Speed, according to the latter, that he had taken part in these robberies and the burglary of a garage from

The Detroit Free Press – June 13, 1921

Fatal Shooting Occurs at McGee Creek, Mono County Finance Company Adjuster Shot As He Attempts to Repossess Automobile.

McGee Creek, CA – September 26, 1932 - Jorie Thos. Medqueaux, age 31 was fatally wounded from a gunshot fired by Chas. Philbrick at McGee Creek Sunday about 8:45 a.m. and died at the hospital in Lone Pine after being brought here for medical treatment at about 4:30 p.m., of the same day. Shortly before he died, he signed a statement accusing Chas. Philbrick whom two of Medqueaux's companions, Clifton Henigan and Donal Roberts, testifying at the coroner's inquest stated that they had witnessed the shooting.

According to their testimony they accompanied Madqueaux, an automobile finance adjuster from Los

While working as repossessors for the National Automobile Insurance Company, Thomas Madqueaux and his driver, A.C. Golsh were arrested for assault and battery after a car chase involving a borrower that ended in an accident. In addition to the $1,000 judgement awarded to the borrower in a November 1931 civil suit, Madqueaux arrest unveiled a long-guarded secret, he had been living under an alias.

Frank Wysocki had been caught. Once the state of Michigan found out, they demanded his return. California Governor Rolf Jr., refused to extradite him claiming that he had been a law abiding and respected citizen for ten years. The state of Michigan didn't press the issue very hard and Frank remained in California living under the alias. But karma tends to get its way eventually.

FRANK WYSOCKI.

Gang leader turned escaped prisoner turned repossessor, Frank Wysocki – (Detroit Free Press, 1921)

Angeles (300 miles away) who was to repossess an automobile from Philbrick for the Auto Bank on which payments were in arrears. Having gone to the house to inform Philbrick, Henigan and Roberts remained as Henigan getting into Philbrick's car to inspect the registration slip to ascertain for sure. Philbrick returned to the car first and dared Henigan out and taking the (driver's seat, drew a pistol from the car pocket, put it in his belt and started to drive away.

Madqueaux stepped on the running board and as he did so as a shot was fired by Philbrick. Seeing Madqueaux fall to the ground and Philbrick alight from the car, revolver in hand, the two companions abandoned their car and ran for safety and gave the alarm, notifying the authorities. Philbrick was placed under arrest and placed in jail at Bridgeport. Madqueaux was rushed to lone Pine Hospital in a critical condition and died only a short time after his arrival, the bullet having entered his left side passed through the body, lodging slightly under the skin on his right side. Madqueaux's relatives residing at Detroit, Michigan, were notified. - Big Pine Citizen (Inyo County, California) -September 26, 1932

After two trials resulting in hung juries, Philbrick, who had claimed self-defense, walked and karma got her way.

Hillbilly Amateur Hour

Lured from by the promise of leniency on his own delinquent auto loan by Elmer Wertz and JC Beecher of United Investigators, Lloyd Shoemaker, his brother and an unnamed "negro", ventured into North Carolina to repossess a vehicle. The borrower, Clyde Archie Bare had skipped from Pennsylvania to rural Ashe County, NC, the shared hometown of Shoemaker. Although, inexperienced in repossessions, they managed to successfully recover the vehicle and handed it off to Investigators Wertz and Beecher.

The investigators then passed the repossessed vehicle over to the unnamed "negro" to drive back to Pennsylvania and deliver it to their office. While they returned to Shoemaker's home in the area to rest before the drive back, as a favor, the investigators allowed Shoemaker to borrow their expensive sedan with the intention of visiting a nearby brother.

Not far from his brother's house, Shoemaker was ambushed by two men with rifles who riddled the sedan with bullet holes. Shoemaker, uninjured, had somehow been informed that the "negro" driver had been killed and the vehicle taken back by the debtor Bare. Beecher and Wertz were then warned that two men were on their way to kill them. Stranded in the country without a car, Wertz and Beecher fled for their lives on foot through the mountainous countryside, in the rain and under the cover of dark.

Finding a car for hire, Wertz and Beecher made their way to a nearby town where they spent the night and requested police protection. Finding their way back to Harrisburg, Pennsylvania, they contacted police to advise of their ordeal and the alleged murder of the unnamed "negro." Unfortunately, police were unable to investigate the story or obtain contact or cooperation from the Ashe County Sheriff who was reportedly "out on an emergency call." - The Gettysburg Times (Gettysburg, Pennsylvania) - October 6, 1932

You can almost hear the banjoes in the background. Like something out of the 1972 film "The Deliverance", this tale illustrates the dangers of country repossessions during the Great Depression. The alleged ambush and killing of an unnamed "negro" hint at a possible set up by Shoemaker, the debtor Bare and even possibly the Sheriff's office.

Public intervention in foreclosures and repossessions have always been common and continue to this day. The newspaper's dismissive mention of the alleged killing of an unnamed black man during the process further reminds us of the openly racist "Jim Crow" society which was commonplace during this era.

A Dynasty in the Making

It was also in 1932 that the third known recorded repossession specialty company was founded, Summs Skip & Collection Service, Inc. Established by Fred G. Summs Sr. and his wife Kathleen O. Summs, for lender convenience, they operated from of the back office of a Norfolk, Virginia Bank. This esteemed company was passed down from father to sons, Fred "Buzzy" Jr. and then Mark, who operates it to this day with his wife Cindy.

Tricks of the Trade

Professionalism in the repossession industry was near non-existent and technology was still evolving. Auto security was minimal and tactics for recovery were still primarily driving it away or towing it with a rope or chain. Locking ignitions were pathetic and easy to bypass with a length of wire (Hot wire.) Door locks were simple five pin cylinder models easily defeated with a piece of bent spring steel through the wing windows or lock picks.

In 1932, Curtis Industries was founded in Cleveland Ohio. On July 2, 1934, W.H. Curtis filed for a patent on his

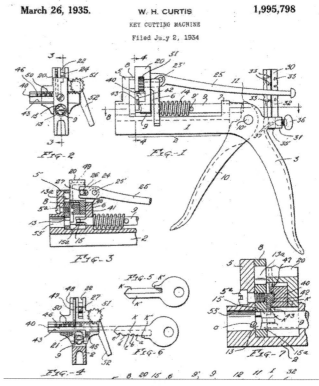

1935 patent diagram for the original Curtis Key Gun – (US Patent Office)

hand held "key cutting machine." Patent number 1,995,798 provided the illustration for the first mobile key cutting device. The "Curtis Key Gun" as it became known, would carry on as a staple of every repossession agency in the nation for well over seventy years.

From 1934 to 1935, GM experimented with a dual sided key but in 1936, implemented a six-cut sidebar lock which remined their staple until 1966. As with prior auto locks, key codes were stamped on the sides of all the lock cylinders to assist locksmiths to whom they sold code books.

With the nation still held in the grips of the Great Depression, repossessors were not difficult to find. They came from all walks of life but varied in experience. As the result, their tactics continued to skate on the edges of the law and often, both they and the public suffered the consequences.

Uncivil Action

Repossessors Held When Car is Taken

Apparently, F.C. Dilbeck of Los Angeles used the oldest break in tool of all to get into borrower N.C. Buchanan's car, a rock. Spotted by the borrower as he fled with his driver, Ed Nance of Redlands, shouts to halt went ignored and local foot cops sprang into action. Commandeering a vehicle, they took chase and opened fire on Dilbeck firing two rounds from moving vehicle to moving vehicle.

Wisely, Dilbeck pulled over and the two were arrested on suspicion of theft. Dragged into the police station, officers discovered and finally believed Dilbeck's assertion that it was a repossession. Dilbeck advised officers that Buchanan was one day delinquent. - The San Bernardino County Sun (San Bernardino, California) – February 2, 1932

One day late. A little impatient, huh? Car dealers notoriously required large downpayments and would repossess the loaned cars on the drop of a dime only to sell the same car again and acquire another large downpayment from the next buyer. Wash, rinse, repeat, this old dealership scam perists to this day.

Have a Drink on Me

With the enactment of the 18th Amendment to the United States Constitution on December 5, 1933, the long dry spell of the Prohibition came to a merciful end and so did the Great Depression, coincidence, perhaps. The United States would continue to struggle to pull itself up from the upheaval of the prior three years and what remaining auto lending remained, was tight in underwriting and still high in defaults.

The Original Bud

W.W. "Bud" Morrison -
photo by the AFA

Long before Harry Dean Stanton played "Bud" in the film "Repo Man", in 1906, Wilson W. "Bud" Morrison was born in Oakland, California. A San Mateo Junior College attendee, he spent his early years employed at the Morton Salt Company before meeting the emerging repossession industry. In 1935, he went to work for a Mr. L.E. Carter who owned and operated the California Adjustment Bureau" located in San Francisco. World War II came and Bud enlisted in the army.

Once the war ended, Bud was back on the streets. While working an assignment for Seaboard Finance in December of 1946, he spotted his unit at Bay Meadows Racetrack and was ready to tow it when first he called the police. Apparently, the debtor, Robert Golladay of Long Beach had warrants against him for passing fake checks. Bud set Golladay up with the police when he came to reinstate his repossessed car. – The Times - (San Mateo, California) – December 2, 1946

Bud went on to serve various positions in the NAAFA and future AFA.

A Shot in the Dark

Hollywood, CA - April 13, 1935 – Looking down from his apartment window at 2 a.m., H. Klein spotted two men in a "tow machine" that he believed to be car thieves. Grabbing his pistol, Klein opened fire on the shadowy figures as they backed their tow vehicle up to his car. Klein failed to hit anyone, but both the repossessors and Klein called the police. Responding officers sent the Repossessors away and let Klein keep the vehicle with no charges filed for shooting at the agents. – Daily Citizen – (Los Angeles, California) April 13, 1935

This outcome and "color of law" attitude toward the industry and repossessions was widely accepted.

A Deadly Thin Line

Repossessor Amos Shulzbach, thirty-years-old, of Brooklyn, New York, was shot by a policeman when the officer mistook him for a car thief. The part-time adjuster and mechanic suffered life threatening injuries and was taken to Bellevue Hospital where he was arrested for grand larceny. It is unknown if he survived. - The Daily Eagle of Brooklyn - (New York, New York) October 8, 1936

This incident illustrates the perils that repossessors encountered by law enforcement who often perceived them to be little more than car thieves.

The Highway Hawkshaws

"The Highway Hawkshaws", as their later New York neighbors referred to them, Met in Hollywood, California in 1930. Hawkshaw is an old term for a detective. Idaho native twenty-year-old Lorna Lou Critchfield was working as a schoolteacher and twenty-seven year-old Ray Barnes was a World War I Navy veteran turned restaurant manager turned insurance adjuster, turned finance adjuster.

Ray and Lorna Lou Barnes – (photos by the AFA)

Their four-month courtship was one where, as Lorna put it in a 1952 newspaper interview; *"I can't remember one date when he didn't ask me to go into some place to ask questions. I wasn't sure if he dated me because he like me or because I came back with the right answers."* Soon after their marriage, the Barnes moved to New York where Lorna's skip tracing skills earned her national notoriety.

Lorna's experience in the repossession industry did not end at skip-tracing. Lorna was skilled with break ins and towing and frequently involved in some dubious recoveries. In one she found a hatchet murder victim in the trunk that almost led her quit. In another, she led FBI agents to a set of stolen secret B-29 blueprints hidden in a vehicle that became the grounds for espionage investigations.

Herding Cats

At this time, the repossession companies were very territorial, and there were rumored occasions where agencies went to extreme measures to protect it. This included criminal acts of extortion, arson, and violence between competitors. These issues would persist, but Ray and Lorna Lou Barnes, with a handful of other adjusters would soon solve the lender issue of credibility and bonding.

Collecting a nationwide group of repossession companies from across the nation, they met in a St. Louis, Missouri hotel with half a dozen small agency owners in the summer of 1936. It was decided then that they would share their lender client networks for marketing. Recruiting new adjusters for a fee for inclusion into their national directory of repossession agencies, they took a portion of the collected fees and secured a bond.

Manually stuffing into envelops hundreds of their thin new directories, they mailed them out all across the country to the auto lending and finance communities. Offering a $5,000 guarantee bond payable to the lenders as protection against loss and providing a trusted national adjuster network, the directory became an indispensable lender resource. This was the birth of the first national repossession association, known then as "The National Association of Allied Finance Adjusters."

Aside from the bond and marketing value of "coast to coast" directory inclusion, the association provided the member companies exclusive territorial rights of 150 miles around certain cities for a membership fee. "The Book", as it was also known, became an essential resource to the lending industry. It took little time for the repossession agencies in its pages to flourish and membership grew quickly. While the new association could provide guarantees of marketing coverage, it could not shut out non-member competition, which was a much larger segment of the industry, just as it is today.

Don't be a Palmer

Thomas D. Palmer, 29, an Investigator for Kelley Kar Company of Los Angeles, left his wife Mrs. Gertrude Palmer in their car and entered a poolroom near Pico and Figueroa streets "to find a man", he told her. That was on a Thursday night and Palmer never came out. Alarmed, Mrs. Palmer called police the next day when he failed to return to their home at 16 Avenue 23, in Venice. Reporting him missing and possibly kidnapped, she told police that her husband had been attempting to repossess a car purchased by a bad man and ex-bootlegger suspected to be in the poolroom at the time of his disappearance. Los Angeles Daily News (Los Angeles, California) – April 23, 1934

No further mention of this missing person case or its victim could be found until three years later.

Two Kidnappers Free Man Here

"This is the end of your ride." one of the two kidnappers allegedly advised before tossing Thomas D. Palmer, now thirty-two-years-of age and considering a change of professions, from his own moving car in the northern California town of Richmond. Walking ten miles, Palmer arrived at the Oakland Police station on May 21, 1937, where he was reported to be *"Unshaven and disheveled"* *"bruised and near collapse"* after his ordeal that started in LA three days earlier. Palmer claimed that the two men leapt into his car at a stoplight in LA and kidnapped him at gunpoint. *"Keep quiet and keep going if you don't want to get hurt."* the thugs advised, stealing his $40 and taking him on a wild ride.

Palmer reported to have been tied to trees in the daytime as they hid his car and travelled by night. He reported that he'd only been fed a sandwich and two bottles of soda over the period of his three-day ordeal. A statewide manhunt ensued that located his vehicle further north in Vacaville, California with switched license plates. Various sources – Sacramento Bee (Sacramento, California) – 21 May 1937 and The Oakland Tribune (Oakland, California) - 21 May 1937

These two events, seemingly connected, were actually three years apart. Both identify Thomas D. Palmer, a collector and adjuster for the Kelley Kar Company of Los Angeles, down to the city, profession, age, and middle initial. Fortunate for him, no further instances of kidnapping or repossession were found in researching newspapers up to the 1950s. He didn't seem well cut out for this profession.

Oliver

In 1937, a World WarI 5th Army Division veteran and investigative finance adjuster from Shreveport Louisiana, O.W.J Reynolds, otherwise known as "Oliver", founded the Automotive Recovery Bureau of Louisiana. A company that is still in operation to this day.

Oliver was one of the charter members of the NAAFA and its President in 1949.

O.W.J. Reynolds –
(photos by the AFA)

Hammering Out Payment Arrangements

Milo Austin; investment company employee, was taken- to Hollywood Receiving Hospital with an inch-and-a-half cut in his scalp after his encounter with a borrower in an attempt to repossess an automobile. Lewis Edward Mann, twenty-three-years-old, provided it with a hammer at 2208 Ewing Street. Mann was charged and plead not guilty before eventually going to trial on June 4, 1937. - Los Angeles Daily News - (Los Angeles, California) - May 26, 1937

Weeds

In 1930, Ford had produced over 1.1 million autos and General Motors 640 thousand. In 1939, Ford had only produced 487 thousand and General Motors, 577 thousand. These muted production numbers were a direct reflection of the post-Depression economy. With reduced auto sales and tighter underwriting guidelines, repossession activity doubtlessly slowed from its depression era peak. The nation was recovering, but the auto industry did not recover to pre-depression levels until 1950.

The 1930's were formulative to the American psyche and culture. Despite the hardships of "The Great Depression", the automobile continued to be an iconic symbol of the American dream. While this decade ended more optimistically than it began, in the next decade, the still growing and organizing repossession industry was set to face its greatest challenge yet.

Pearl Harbor – (photo courtesy of the National Archives)

CHAPTER 4 – THE 1940'S – SACRIFICE AND SURVIVAL

"Do not accustom yourself to consider debt only as an inconvenience; you will find it a calamity."
— Samuel Johnson

In 1940, the growing American population now stood at 132 million and continued to struggle economically. The average annual income sank to $956 per year. Democratic President Franklin Roosevelt, now in his seventh year in office, watched on as Adolf Hitler and the Nazi army reigned over much of Europe. Auto manufacturing remained low with only 2.7 million automobiles produced, a minor increase of 300 thousand vehicles over 1930.

The Drums of War

While the Great Depression ended in 1939, auto loan underwriting remained tight and with it, repossession volume was light. The winds of war in the air, the United States instituted the Selective Training and Service Act of 1940. With it, all men between the ages of twenty-one and forty-five became required to register for the draft. This was the first peacetime draft in United States history.

On October 17, 1940, the first federal hinderance to repossession activity became law. The Soldiers' and Sailors' Civil Relief Act (SCRA) (codified at 50 U.S.C. §§ 3901—4043) provided civil protections against collections, foreclosure, and repossession activities. The SCRA required judicial approval for repossessions against service members and their dependents. With 9 percent of the population, enlisted or commissioned in one of the branches of the armed forces, the recovering but evolving repossession industry was back on the ropes.

Straw Men

America's first recorded "straw buyer" auto fraud case surfaced in 1941. A fraud enterprise named "Choice Motor Sales, was run and operated by used car dealer, Michael Boras of Brooklyn, New York. Choice Motor Sales was located at 1743 Bushwick Ave., Brooklyn, New York.

Boras recruited a vast array of straw buyers, ranging from street vendors, bartenders, truck drivers and even five NYPD cops. For a paltry $10-$15, these "straw buyers" would sign on the dotted line for auto loans with the assurance that they would be paid off shortly. Meanwhile, Boras received his customary $600 dealer commission from the finance companies. Boras would then sell the financed vehicles for cash, which he would then use to make payments on the loans and perpetuate the scheme, a traditional "Ponzi Scheme."

Of course, like all Ponzi Schemes, it all finally came crashing down. Twenty loans and two years later, the three defrauded finance companies noticed the common threads in their losses. Boras and the fact that their defaulted loans were not in possession of the alleged borrowers. $100 thousand in losses later, the District Attorney uncovered Bora's "straw buyer" scheme.

Boras pleaded not guilty of the charges and made bail of $2,500. Five NYPD officers involved were reprimanded internally for their participation. At the time of this writing, he location of Choice Motor Sales is still a car dealership. Obviously, the current owners are unrelated to Boras.

A Trigger-Happy Ending

Driving down from New York and arriving in New Jersey just after midnight on March 11, 1942, thirty-two-year-old Wilbur Critchfield spotted his target. Climbing into the vehicle, he was greeted by a .38 round in the leg from an unnamed borrower. Critchfield was quick to explain what he was doing. The man apologized and Critchfield drove the repossessed vehicle to a Dr. Heller in Elmhurst who extracted the bullet while Critchfield reported the incident to arriving police at 4.am. – Daily News (New York, New York) - March 11, 1942

Officers did not immediately file charges on the borrower and were waiting for Critchfield to heal to determine the extent of injury. Critchfield was mentioned as working for *"a Queens firm specializing in repossessing autos."* Perhaps all a coincidence, but The Barnes Detective Agency, owned by Ray and Lorna Lou Barnes, was also in Flushing, Queens, New York. Lorna Lou's maiden name was also Critchfield, and she had a brother listed as W. Ray Critchfield.

A First for Houston

One hot Texas Friday afternoon, W.C. Edsall, a twenty-six-year-old welder, angry because his car had been repossessed, shot a Houston automobile agency employee to death. Several hours later as he was trying to make his getaway, he was shot near Brenham by the Brenham Chief of Police. He was hospitalized and listed in critical condition and charged with murder. The repossessor killed was twenty-year-old Alvin S. Ablon. - The Eagle - (Bryan, Texas) – August 1, 1942

Had this happened after dark, Edsall may have fared better with Texas law. This would by no means be Houston's last repossession murder.

America Shifts Gears

Just before 8:00am on Sunday December 7, 1941, Japan attacked Pearl Harbor. Four days later, the United States declared war on Germany and Japan and the world would never be the same. By February of 1942, Detroit had transformed into an "Arsenal for Democracy." There were no new automobiles manufactured for personal use in the United States again until 1946.

In 1942, the draft age was lowered to eighteen and Americans enlisted into the armed forces in droves. Peer pressure and societal perceptions of persons, who of age were not in the service by choice or draft, were viewed as suspicious, unpatriotic or cowards. This was so extreme, that many men classified "4F" or physically unfit to serve, committed suicide. It is most probable, that during this era, only men over the age of 45 and those classified as unfit to serve "4F" would be available to repossess what few assignments were available.

Rationing and Repossessions

With America mobilized for war, austerity measures were introduced to conserve just about every commodity possible. From milk to meat and gas to rubber, you needed a ration card or certificates to acquire much of anything that might be needed for the war effort. With new car production frozen and replacement parts scarce, the public often relied on black market suppliers to fill their needs. The repossession industry, long accused of stealing car parts and property, came under the focus of the Rationing Boards.

In July of 1942, the rationing boards issued a new law requiring "all sellers of tires and tubes, sellers of motor vehicles and Repossessors: (a) at the close of business on the last day of every month, take an inventory based on a physical count of all new tires and tubes, retreaded and recapped tires and used tubes and tires in his possession." - The Town Talk - (Alexandria, Louisiana) - July 11, 1942

Of course, this left a lot of room in the middle of the month to do business and one can easily imagine many spare tires went missing. Unfortunately, seeing the opportunity to make a buck while the repossession volume died, Harry R. Keifrieder, an adjuster for an unnamed finance company, took it a step further and got involved in a black-market tire ring. On September 10, 1942, he was arrested by Federal agents for "accepted transfer and delivery of 175 new passenger automobile tires on or about August 1st, without rationing certificates. - The Wilkes-Barre Record - (Wilkes-Barre, Pennysylvania) - September 11, 1942

As patriotic as everyone seemed, people needed things and people needed to make a living. Law or no law.

The Unsinkable Frank Mauro

The USS Hornet sinking, Battle of Solomon Islands on October 26, 1942 – (US Government)

After Pearl Harbor, a bulky eighteen-year-old, six-foot-one- and 275-pound Frank Mauro Gesualdo rushed to the recruiting office. Choosing the closest office to his home he tried to enlist in the Air Force. But the recruiters took one look at him and said, "'*We're looking for fliers, not bombs.*'" The next closest recruiting office was the Navy, and that's where fate took him.

On the morning on October 27, 1942, the USS Hornet was sunk by a pair of Japanese destroyers in the Battle of the Solomon Sea. With it, Frank and his crew members were sent adrift in lifeboats. Frank and his fellow sailors took turns hanging from the side of the overcrowded raft. Watching his fellow exhausted sailors slip beneath the waves or succumb to the swarming sharks, he clung to the only thing he could grab before his ship compartment was hit, the same rosary beads that his father carried into World War I.

Seventy-two-hours later, Frank's prayers were answered, and they were rescued. This is an account that one of his sons made of his navy years. His faith, tenacity and conviction forged during these days would later serve him in an industry he had probably never even thought of before in his still short life.

The Other Bud

At just about the same time as Frank Mauro went to the recruiting office, the Krohn brothers were doing the same. Out of the odd chance that tragedy could befall them both in combat, sixteen-year-old Allen M. Krohn opted for the Merchant Marines while his brother went to the Navy. Allen, "Bud", as he was later known, spent the war as Japanese submarine bait on lightly armed tankers loaded with highly flammable aircraft fuel through the thousands of Pacific Atolls. Spared the Japanese kamikaze, submarine and manned torpedo attacks, Bud made it through the war and stayed with the Merchant Marines until 1953, when he chose another calling on land.

Fourteen and Fit to Fight

In 1940, at the age of fourteen, Edward Francis Dunleavy of Scotia, New York joined the National Guard. When the war in Europe began, he was already eighteen. "Eddie" became attached to the 811th Tank Destroyer Battalion, a specialized unit whose purpose was to slow enemy armor advances, often behind enemy lines. The 811th was attached to numerous Divisions and saw heavy action on many fronts including the Battle of the Bulge, The Siegfried Line, and the crossing of the Rhine.

Edward served honorably and upon discharge, met his wife Beverly Anne Snyder whom he married in 1949. Coincidentally, the same year that his career in the finance world as a manager at Domestic Finance Company. In the years that followed, Ed began to develop a vision of another career.

The Mob Rules

Crowd Resents Car Seizure

Police Called to Disperse Throng Booing Repossessor

Traffic was tied up in the heart of the Long Beach business district and police reserves were called out to disperse a crowd estimated at 3,000 persons. The crowd gathered at Fourth St. and Pine Ave., booed and taunted an unnamed man attempting to repossess an automobile, he had sold to another. The borrower, who claimed to owe $150 on the car, challenged the man's heavyhanded tactics, as did the gathered crowd. Passing a hat in the crowd, a collection of $50 was taken and the money handed over to the would-be repossessor.

Wisely, the man agreed to drop the matter and police dispersed the crowd with no further incident. The Los Angeles Times (Los Angeles, California) – November 11, 1942

Reporting has always been somewhat haphazard, vague, and often inaccurate in identifying the difference between lenders, adjusters, and private parties in repossession matters. As mentioned earlier, during and after the Great Depression, repossession and repossessors were not viewed in a favorable light by most Americans. World War II did not soften these sentiments one bit.

More Mistaken Identities

While the boys were fighting overseas and shooting at the Japanese, Germans and Italians, Mrs. Mildred Emmons of Upper Darby, PA was shooting at a repossessor from her second-floor window. Mistaking forty-nine-year-old Edward Gray "a negro" the newspaper article adds, for a car thief, this former President of the Upper Darby Council of Republican Women, grabbed her rifle, locked and loaded and took the law into her own hands. Gray was taken to a Delaware county hospital and treated while Mrs. Emmons was charged with assault and battery. – The Times Tribune - (Scranton, Pennsylvania) – September 23, 1943

This all-too-common claim of mistaken identity has been a common issue and defense in many, if not most repossessions, even to this day.

A Long Wait

As if the repossession industry image wasn't bad enough before the war, "Adjusters" during this era were shunned, which may not mean a lot to us in the modern era, but at that time, reputation extended into many aspects of the lives of the Adjusters and their families. With the cessation on new automobile manufacturing, what was left were used car loans to an impoverished nation, whose sole bread earners were in many cases in military service and protected by 1940's Soldiers' and Sailors' Civil Relief Act (SCRA.) The war machine at home was keeping employment high and with no new cars, no new loans and SCRA protections, the still young repossession industry was essentially dead.

VJ Day, Times Square – (photo by National Archives)

With sixty million killed worldwide, on August 15, 1945, Japan surrendered, and World War II came to a merciful end. Returning service members came home with a renewed demand for auto loans and the American love affair with the automobile recommenced. It took Detroit awhile to switch back to auto production, but by the end of 1946, auto sales more than doubled their pre-war levels of 1.1 million with over 2.2 million automobiles manufactured.

Meet Al

Discharged from the service in 1946, World War II veteran, Alvin "Al" Michel went to work for the Bank of Ohio as a Collections Officer. While working at the bank, Al made friends with Paul Leleu, an NAAFA member. Paul suggested that Al apply for membership with the NAAFA as a repossession agent for an opening in their Cleveland market. Al applied and was approved, leaving the bank to start his office in Cleveland and Youngstown, Ohio in 1952.

In 1957 the then, AFA membership territory for Detroit became available. Al applied and was accepted. Al operated AFA repossession agency offices in Detroit, Cleveland, and Youngstown until 1960. Selling the Cleveland and Youngstown locations, Al moved his family to Detroit in 1961 where he operated Midwest Recovery and Adjustment Service for many years to come. Unfortunately for Al, Detroit became a new battle ground with more casualties in the years to come.

Al Michele –(photo by the AFA)

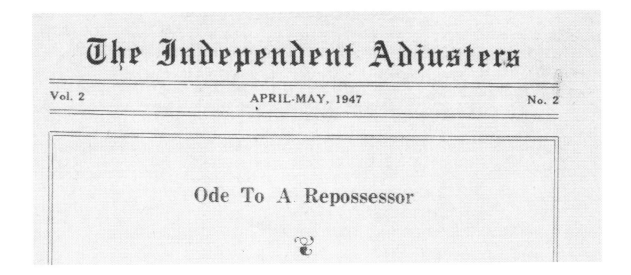

The Independent Adjusters

Vol. 2   APRIL-MAY, 1947   No. 2

Ode To A Repossessor

Self Consciousness

With the rebirth of the auto industry, it was a new era for the repossession industry. For most, SCRA protections had expired, and, with a rebounding auto industry, the repossession industry was back in business, but painfully aware of their public image problems. This self-perception is well articulated in the form of a quaint poem published in the April-May 1947 "The Independent Adjusters" newsletter.

There's a man in every town,
Yes, and this man gets around
Rain or shine
He's on the find.
No, he's no policeman with a gun
And shiny badge,
Or a doctor with a little black bag.
It's true he has a profession
Which is hunting and guessing
And at that he must be good
Altho with most folks, his job
Is misunderstood.
He searches far and wide on the plains,
The hills and in the woods.

He's lied to and lied about.
He's accused, excused and kicked out.
But he never stops to fret and pout.
He may get tired, but he never gives out.
He knows all the crooks, cheats, deadbeats
And their hangouts.

It's true he'll snoop around.
In every alley, garage and hole in town.
He takes chances with his life
Which causes worry to his loved ones
And wife.

He's on the alert to all remarks
He grasps every conversation in every part
He never loses faith or heart
He's shown very little respect
But even that he doesn't expect.
But, after all he's to be admired –
For his prompt and efficient services
Are much desired.

So, in closing may I say
Don't forget in some way to pay
Our faithful Repossessors and investigators
Their due respect and praise
For you are sure to need one of them
Some of these days.
S.C. DeWeese;
Allied Finance Adjusters, Agency Owner

This poem had repeatedly circulated through the repossession industry for decades. As antiquated as it may seem now, these perceptions and issues are as relevant now as ever.

Harvey and the Sea Monster

Attached to the 49th General Hospital in postwar occupied Tokyo, Japan, a nineteen-year-old Army PFC Altes wrote to his parents of an incident "*which he'd remember all his life.*" According to Altes letter home, troops in the Tokyo-Yokohama area were listening to an Armed Forces Radio Station (AFRS) broadcast about seven o'clock on the night of May 29th, 1947, when an excited reporter interrupted. The broadcaster went on to make an alert to all soldiers in the area that there was a disturbance in Tokyo Bay and two U.S. ships were missing.

PFC Harvey Altes, son of Mrs. Michael Altes, eight Genung street, described the incident in a letter to his folks as one which he'd remember all his life. Altes is attached to the Forty-ninth General Hospital in Tokio.

Red-faced Army brass told part of the story, too. It seems that the Armed Forces Radio Service, looking around for some unusual way to mark the fifth birthday of its establishment, perpetrated the hoax.

According to Altes' letter home, troops in the Tokio-Yokohama area listening to an AFRS broadcast about seven o'clock one night, when an excited announcer broke in to alert all troops in the area. He mentioned a mystery disturbance in the bay, and said two U. S. ships were missing.

A few minutes later, wrote Altes, the program was interrupted again by a report that an undescribed sea monster had crawled from the bay onto land. All persons were ordered to get off the streets and stay off.

The next bulletin reported the monster as being twenty feet high, apparently a prehistoric freak driven ashore by some subterranean eruption. The monster, the announcer said, had wrecked a train, injuring some passengers, and had crushed a police box in a Tokio suburb. One soldier, injured by the monster's thrashing tail, was being sent to Altes' hospital for treatment.

By that time, Altes noted, "there was no doubt in our minds. We thought the monster must exist if it came over in such apparently authentic reports. We had no reason to suspect anything but an historical event in the making."

The stream of bulletins came faster. Military police were reported firing futile shots into the monster as it lumbered toward municipal Tokio, leaving a trail of destruction. Meanwhile Army planes roared low overhead, apparently searching for the monster.

Then came another report. The beast was cornered in a downtown alley and an AFRS mobile radio unit was on its way there to continue the stream of reports. A new, excited announcer, possessed of a vivid imagination and a facile tongue, described the overflowing crowds, the green smoke of phosporus bombs, and the tear gas of a chemical mortar battalion combining with the intermittent roarings of MP flame-throwers holding the creature at bay.

Then the troops moved in for the

PFC Harvey Altes (right) – (photo courtesy of Nicki Merthe-Altes)

Middletown Times Herald, 17 June 1947 - © Middletown Times Herald — USA TODAY NETWORK

"A few minutes later" wrote Altes, *the program was again interrupted by a report of an undescribed sea monster that had crawled from the bay onto land. All persons were ordered to get off the streets and stay off! The next bulletin, according to Altes' letter, reported the monster as being 20 feet high, apparently a prehistoric freak driven ashore by some subterranean eruption. The monster, the announcer said, had wrecked a train injuring some passengers, and had crushed a police box in a Tokyo suburb. One soldier, injured by the monster's thrashing tail, was being sent to Altes' hospital.*

By that time, Altes noted, *"there was no doubt in our minds. We thought that the monster must exist if it came over in such apparently authentic reports. We had no reason to think that anything other than an historical event was in the making."* The story carried on, getting worse and worse until they broke character and broadcasted that it was just a joke performed to celebrate the AFRS 5-year anniversary. - Middletown Times Herald - (Middletown, New York) – June 17, 1947

Harvey Altes was just one of tens of thousands of occupying troops in Japan, including General Douglas MacArthur, fooled by this one-hour hoax and MacArthur was not at all amused. This broadcast had caused widespread panic even amongst the top brass. The next day, five of the soldiers responsible were relieved of their duties, pending an investigation and several allegedly transferred to Korean as punishment. The idea for "The Tokyo Hoax" was obviously based on Orson Wells' "War of the Worlds" broadcast and while this sounds like the inspiration for "Godzilla", but the film's Japanese creators seemed to have had no knowledge of this event.

PFC Harvey Altes would be discharged and back in his hometown of Middletown, New York in no time. Harvey married Joan Marie Kinney of Port Jervis, New York, and moved to Daytona Beach in 1951. The rest is repossession history, but we'll get to that soon enough.

New Blood

Plucked from sea and with the war behind him, Frank Mauro returned to his native Chicago where he'd grown up in the old Italian neighborhood near Taylor Street. The son of immigrants from their namesake town of Gesualdo, Italy, he attended Crane Technical High School before the war. Now back on the block, Frank began working on cars, repairing, fixing, selling, and of course, eventually repossessing them.

In time, Frank's talent for repossessions grew and he opened his first collection agency one block from Wrigley Field. Armed with his license as a private detective he soon joined the National Association of Allied Finance Adjusters (NAAFA). Frank had survived the Japanese, sharks, and the mean streets of Chicago. He was a natural fit for the repossession industry.

1940's NAAFA Conference Meeting with Map – (photo by the AFA)

A Friendly Divorce

With the World War II behind them, they industry saw a resurgence and In 1948, the NAAFA found itself torn in what direction to take the, then crowded fifteen-year-old association. Who exactly led this revolt and why is unknown, but by joint agreement, the NAAFA split into two separate associations. The Allied Finance Adjusters (AFA), who retained the original bylaws and standing, and the National Finance Adjusters (NFA.) Ray Barnes, one of the founders of the NAAFA from 1936 became the NFA's first President.

The exact timing of this is also unclear. The AFA incorporated in 1951 and the NFA's 1962 Directory states their origin at 1948. Even more peculiar is a photo, supposedly from 1951 per Chuck Cowher, that shows the AFA leaders before a coverage area map that still used the NAAFA header on it.

By agreement, both associations allowed members to retain their membership in both organizations. Following Ray Barnes' presidency was Frank Hyde, Tom Wolfe, George Turner, Louis Light and industry newcomer Frank Mauro. At Frank's side were some colorful characters like his longtime friend Art Lamoureux of Detroit who was its twelfth President.

Art, a fellow repossession agency and auto auction owner from Detroit, was a US Army World War II veteran and Frank's right-hand man in the NFA. Between Frank and Art, they allegedly, each owned a 3 percent share of "The Sands Hotel" in Las Vegas. Also, in the new NFA were Burton Greenwood, son of William Greenwood, founder of "Greenwood's Garage", in Baltimore. Burton was the longtime front man for the NFA. A well dressed and true gentleman, according to all that met him, much like his son "Buzz."

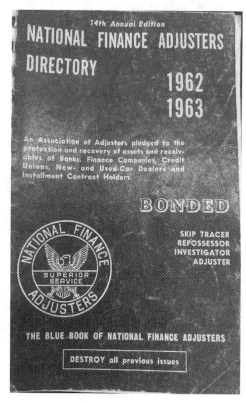

1962 NFA Directory – 14th Annual

In the Dash

In 1949, Chrysler introduced the first technological challenge to the repossession industry since it began. The introduction of the key locking ignition switch quickly grew into a product standard feature in all makes and models over the next several years. While door locks had been around since 1920, steering wheels remained unlocked. Bypassing these locks from behind the dashboard using a classic technique later termed "hot wiring", Adjusters quickly adapted and learned to overcome these locks.

Regardless of its shortcoming, in April 1949, Popular Mechanics wrote: "*Among the innovations of primary interest to the driver is the combination ignition and starter switch which eliminates the starter button. The car starts by turning the ignition key slightly beyond the 'ignition on' position. When released, the key automatically returns to 'ignition on'. Aside from the convenience to the driver, this starter makes it impossible for children to move a car which has been left in gear by pushing the starter button.*"

Soon to follow, Chrysler introduced the first matching sets of door and ignition keys.

Tales From the Field

In 1949, an article titled "*We Stole 10,000 Cars*", appeared in the Washington DC Evening Star. NAAFA founder Ray Barnes, shared several "war stories" from the repossession field. According to the writer, smooth faced Barnes sported a pair of scars, one on the chin from a borrower in Boston and another from a wrench in Cleveland that came with a fractured skull. In the article, Barnes shared information that much of the usually secretive industry, would probably have preferred he had kept quiet.

This included tactics employed by him and others of the era. Barnes claimed to often use a device known as a "Phantom Tow Bar". This device is described as a thin, strong steel rod so inconspicuous that the car towed appeared to be following without a driver. He mentions an occasion of having to employ a forked stick and a canvas bag to capture a rattlesnake kept in a target vehicle to thwart his efforts.

Of course, the snake being personal property, he had to store and return it to its owner is safe condition. Ray spoke of having to return property as odd as a stuffed owl, a mink coat, and a cheese sandwich. On another situation, Ray had attempted to return a pair of rubber boots to their owner in Pomona, California where things got out of hand.

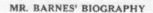

1947 NAAFA Directory
Ray Barnes Biography

The borrower owned an almond orchard and had not noticed the vehicle missing when Ray arrived. Handing the boots over as the man was sharpening a long pruning blade, Ray advised the man of the repossession. Ray remarked at being caught off guard by the man's lack of emotion and silence, which was suddenly broken by a swing of the blade to his head. Having missed, the man's anger grew, and he stood poised to take another swing, but not before Barnes drew his revolver and shot the man in the leg.

Ray claimed to have once recovered ten vehicles financed by notorious members of the Brooklyn based mafia enforcement gang, "Murder Inc." After recovering several of the vehicles, Barnes claimed the death threats began coming in. By then, Murder Inc. was already on the police radar and they moved in on them, possibly saving Barnes' life.

During both his early years in California and his later "Barnes Detective Agency" years in New York, Ray spent extensive time on the road. At that time, he claimed to make $35 to $250 per recovery ($378 to $2,700 in 2021 value.) These news stories by Ray and Lorna Lou carried on for decades. How these were received within the young industry is unknown, but these seemingly dime store novel accounts, are some of the best and earliest accounts of the lives and tactics of repossession agents and skip tracers from the era. - Washington DC Evening Star - (Washington DC) - September 18, 1949

Barnes' statement on repossession fees is fairly consistent with that of an Oakland, California agency owner, Charles Clark of National Auto Recovery Bureau (NARB) from a March 20, 1949, tell all posted in the Star Press of Muncie Indiana, where it is stated *"His fee ranges from $10 to $500 depending on the amount of effort involved."*

1953 NAAFA Convention, Chicago – (photo by the AFA)

CHAPTER 5 – THE 1950'S
– THE GOLDEN AGE

"If you think nobody cares if you're alive, try missing a couple of car payments."
- Earl Wilson

If ever there was a "Golden Age" of the repossession industry, this was probably it. The average annual income of the population of 152 million had almost risen back to its 1920 level of $3,300 a year. With wartime austerity measures long gone; the rebounding auto industry had soared to new record highs in production with 6.5 million vehicles produced for an average sale price of $2,201. Harry Truman was President and the national unemployment rate was a healthy 4.3 percent.

Bigger, Faster, Stronger

The horsepower race began in the late 40's with GM's overhead valve V8 engine and in 1951, Chrysler produced it's first Hemi engine. Cars were getting longer, wider, and lower with space-age styling. Characterized by rocket shaped taillights, chrome plating and two-toned exterior paint, they mirrored the optimism of the post-war era. Throughout the years, auto manufacturers came and went with names like Kaiser, Fraser and Crosley eventually fading to extinction to the dominant titans of Detroit, namely GM, Ford, and Chrysler.

Massive technological developments had entered the auto industry, including air conditioning, power steering and brakes, seat belts and the automatic transmissions. Despite these developments, recovery tactics had not changed dramatically from the previous decade. Hot wiring, lock picking, strongarm threats and towing continued to be the primary methods for involuntary repossession.

With World War I veterans getting "long in the tooth", and a massive population of World War II veterans back home, there was no shortage of fresh testosterone in the ranks of the industry. Easy as it was to find men brave enough to creep around in the middle of the night and repossess vehicles, with employment rates high, the character of the men in the field varied dramatically.

Joined at the Hip

As the auto industry and the economy grew, the repossession industry grew at its side. The number of repossession agencies expanded as did the memberships in repossessor associations. These growing associations met annually in large national conventions hosted in four-star hotels in major metropolitan cities. With air travel still in its infancy, they travelled by car or train for days and weeks, often accompanied by their wives and children.

Some of these agency owners, like the Greenwoods and Summs, were already second-generation owners by then. Their children, in many cases, would grow up to carry on the family business in the decades to come. These conventions created lifelong bonds between these owners as well as their families. This is an industry tradition that carries on to this day.

Harvey Heads South

The transmission on Harvey's car went out and he didn't have the money to fix it. Talking with the owner of a car dealer in Daytona Beach, Florida, he proposed a solution. The dealer had a bad check written to him on a sale and wanted the car back. Long story short, Harvey got the car and the seed was planted.

Complexion "Ruddy?" - Harvey Altes' state investigator ID. (photo courtesy of Nicki Merthe-Altes)

In 1951, twenty-three-year-old Harvey Altes took over a small Daytona Beach,

Florida detective agency. Soon after, a lender in North Carolina assigned him to repossess a truck in neighboring Bunnell. Harvey located the truck in a field and recovered it for a whopping $35 ($378.16 in 2021 value.) His first professional repossession.

From that moment, Harvey was in the repossession business and for many decades to come. Harvey would become one of the most influential characters in the industry as well as the state of Florida. In addition to his success in the recovery and investigation industry, he served as a special investigator for the state Attorney General and served many years as a Constable throughout the 1960s. Harvey earned the nickname "*The Godfather*" and with it, the respect, and influence that came with it.

The Rolling Jewelry Box

One of the earliest found legal judgments against the repossession industry over personal property occurred in Florida of July of 1952. The Key West Citizen reported that Circuit Judge Stanley Milledge ruled against the General Motors Acceptance Corporation (GMAC) for a claim of damages by a professional dancer named Shirley Ramun. According to Ramun, the Repossessors took her vehicle when she was only two months delinquent, and the check was already in the mail when they arrived. She sued for $33K in claimed damages for physical damage to herself as well as lost cash and jewelry from inside the repossessed vehicle, a claim that resonates to this day and plays itself almost daily.

Who doesn't keep their cash and jewelry in the car, when they know they're behind on payments, right? The judge ruled against GMAC stating that a court order is required for repossessions, even on conditional sales contracts. GMAC appealed the ruling with unknown results.

Blood and Fire on New Years Eve

Temperatures had dropped near freezing on New Year's Eve as the taxi driver spotted the burning car parked on an east Dallas side Street. Flames glowed through the charred windows illuminating the dark street sending the cab driver to call the police, unaware of the car's macabre contents. Arriving fire and police soon stumbled across the most heinous repossession murder in the industries history and at the time, one of the worst in the history of Dallas.

Having extinguished the fire in the car, it became immediately apparent to the firefighters that there was something laid out on the floorboards of the sedan. Upon closer examination, they discovered it was a someone, but with no identification on the body, they could only assume who it was based on the vehicle registration.

The torched car of Edwin Joe Campbell, on the backseat floorboards, his burned body - (NBC5/KXAS Television News Collection, University of North Texas Special Collections.)

Twenty-five-year-old Edwin Joe Campbell had been working as a collector and skip tracer for the Pacific Finance Company for three years that night. He had developed into a skilled skip tracer and was in the process of closing in on a debtor who'd skipped out three months behind on loan payments for a 1947 Buick Sedan. Unfortunately, he found him.

Investigating officers pulled Campbells burnt body from the charred wreckage to find four .25 caliber bullet holes in the back of his head. Coincidentally, the cab driver carried a pistol of the same caliber and was arrested as a suspect, but soon released. The Coroner later discovered that Campbell had also suffered a broken jaw and had several teeth knocked out showing evidence of a severe beating. Digging in deeper to Campbell's activities of the early evening, they soon discovered that Campbell had been hot on the trail of unemployed bus driver and debtor, twenty-four-year-old Donald Hawkins Brown.

Police soon discovered that Brown had recently been living in boarding house with his wife and two small children three blocks away from where the burning car was found. Arriving at the flat, they found Brown's room vacant and empty, except in the attic where they discovered a pair of mens pants covered in blood and smelling of gasoline. Also found, was Campbell's wallet and some personal belongings.

A nationwide manhunt ensued with much of the nation on the lookout for the 47' Buick Sedan, Texas license plate JVT801. But Brown hadn't gone far and had assumed the alias surname "Gross" the day after the crime. Investigators moved on a tip that Brown had recently applied for a job at a taxidermy shop in Fort Worth and swooped in on him when he came to discuss the job with the shop owner on January the 14th.

Once in custody, Brown denied having killed Campbell, but did admit to knowing who he was. Asked where he was that evening, Brown just lowered his head, wrung his cuffed hands and replied "No, I don't." Also arrested as an accomplice was Brown's wife, Billie Joe, who furiously denied any knowledge of the crime and claimed to have no idea why her husband, she and her two children, eight-months and two-years-old were taken into police headquarters.

Campbell, a Texas Tech graduate and son of a Texas Ford dealer, was laid to rest on January 3, 1953, at St. Rita's Catholic Church. Campbell left behind a widow, Helen and an infant son.

Justice was swift once upon a time, and by April 20, 1953, the trial against Brown commenced. Although the murder weapon was not located, during the trial, the District Attorney presented four key pieces of evidence. Brown's bloody trousers, Campbell's personal items found in the attic of Brown's rented flat, testimony from his landlady that he, his wife and children had moved in the middle of the night the night of the crime and witness testimony by neighbors who had seen Campbell and Brown meet at the boarding house and in an argument over the past due payments and that Campbell had threatened to repossess the car then.

On the defense, Brown's wife, Billie Joe, testified that he had been home all night long. Explaining the blood on his trousers, she testified that he'd broke a tooth and cut his lip changing a tire that night. Mrs.'s Brown's perjury was quickly dismissed as the DA had already tested the blood on the trousers and some found in the driveway which were determined to be O positive, the same as Campbell. Brown, nor his attorney had an answer for Brown's blood type.

It took six days to pool the jury and about three days of trial, but on April 29, 1953, after less than two hours of jury deliberation, the jury had reached a decision. Before a packed courthouse and, unusual for the era, filmed for television, the verdict was read. Campbell was sentenced to death.

Brown, appeared unphased and simply stated "All right." Brown's wife and mother broke into tears and clung to him until ultimately, he was dragged away into custody from the courtroom.

Also present at the trial was Campbell's twenty-three-year-old widow, Helen. On May 7th, while visiting her sister and brother-in-law in Odessa where she was looking for work, she was sharing a soda with them, when she went to the bathroom. Soon after, Helen was discovered dead by suicide on the bathroom floor. She was buried in Ranger, Texas alongside Joe Campbell. They left behind a two-year-old orphan son, Stephen Allan Campbell.

Brown professed his innocence and managed to receive reprieve after reprieve until justice had run out of patience with him. On his last night on death row, Brown refused his final meal and told a reporter that; "It's their show, I hope they enjoy it." Brown was executed in the electric chair at midnight on January 12, 1955. He never confessed.

In an industry with many murders, and some unsolved, this one goes down as probably the most violent, gruesome, and callous.

Bud's New Calling

The Merchant Marines kept Bud at sea and away for months at a time. These periods were often followed by long periods on land, where a twenty-seven-year-old Bud Krohn found himself working part time repossessing cars in the San Francisco Bay Area. By 1953, Bud had quit the Merchant Marines and began his new career as an Adjuster repossessing cars and other chattel for the "Modern Adjustment Bureau" owned by William Orisman and Robert Steinert. It was here that his son, Ken, earned his way into the trade sweeping floors and making keys in the years to come.

Road Block

Patrick J. Collins and Edward Martin of the C.I.T Credit Corp. had just repossessed Mr. Harry Stevens' car from a Viers Mill, Maryland residence at about 10 p.m. and all was going well. That is, until about ten minutes later when they encountered the Montgomery County police road block. Stevens had called police and they sprung into action. Maryland required a writ of possession for repossessions and did not look kindly upon Repossessors attempting self-help repossessions.

Both men were arrested and released on $500 bonds pending trial. Evening star - (Washington, D.C.) - September 16, 1954

Since the dawn of the repossession industry, America has been a patchwork of different laws regulating the repossession process. It was not uncommon for adjusters to slip back and forth across state lines skirting the replevin process. Much to the dismay of law enforcement and the public, this "anything you can get away with" attitude was common for decades to come.

The VIN

In 1954, the US government collaborated with the auto industry and the Automobile Manufacturers Association in the creation of a standardized vehicle identification numbering system. The Vehicle Identification Number (VIN) now had a standard digit sequence as well as concealed chassis markings. Prior to this, states used the engine number to register and title vehicles, which was a common problem at that time when engines were replaced. Soon after, lenders began requiring VINs before approving and funding auto loans.

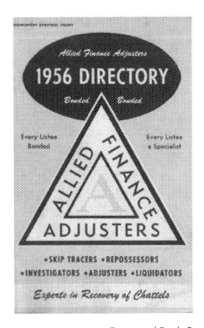 

Front and Back Cover the 1956 AFA Directory

1958 AFA Convention, Chicago

Born for the Business

Hank Leleu's long life in the repossession industry began in this decade. Hank, a second-generation agency owner, claimed that he cannot remember a time when he was not involved in the repossession business. His father, Paul Leleu of Chicago, was one of the founding AFA members since 1936.

Hank has fond memories of sitting in the backseat of his parent's car with brother Paul Jr. as his parents drove around Chicago locating and recovering "chattel", the common term for "collateral" in the early decades of the industry. In time, Hank would follow his father to work where he learned how to sweep floors and clean bathrooms. Eventually, he advanced to light filing and other duties such as cleaning up the storage lot and picking up the guard dog's droppings.

Graduating to the honor of conducting the inventory and removal of personal effects from the recovered vehicles, he eventually moved up to filling out vehicle condition reports and other office functions. Finally coming of age, Hank received his

ALLIED FINANCE ADJUSTERS CONFERENCE, INC. PLEDGE 1936-1985

Allied Finance Adjusters Conference, Inc. is pleased to send you this current, up-to-date directory for 1985-86. We wish to direct you to Pages 1 through 12 of this new directory and urge you to become familiar with their contents. Within these pages, you will become familiar with how Allied and its adjuster members work; thus, smoother recoveries for you.

Every Allied member is bound by the strict code of ethics inside the cover of this directory. He is required to advance his knowledge of any changes in his state's repossession, title and credit laws and to be at all times in strict compliance with those laws.

On behalf of the entire membership of Allied, I wish to extend our hearty thanks to our many client friends for your past trust and loyalty to each of us. We look forward to servicing your delinquent accounts for many more years to come. Remember, Allied is the oldest and most trusted name in the finance adjustment field. We are the cornerstone for the industry.

In closing, I would like to invite all Allied clients and members to our 49th Annual Convention in Boston, Massachusetts at the Westin Hotel — Copley Place — from July 30th through August 2, 1985.

Respectfully,

Henri Leleu
President
Allied Finance Adjusters Conference, Inc.

Henri "Hank" Leleu - from a 1985 AFA Directory

learners driving permit, and the rest of repo industry was opened wide to this teen. Now allowed to ride with the repossession agents in the field, he perfected the basics of hot wiring ignitions, picking locks, making door calls for payments, and skip tracing.

At the tender age of sixteen, Hank repossessed his first car, a 1961 Ford Starliner. He could even remember the location it was recovered from, North Avenue and North Austin streets in Chicago. Hank's endearing story is not altogether unique in the repossession industry, it is one of a hardworking family business with blue collar work values. This shared sense of tradition carries on amongst many agency owners and their families to this day.

The Firsty Handoff

In 1956, William "Frank" Greenwood of Greenwoods Garage, passed down the family business to his middle son Burt Greenwood. Burt had already served two years in the army and earned a degree from John Hopkins University at this point. The family business had grown so much that one lender set up an outpost in their office. This was the second generation to carry on this now almost one-hundred-year-old business.

A Pioneer Passes

Unexpectedly, on February 13, 1956, Ray L. Barnes, husband of Lorna Lou Critchfield Barnes and co-founder and ex-president of the Allied Finance Adjusters passed away of a heart attack at the age of fifty-three in their hometown of Flushing, New York. Ray and Lorna had no children and spent much of their free time on their 30-foot cruiser christened the "Lorna Lou" moored at the Bayside Yacht Club, where Ray was the Club Commodore and Lorna later served as a Chairperson. In their era, Ray and Lorna Lou were the closest thing to celebrities that the repossession industry had ever had.

Ray may have passed, but Lorna Lou was far from done with the repo industry.

The Teen Kings

"The Wink Westerners" had already been around since 1949, when its founder, then thirteen-year-old Ray Orbison, founded them. Sporting cowboy clothes and bandanas around their necks, they played Slim Whitman and Glen Miller covers on a local radio show with startup acts like Elvis Presley and Johnny Cash warming up for them. By 1955, Ray had discovered Rock and Roll and changed the band name to "The Teen Kings." It was soon after that when they recorded their first hit, "Ooby Dooby."

In 1956, the song was played by a record store owner friend of the band over the telephone to Sam Phillips of Sun Records. By late March, the band was signed to a contract. That meant that they would have to travel to Memphis. The Teen Kings had a number of changes in the band lineup and it was then that a local Lubbock guitarist and bandleader from Oklahoma whose band just had quit him was asked to come to Memphis with him. Nineteen-year-old James Golden of Lubbock wasn't that interested in this new rock and roll thing or moving out of state and declined to join him.

Eventually Ray Orbison went solo and became a music legend. About the same time, an unemployed James "Jim" Golden was sitting in his Lubbock motel room when he received a knock on the door. It was thirty-three-year-old World War II Army veteran Forrest D. "Frosty" Thomas and he was there to repossess his car. Seeing Golden dejected and down on his luck, Frosty asked him if he wanted a job.

This is the story of Jim's entrance into the repossession industry according to former ALSCO office owner and RSIG President, Ed Marcum, who heard it at dinner tables in the early days at ALSCO meetings.

More Mistaken Identities

Repossessor Taken for Thief, Shot

In the wee hours of the morning, Jules Spindler, twenty-eight, was behind the wheel of the car as he and Joseph Roth of the National Adjustement Bureau were "drifting" the car down the driveway. The repossession was going as planned until he accidentally struck the picket fence of thirty-five-year-old Willie W. Williams with the sedan. Awakened, Williams claimed to believe that someone was stealing his car when he grabbed his .45 caliber automatic pistol. Williams fired one round and struck Spindler in the back.

Spindler was listed as being in critical condition following surgery that day and it is unknown if he recovered. Williams was booked on suspicion of assault with the intent to commit murder. San Bernardino Sun – (San Bernardino, California) December 8, 1956

A New Barnes in the Industry

Also in 1956, another Barnes, unrelated but coincidentally also from Tulsa Oklahoma, like Ray Barnes, entered the repossession industry straight out of high school at the tender age of eighteen. After a short stint in the air force, Jack Spencer Barnes returned to Tulsa following in his father's footsteps and taking over his father's company

1959-1960 TFA Directory

after his passing. Barnes became a longtime leader in the NFA and mentor to many in the industry through his books. Jack's exploits, like Ray Barnes' are the stuff of legends, and almost as colorful.

Pregnant and Dragged

Thirty-year-old pregnant housewife Minerva Lee of Norwood Maryland was startled when she heard the sound of her station wagon's engine start in her front yard that Saturday afternoon at about 5:20pm. Rushing outside, she attempted to block it being driven away and only succeeded in getting her arm stuck in the side window as it passed by. At the wheel, just kept backing up, dragging the pregnant Minerva lee alongside him until hitting the street where she fell, suffering cuts, bruises and abrasions to her arms and legs. Mrs. Lee was admitted to the hospital and treated while police searched for the culprit.

Thirty-six-year-old Emory Harmon, an adjuster for the Eastern Acceptance Corp., soon after called police to report the repossession, making no mention of the incident. Police soon arrived at his lot and took him in custody. Harmon was charged with assault and battery, repossession by use of force and, auto theft since he had not received a writ of possession from the court before repossessing the vehicle. - Evening star - (Washington, D.C.) October 01, 1957

Stories of people being dragged during repossessions was not uncommon. The notion of breach of peace was not widely recognized by many. The Maryland State police had to be getting seriously tired of their writ of possession laws being so frequently ignored.

Murder Without Malice

On December 9, 1957, Repossessors, Robert Lumpkins and Thomas Ganoe, arrived at the Ponder, Texas farmhouse of Burnell Malone. Sent by an unnamed lender to repossess a sedan from Malone's son-in law, Boyd Fuller, they found their target vehicle in the driveway, but Fuller was not home. Discussing the the delinquent loan status with the farmer, Malone chose to remedy the situation and went to a back room to write a check. Lumpkins chose not to wait and took Fuller's car.

They hadn't gotten more than a few miles south to the town of Justin when Malone caught up to them. Cutting off Lumpkins driver, Ganoe, Malone dragged him from the chase car at gunpoint. Seeing what had developed behind him, Lumpkins turned the repossessed car around and sped to the rescue. Malone was beating Ganoe over the head with the pistol when Lumpkins emerged from the car and drew his pistol firing one deadly shot into forty-year-old Malone.

Lumpkins and Ganoe fled the scene as witnesses rushed to the dying farmer's side. Both men turned themselves into authorities immediately. No charges were filed against Ganoe but Lumpkins went to trial for "murder without malice" the following year. Lumpkins was acquitted of all charges. - Fort Worth Star-Telegram - (Fort Worth, Texas) November 26, 1958

Time for Another One

Dissatisfied with being shut out of the market by the AFA and NFA's exclusionary tactics, unaffiliated agencies united in discourse began banding together. In 1957, a suggestion from Frosty Thomas to "Dan Grey" of Fort Worth, Texas, led to the formation of the "Time Finance Adjusters" (TFA), incorporated on August 26, 1958. With the creation of yet one more association, competition in the local markets caused additional division to the already fractured industry. This division of unity within the industry only increased with time.

A Hot Car

Oil Geologist Amner Petty of Pasadena had gone out of town overnight only to discover his 1956 sedan missing from his driveway the next day at 1:40 p.m. Also missing was an innocent looking denim bag containing what Petty described as "highly dangerous" radioactive materials used in his work. The repossession was misreported in Los Angeles, but Burbank police tracked down the repossession as having been performed by San Fernando Recovery Bureau of Burbank. Police checked both the agency lot and the dealer, Lincoln-Mercury of Beverley Hills, but were unable to locate the car.

After several hours, police located the unnamed repossessors. Despite being told of the danger lurking in the trunk of the car, they still refused to disclose the whereabouts of the vehicle and advised that they would notify their company office of the radiation when they delivered it later in the week. - Pasadena Independent (Pasadena, California) – June 9, 1958

The article does not indicate if they were threatened with arrest, but their apparent ambivalence, naivety or ignorance of the dangers of radiation, even for the 50's, is amusing, if not a little startling. The danger of radiatioactive materials in the trunk of a repossessed car would later, by pure coincidence, reappear in film in 1984.

A First Generation

Ten years after starting at the Domestic Finance Company, Edward F. Dunleavy broke free and founded the "Professional Adjustment Agency" in a small office in Schenectady, New York in November of 1959. In the beginning the company's primary service line was third party collections, but soon after opening,

Edward F. Dunleavy, Founder of TCAR – (photo by Chris Dunleavy)

Ed diversified the company's offerings into Repossessions and credit reporting. Over the next twelve years Ed continued to build the company and then in 1973 he became the first company in the state of New York to contract with and automate his credit reporting services with TRW, now known as Experian.

Edward joined the ARA in 1966 and later in the 1970's, son Chris remarks that it took a good word from Art Christiansen to get him into the TFA.

Racketeers, thugs, wildcatters, Ex-Convicts and Muscle Men

California Secretary of State Frank M. Jordan came under fire in a state Senate Committee hearing with allegations that under his watch, California's $100 million a year collections industry was running amuck. Testimony of beatings, intimidations, bomb threats, and injury to children were laid out before the committee complaining that under Jordan "*conditions are growing worst in the fast-growing field of auto repossessions.*" The committee went on to add, "*Free from state regulation and with no state license required, it has provided a hunting ground for petty racketeers, thugs, wildcatters, ex-convicts and Muscle Men.*" The San Francisco Examiner (San Francisco, California) April 23, 1959

Darn those muscle men and their muscles! In California, these complaints carried on for years with no action as the west was very much living up to the "Wild" part of the "Wild West" image.

Repo Jobs

Paul was a tattooed World War II Coast Guard machinist veteran who didn't know how to swim. Clara was a young World War II widow and child of Armenian refugees living in San Francisco. After the war, when Paul's ship was decommissioned in San Francisco, he met Clara, and ten days later in March of 1946 they were married. By 1952, Paul had settled down and found a job working for San Francisco based CIT Financial as an automobile Repossessor.

Unable to have children, in 1955 they adopted a baby boy, and named him Steven Paul Jobs.

According to Steve Job's biography, in addition to repossessing cars, Paul Jobs bought, fixed, and sold cars. Jobs claimed that his college fund was paid for with broken down for $50 cars that he would fix and sell for $250. Through trips to the junkyards and dabbling with his father on cars, Paul gave Steve his first exposure to electronics.

Jobs claimed that his father did not have a deep understanding of electronics, but he managed to fix a lot of automobiles as he learned along the way. He claimed that his father had showed him the basics of electronics and through that spurred his interest. From the leathery loving hands of a San Francisco Repossessor was spawned one of the greatest innovators and technological leaders in world history.

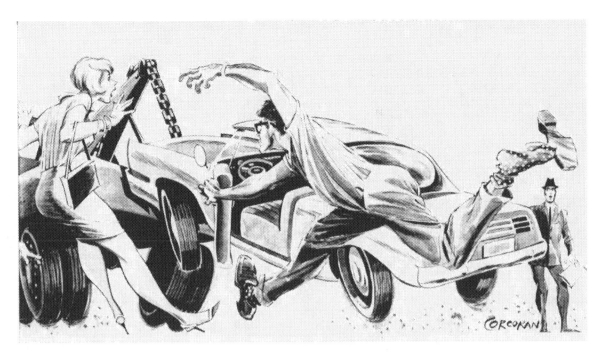

Photo by - © Baltimore Sun, drawing by Joseph Corcoran, article "Legal Car Snatch" by Malcolm Allen - October 9, 1966

CHAPTER 6 – THE 1960'S – AN ERA OF CHANGE

In 1960, former Five Star General Dwight Eisenhower was president of a United States population of almost 181 million people. Unemployment was high at 6.6 percent and GDP stood at 2.6 percent. Over 6 million vehicles were produced in this year with an average price of $2,752, more than a $500 increase from a decade earlier. The average annual income across the nation climbed to $5,600 a year, up from $3,300 ten years earlier.

On the guitar, Art Christiansen, top center, 1960. According to Art, this picture was
taken just a month before starting his first repossession company

Art Rocks

It was in this year that a young Art Christiansen left he the Navy and took a job for a New Jersey
Finance company. Soon after, he went out on a Friday night repossessing cars with a coworker, an
ex-Navy SEAL with a dotted line tattoo on his neck that read "Cut Here." Art was hooked and the
following Monday morning, he started Commercial Services Company, and within a couple of years,
became a Constable and made a name for himself as a gentleman repossessor in an industry that
still more resembled the "Wild West" than an arm of the financial services industry. Art would go
on to leave an indelible imprint on the industry for decades to come.

The NFA in Miami

Sheltered from the humid August Miami Beach weather, about 125 members of the National
Finance Adjusters met at the Deauville Hotel on August 20th. Then President, Jess B. Krug, a St.
Louis agency owner gave an interview to the Miami Herald stating that the repossession industry
welcomes the influx of compact cars onto the American roads because they add to the volume.

"*When dealers go in for volume, they start accepting marginal cases as credit risks in financing cars. That means more business for us.*" He was quoted as stating.

Krug reported that he was paid $35 ($322.81 in 2021 currency) for repossessing cars, $50 ($461.15) for light trucks and $75 ($691.73) for heavy trucks and trailers. Krug boasted of modern technologies growth in the industry touting portable key-cutters (Curtis key gun). "*Tumbler-jumpers" (shaker picks) and advanced models of "jump wires*" as evidence. Krug concluded the interview bewailing the industries "*lack of skilled qualified Repossessors.*"- The Miami Herald - (Miami, Florida) August 21, 1960

These fees were the association set fees and included $.08 cents a mile ($.74 in 2021 value.) These fees were later stated in a newspaper interview with Jack Watson of Atlantic Adjusters in New Jersey, also an NFA member. Interestingly, although unlikely, the article also says that there were 2,100 member firms in the NFA.

The Sieges of the 60's

Failing to receive an extension on his auto loan $300 behind in payments, Anthony Jones, a carpenter, had just left the finance companies office unaware of what the evening had in store for him. Armed with a tip that Jones was getting ready to skip town, on that same afternoon of September 18, 1961, at approximately 4:30 p.m., repossession agents spotted Jones' station wagon in an alley near the finance company office. Inside was Jones, his wife and five children, ages seven, six, four, two, and ten months. With a pair of cars, they blocked them in and the waiting game began.

Surviving through the night on milk and food provided by sympathetic passersby, the Jones family was still there in the morning. So were the unnamed repossessors who had refused to provide the press their names or company name. By 9:00 a.m., the Assistant Chief of Police had arrived and declared the situation first, a civil matter and second, an endangerment to local property. Citations were issued to all, and the threat of a tow truck was enough to get the agents to move their cars.

Jones and family then fled back to their rented North Highlands home with the agents on hard on their tail. Parking behind the house in a field, the agents blocked them in again. With family still in the station wagon, Jones pitched a tent and ordered a portable toilet to sit out the situation. The siege ended later that day when the finance company received a court order for the vehicle. Sheriff's deputies talked Jones into surrendering the vehicle. Sacramento Bee - (Sacramento, California) September 19, 1961

The Humboldt Holdout

Armed with a writ of possession over a $60 judgement, Humboldt County Sheriff's Deputies were ready to seize unemployed timber laborer, Louis Crosswhite's white and yellow 1956 station wagon. Fifty-year-old Louis claimed that he'd paid the judgement and refused to surrender the vehicle and deputies arrested him for obstruction. So, like any good father, he ordered his eleven children to lock themselves inside and let no one in. The children took shifts and kept the deputies at bay.

The Sherriff sent for a tow truck, but eventually left empty handed when the children still refused to exit the vehicle. Later that night, deputies again attempted to talk the kids out, but failed and pasted a Sherriff's hold sticker on the window. This was on a Wednesday.

Three days went by and still the children, led by Louise, his nineteen-year-old Humboldt State College daughter, remained unmoved. In the meanwhile, unable to afford bail, Crosswhite remained in custody with a plea hearing set for the following Tuesday, nearly a week after the ordeal began. Undaunted and firm in their conviction, the children sang hymns and read bible verses while vowing to sit it out until their father's hearing at the earliest.

Back Cover of the 1961 AFA Directory

"Daddy has lost everything he's worked for all his life. If I can help him now, I'm going to do it. We are going to do as God provides." stated Louise.

Complicating things, the judge had to disqualify himself because he had prior timber deals with Crosswhite and another judge was not available for an entire month. Eventually, it was discovered through the press, that, as Crosswhite claimed, his judgement was paid in the neighboring county it was issued in, but they were slow to notify Humboldt County. Vindicated, Crosswhite was released from custody and was allowed to keep the car.

For more than a decade afterward, Crosswhite continued to be a pain to the Humboldt County authorities, filing a $75,000 lawsuit for false arrest amongst other acts of contempt. For those who argue that repossessions should only be performed by law enforcement, this situation illustrates that even for police, this is not as simple as it seems. - The Pantagraph - (Bloomington, Illinois) June 23, 1962, and Star Tribune - (Minneapolis, Minnesota) February 27, 1966

Hank and the Human Hood Ornament

Repossessors Win = Woman's 13-Hour Car Hood Sit-On' Fails

LOS ANGELES (AP) - Mrs. Josephine Genit, a real estate saleswoman, ran to her car when she saw repossessors, Hank Harrison, forty, and Ron Moore, twenty-three, climb into it. One of them yelled, "I got it, I got it." "We'll see about that," said Mrs. Genit, as she jumped onto the hood. That was 4:30 p.m. on a Monday, and on the hood, Mrs. Genit remained all night.

Unresponsive to the agent's pleading for her to get off the car, three payments behind, she laid out flat on the hood. Eventually, neighbors came to her assistance with a mattress, blankets, a hot water bottle and food. Said Mrs. Genit; "The conduct of the Repossessors was gentlemanly. The hood was nice and warm. They started the engine up every once in a while."

At 5:30 a.m. the following Tuesday morning, they started the car up and drove away, slowly, with the blanket swathed Mrs. Genit still aboard and clinging to the windshield wipers. Three miles later they were at the storage yard and Mrs. Genit had lost her car. "It's a great blow," she said. "I have to drive clients around in my work." she admitted and acknowledged that she was behind in her payments. - San Bernardino Sun - (San Bernardino, California) January 14, 1965

This was not Hank Harrison's last brush with the press for the year.

While extreme in lengths, strongarm tactics like these were relatively and unfortunately common and would continue to be for years to come until cell phones and stronger breach of peace standards came to be. No respectable agency owner or lender would tolerate such dangerous and litigious antics today.

Don't be a Hank

Forty-year-old Hank Harrison was working solo on a Monday night. Driving off with a repossessed vehicle, he left his car behind to pick up later. Soon after, Hank returned to pick it up and found it missing, stolen. Reporting it to the Los Angeles Police, he reported losing the car, over $1,000 in tools and, his front teeth.

The unnamed original reporter made a point of reminding readers of Hank's January stand-off with Mrs. Josephine Genit. - Oroville Mercury Register - (Oroville, California) UPI Story - March 23, 1965

A few years later in 1968, Andy Warhol declared that in the future, everyone would have fifteen minutes of fame (paraphrased). In 1965, Hank Harrison had at least fifteen minutes of shame. Unless Hank had a good sense of humor, this was, at very least embarrassing and probably not good for business. Both stories were reported nationwide.

Also in 1968, March the 21st to be exact, Action Recovery Bureau posted an announcement in the classified ads on page 107 in The Van Nus News. "the following are no longer employed by the agency, are not authorized to represent the agency in anyway. Henry R. "Hank" Harrison, Paul Irving and Raymond Zielski. Signed Michael D. Cohn, DBA Action Recovery Bureau. Apparently, Hank's employer was fed up with his antics as well.

No Average Joe

Honorably discharged from the Air Force in 1959, young Joe Taylor became a police officer. Soon disenchanted with the "good-old boy" politics of a small-town police department, he took a job as an employee of Associates Finance Company in 1961. Below is Joe's recollection of the repossession industry of the 60's from a 2017 interview in CUCollector.com.

"Associates had an iron clad policy that their employees who handled repossessions were not allowed to repossess a customer's car until you actually sat down with the debtor, looked at his income and determine whether he could actually pay for the car. Only after determining that the debtor could not afford the payments were you allowed to take the car. Could you imagine that process in today's society? This training taught me the very important communications skills that served me well in the coming years when I had my own repossession agency."

"Tow trucks? Didn't need one. We either drove the car in or towed it with a chain hooked to our company car. Only if the tires were missing did we call for a roll-back. And, with a mostly non-transient society we didn't hear much about skip-tracers."

Joe Taylor, late 1960's per Joe

"It seemed that debtor's "back then" realized that if they couldn't, or wouldn't pay for their car, they understood that repossession was the alternative and the potential for violence during a repossession was virtually non-existent. Two instances I remember well. One, we had a delinquent debtor in Daytona Beach, some 75 miles from our office. I got to Daytona on a Greyhound bus and caught a taxi to the debtor's address. The debtor did not know I was coming and when I arrived and told him what I was there for, he gave me the keys to the pick-up truck."

"In the other instance, the debtor lived in West Palm Beach, some 200 miles from my office. This time I contacted the debtor and advised my purpose for calling. The debtor advised that the car would be at his residence address. Again, I rode a Greyhound bus to West Palm Beach, caught a taxi to the residence where I found the car with the keys inside and I drove it back to my office. As I said, the industry was so very different "back then."

In the years that followed, Joe would carry on becoming a pioneer in the emerging field of legal compliance. It could almost be argued that Joe invented it. Regardless of Joe's more peaceful experiences in the field, conflict was never far away for many.

As previously discussed, throughout the history of auto lending, lenders and car dealers have conducted their own repossessions with great regularity. In the banking industry, collecting on your own loans was a standard that carried on well into the 1990's. Of course, this practice was not without its own obvious perils, especially in the hands of untrained and inexperienced persons. These risks, also extended to the general public with private party transactions, and often with tragic results.

A DIY Fail

An unidentified man reported to police that despite his best efforts, the finance company won. Knowing that his lender was trying to repossess his car, he locked it in the garage. As a do-it-yourself car alarm, he tied a bicycle pedal to it, placed a tricycle under it, a steel barrel behind it and tied the garage door shut with thick steel wire and locked the garage door confident that with all of his obstacles attached to it, he would hear something should anyone attempt to take it. Entering the garage to go to work, the next morning, his car was gone. - La Habra Star - (La Habra, California) April 7, 1961

Legal? No. Common? Yes, especially in the past.

1960 AFA Convention, Philadelphia

Fatal Force

October 1962, Golansville, Virginia; used car dealer William Hodges, fifty-five, and his associate, Elliott Muncey, thirty-six, both white, set out to repossess a red 1950 sedan. Unable to find the vehicle, they waited until the borrower, Cariol Tolliver, a twenty-one-year-old black man, emerged from his residence. Seeing Tolliver approaching, Hodges and Muncey stopped Tolliver at gunpoint and forced him into their car. According to Tolliver, Hodges held the barrel of a .38 caliber pistol on his ribs while Muncey struck Tolliver across the face with his own .38 pistol.

In the process of the pistol whipping, Muncey's pistol fired and struck Hodges, killing him on the spot. Muncey demanded that Tolliver drive them to the hospital where Hodges was officially declared dead. Muncey fled but was later arrested and charged with the murder of Hodges and felonious assault on Tolliver. – Richmond Times Dispatch - (Richmond, Virginia) October 10, 1962

Stories of this type are not uncommon, and I hope to serve as cautionary tales for overzealous novices and car dealers who believe they can do it themselves.

A State of Unity

In 1961, the California Association of Licensed Repossessors (CALR) was incorporated. CALR stands as the longest standing state level repossession association in the nation. Through industry and political engagement, they have helped shape the states repossession and licensing regulations. CALR is perhaps the nation's best example of a state level association, one emulated nationwide.

One of its current Board members is co-founder Richard Egley's daughter Marcelle Egley.

Make That Four

1n 1962, the American Collectors Association, Inc. (ACA), formed the "American Finance Adjusters" (AFA.) Yes, another one and that wouldn't last long. Formed to serve the numerous collection agencies within the ACA ranks who also owned repossession companies, this association was a wholly owned division of the ACA and headquartered in Minneapolis, MN. The ARA provided directories to its members and was later renamed, the "American Recovery Association" (ARA) in 1965.

The industry now had four major national associations, the AFA, NFA, TFA and the ARA. By then, all the associations carried bonds, which had gradually increased to $100,000. All four circulated directories, and the offer of secured agency territory within the associations and little significant difference existed in membership benefits. None of these were established as "trade associations" and none took much action in the way of attempting to affect public policy or garner political support.

The growing numbers of associations gives the appearance of a continuously fracturing industry, but in reality, with most agencies belonged to two or more associations, the industry was actually very united in many ways. The common member bases kept fees fairly similar between them. This cohesion would eventually become a major issue and change the value and power of the associations dramatically.

1963 ACA School of Repossessions Manual

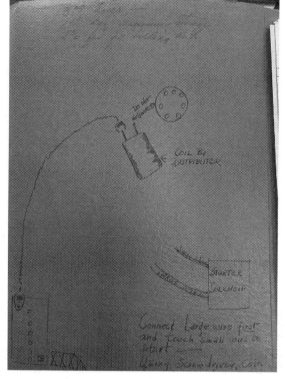

Hotwiring notes on the inside of the manual's cover

A Father and Son Act

On a sunny Saturday morning in 1963, a sixteen-year-old Ken Krohn was running accounts with his father, now a seasoned repossessor of ten years, A.M. "Bud" Krohn. Driving down the gravel streets of Pacheco, California they rolled up to the flat-topped house with a car port. Under its awnings sat the assigned 57' Chevrolet, Nomad. Exiting their car, Bud went to the door and knocked while Ken went to the car.

Still waiting for the door to be answered, Bud waited on the porch as teenage Ken entered the Nomad. Reaching behind the dashboard, Ken unplugged the ignition switch and went to work. With a paperclip and a pocketknife, Ken had the V8 engine humming as the borrower's front door swung open. "I've got it. Let's go!" he shouted as he backed down the driveway leaving Bud on the doorstep with the borrower.

In the years to come, Bud and Ken would become fixtures in the national repossession industry. In 1969, Bud had co-founded AOC Adjusters with fellow agency owners Tony Tomasello, Walt Burleson and Derrell Biddy.

Jack and the Bear

While Jack Barnes of the NFA was still running his repossession business, he was also performing as a professional wrestler. Allegedly performing under the names "The Great Bolo" and "Dr. X", Barnes once wrestled a bear on live TV as a publicity stunt. In 1964, Jack took a swing at politics with a run for Senate. It was during the 1960's that Jack's diverse skillset came into play, where his auto, aircraft and commercial recovery experience earned him industry respect launching him into various lofty roles within the NFA.

Lorna in the Blade

On August 18, 1963, the "Toledo Blade" published another anecdotal repossession agency story where a name from the past resurfaces. This one hails from the origins of the Allied Finance Adjusters, Lorna Lou Barnes, the brash red-haired widow of Ray Barnes, and co-founder of the AFA. Erroneously referred to as "Lora", she tells a story of how in 1946, when operating out of their Flushing, New York office, she was assigned to repossess a car being driven by former heavyweight champion, Jack Dempsey. According to Lorna, "Jack had a fondness for transporting girls across state lines in the car and the repossession especially nettled him."

According to the story, he told Lorna "You're a thief and I'm going to kill the guy you sent out to take it!" Lorna allegedly talked Dempsey down but is reported to have said that she "has been shaky about repossessing from heavyweight champions ever since. Congressmen are easier. We've had them too, you know."

A second, and apparently unrelated person in the story was reported as Johnny Kirkman. Johnny, a brash adjuster who claimed to also work in Brooklyn as a waiter until midnight, tells several repossession stories. Kirkman claimed to be "one of the finest repossessors in the land." and further claimed that "If the price is right, I'll repossess a lion!"

Later in the story, Johnny reports that he averages about $20 per repossession. That's about $170 in 2021 value. It is unknown what became of Johnny, but Lorna Lou Barnes had already broken down the gender barriers of this male dominated industry and was becoming a legend in her own right. But she wasn't the only one.

The She Devils of the Desert

The press has always had an interest in the repossession industry and in July 4, 1965, the Arizona Republic newspaper published an article title "The Repossessors." It was in this article that we first learn the name of two more women in the repossession industry and one whose history goes almost as far back as Lorna Lou, Priscilla Bouchey of Ace Adjustment Agency of Phoenix, Arizona. Priscilla claimed that she had started the company with her unknown and unnamed ex-husband in 1938.

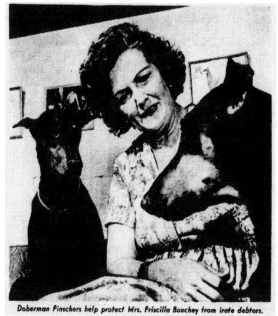

Doberman Pinschers help protect Mrs. Priscilla Bouchey from irate debtors.

"Doberman Pinschers help protect Mrs. Priscilla Bouchey from irate debtors." -Arizona Republic - 7/4/1965 - © Arizona Republic — USA TODAY NETWORK

Being in Arizona, she discusses the large number of skips that would arrive there from Texas and California. In particular, she recalled an instance where her agents had recovered a car from a skip from California. The young man's parents had enlisted an attorney who had been threatening her, but things came to a boil when the boy and his mother showed up at her front door.

Brazenly, the boy threatened to "knock her down" right in front of his mother, who advised him that whatever he did to "this woman" she wouldn't testify against him. Priscilla then opened the door all the way to introduce her four Doberman pinschers who never strayed far from her side. The boy and his mother fled and never got the car back. How were they to know that Priscilla was a founding member of the Desert Valley Doberman Pinscher Club?

Thirty-eight-year-old, 5' foot 2" brunette, Eileen Senerchia, operated a company simply known as the Auto Recovery Bureau in Phoenix with her husband Arthur and her unnamed brother-in-law. Eileen characterized the majority of the debtors they repossessed from as "boozers" and that they recovered many cars from bars. Like her husband, Eileen also worked in the field recovering cars, but admitted to bringing a male assistant with her at times when going to rough locations. On the subject of hotwiring ignitions, Eileen confessed to not doing it because of her fear of sparks.

Eight years later in 1973, Eileen and Arthur were named in a lawsuit titled Bible v. First National Bank of Rawlins. The basis of the lawsuit was that the recovery agents had shouted an obscenity overheard by Mrs. Bible during the repossession. In testimony they stated that they had been in business for thirteen years and that on only two occasions had violence occurred to any of their agents, but neither had every been injured. One was shot at by a borrower and another had a pitchfork thrown at him.

Court testimony by the Senerchia's claims that they earned between $40-$50 per recovery ($351-$439 in 2021 value.) Arthur and Eileen's son Gary, an agent for Able Adjusters, was killed in a motorcycle accident in 1981. Eileen passed away at seventy-eight years of age on March 23, 2005.

Also included in the story was Tom O'Grady of Arizona State Recovery Bureau and Harold Chapman of Arizona Repossession Bureau who share very similar accounts of repossessing in Arizona during this period. O'Grady kept a trophy wall of weapons taken from under the front seats of repossessed vehicles on his office wall and told of one of his young agents having been shot at two weeks earlier with the bullet passing through the truck window and narrowly missing his head. Arizona Republic - (Phoenix, Arizona) July 4, 1965

While the early years of the repossession industry are dominated by the names of men, this was a different era. As we can see from the tales of women like Lorna Lou Barnes, Priscilla Bouchey and Eileen Senerchia, women had been very present and very active in the industry, likely since its inception. So much so, that if you look at the early association convention photos, you can very easily imagine that many of the women in those photos were a lot more than just some agency owner's wives. Ask anyone in the industry now and they will tell you that women are some of the most influential and dominant characters in it, and I imagine that was the case even then.

Locking the Wheel

Throughout the early 1960's, repossession tactics and techniques remained fairly consistent with the decade before. Hot wiring ignition switches, using dealer of lender provided keys, lock-picking, key impressioning, lock slamming and the occasional use of a tow truck were still the primary methods of auto recovery. But with car theft and "Joy Riding" being blamed as the cause for many vehicular accidents, the repossession industry was soon challenged with new obstacles.

Federal Motor Vehicle Safety Standard 114 was introduced in 1966. This technological hurdle for repossession agents mandated that manufacturers equip new passenger cars with a key-locking system that prevented the automobile from being steered or navigated without the ignition key. Although the mandate did not go into effect until 1970, by 1969, all the major auto manufacturers were in already compliance.

Pin locks were still the standard in 1965, but Ford was the first to introduce the double-sided cut key which enabled the user to insert either side of the key in the lock or ignition.

California Makes it Legal

In 1963, California codified the lender's right to self-help repossession under California Commercial Code 9503. Prior to this, the right had existed in common law and by contract. Throughout this decade and well into the future, this right had been challenged by claims of unconstitutionality under the fourteenth amendment. Specifically, the due process clause.

THE ROSE SERIES P. 14653   PARKING AREA, HAMILTON PLACE, MT. WAVERLEY, VIC.

1960's Volkswagen Beetle- (Photo courtesy of the National Archives)

The Winds of Change

On November 23rd, 1963, thirty-fifth President of the United States, John F. Kennedy was assassinated. This event seems to have triggered one of the most transformational eras in our nation's history. America's involvement in the war in Vietnam escalated alongside the anti-war movement as societal change began to take hold.

Slowly creeping into the American driveways in the 1950's, foreign vehicles now made up just over 10 percent of the vehicles on America's roadways. None was more popular than the Volkswagen Beetle, who entered the market with a sales price as low as $1,565. According to a repossession agent interview in the Baltimore Sun on October 9, 1966, the unnamed Baltimore agent complained that a tow truck was a virtual necessity since they all allegedly had a steering lock. He further claimed that "*the lock is so 'gooped' up that no one across the country has been able to figure out how to open it.*"

Keeping the Peace

In an industry still running wild, it took its cousin, the collections industry to lead the way to safety and professionalism. Through the ACA International, founded in 1939, the new American Recovery Association (ARA), launched in 1962 set forth a training class "*to perfect techniques in the peaceful repossession of goods and chattels sold on conditional sales contract, or chattel mortgages on which payments have become delinquent.*" Scheduled for April 29th and 30th of 1966 at the Oshkosh Wisconsin, Howard Johnson's Motor Lodge, it provided training to ARA members from the states of Minnesota, Iowa, Wisconsin and Illinois. Training was conducted by AFA co-founder Paul Leleu of the Automobile Recovery Bureau of Chicago. The Oshkosh Northwestern - (Oshkosh, Wisconsin) – April 27, 1966

While their first repossession training event was held in 1963, this is from all evidence, the first known repossession training event that brough the issue of safety and peaceful repossession to light. While the other three repossession associations focused primarily on marketing and territorial expansion and control, the ARA, with John Johnson of the ACA in control, focused heavily on professionalism and client outreach. This model would carry forward and eventually become adopted by their fellow three associations.

Bill Bowser, consummate Cadillac aficionado and collapsible tow boom pioneer
(photo courtesy of Bob Lyons, The Dagmar – Cadillac & LaSalle Club)

The Cadillac Repo Man

As a young man, Bill Bowser saw his first Cadillac and told himself that one when got rich he would buy one. While he was never able to afford a new one, he did eventually own several used ones that he was proud of. One of which was a 1949 that he used to pull repossessions with by chain as early as 1955. It wasn't until 1964 when he started the Denver Repossession Bureau that he combined his love for Cadillacs with repossessing.

While most recovery agencies worked by hand and only sparingly used tow trucks, Bill spent much of his time in tow trucks and lamented to his mechanic, Keith Pickett how he wished the tow truck drove like a Cadillac. Pickett said; "We could do that." And just like that, the two designed and built the first known collapsible electric tow apparatus. Stuffing it into the massive truck of a 1963 Cadillac which he used it successfully until 1966 when they opted for an upgrade.

Taking a wrecked 1966 Cadillac sedan, they cut off the back set roof, beefed up the suspension and created basically a Cadillac-El Camino, which they referred to as a "Cad Camino." This was only the second of what became a novelty item that Bill had became known for clear into the 1980's. Bill's 1965 Cadillac tow truck was on display at the International Towing and Recovery Hall of Fame and Museum in Chattanooga, Tennessee from 2009 to 2011. It was also displayed at Forney's Museum of Transportation in Denver, Colorado in 2013. Bill kept driving these Cadillac tow trucks as recent as 2014. – The Dagmar – Cadillac & LaSalle Club newsletter – September 2014

Bill never did get rich, but he did get a lot of Cadillacs. He probably didn't realize it at the time, but his joint invention of an electric collapsible tow boom would go on to change the way the entire repossession industry would operate decades later. In 1972, Bill published his autobiography "The Man came and Took it Away" which was published under his pen name, W.G. Bowser.

Bill passed away at the age of 82 on September 19, 2014. Upon Bill's passing, Pratt Adjustment Bureau owner Jeanne Lewis stated; "Bill was always quick with a laugh and a smile. He always had a new joke or a good story to tell. I am grateful I got to hear some of them first hand. I will miss you, Bill."

A Long Walk in the Woods

When Camden County Sheriff's deputies found an abandoned car hidden deep in the woods of Kingsland, Georgia on February 26, 1966, they knew something was wrong. Checking the registration and making a few phone calls, they found it registered to twenty-six-year-old Buster Wainwright, a collector for General Motors Acceptance Corporation (GMAC). They soon found that the day before, Wainwright had come to the area with fifty-year-old car dealer Troy Connor to repossess a 65' Oldsmobile from thirty-three-year-old Robert Felton Moore of Folkston and no one had heard from them since. Suspicious, deputies went to Moore's home and found that he had already fled and his car was gone.

A manhunt was launched and soon after, Moore was spotted in the Oldsmobile and a chase ensued when he refused to pull over. Deputies were forced to shoot the tires out of the car until he came to a stop. Once in custody, Moore confessed the grisly truth.

The day before, Moore had agreed to surrender the vehicle, which he volunteered to drive back to Woodbine following Wainwright and Connor. Along the way, Moore pulled the car over to the side of the road and claimed to be out of gas. Climbing into the back of Wainwrights car to get some gas, Moore pulled a gun on them. Leading them down a rarely used forestry department road, he ordered them to pull Wainwright's car over.

Once there, he marched them off into the woods at gunpoint and ordered them to strip to their underwear. Somewhere in the process, Moore beat one of the men with a tire iron before shooting both to death. Moore buried them in a shallow grave, hid Wainwright's car and fled. Moore showed deputies the location of the men's bodies and was charged and convicted of murder and later in April, sentenced to die in the electric chair. - The Daily Independent - (Kannapolis, North Carolina) February 27, 1966

The Godfather Takes Over

By 1966, the Time Finance Adjusters (TFA) had found themselves less successful than their competitors the AFA, NFA and the newly formed ARA. Five years in arears of state and federal taxes, they were in trouble. Reaching out to one of their most prominent members, their problems were solved. Harvey Altes, then owner of Falcon International, Florida District 12 Constable, and amateur Jai Alai player, bought the TFA and paid their back taxes reinvigorating the then floundering association.

Jai Alai Harvey, 1960's – (photo courtesy of Nicki Merthe-Altes)

Focusing on growth, Harvey took in the outcasts and riskier elements of industry. People who were turned down by AFA, NFA and ARA, of whom he was a member of all three as well. Harvey was an advertising professional, probably the best the industry had ever seen bu some accounts and was an adept industry politician who garnered either fear or respect from the players in every association. Harvey was just getting warmed up.

The Riots of 68'

On April 4, 1968, Martin Luther King Jr. was assassinated in Memphis, TN. This sparked riots nationwide and in Chicago, they were especially violent. In forty-eight hours, eleven died and forty-eight were wounded by police gunfire as mobs swarmed the streets. Day and night, the city suffered police clashes with violent and looting protestors who started 125 fires and damaged 210 buildings. Sitting right in the middle of the mayhem on Chicago's southside was Frank Mauro's auto storage warehouse with over 200 cars inside.

Watching the neighborhood explode, Frank gathered a crew of armed men and arrived at the warehouse in the midst of the chaos determined to stand their ground. After three days and two nights, the city calmed down. When the dust settled, half of the neighborhood around Frank's warehouse was in ruins. Over those three days they withstood the siege with armed force and none of the stored vehicles nor the warehouse were damaged.

In this same year, Frank's relationship with the auto franchise dealership industry began, one for which he would better be known. In September Frank was granted his first auto franchise, an Oldsmobile dealership at 105th and Michigan Ave. Frank went on to become a legend of the auto industry and the family auto empire eventually expanded to twenty-four dealerships in three states.

Meet Jim

Through the decades, breaking into cars had employed a wide range of methods from lock picks to coat hangers and butter knives. It was in 1967 that the Hudson Lock Company from Hudson, Massachussets, introduced the auto break-in tool whose name is synonymous with break in tools. Using a strip of spring steel about twenty-four inches long and about an inch wide, they cut three-inch long tapered notches with hooks on the end of each side.

This was the birth of the "Slim Jim." A term for auto break-in tools of all kinds and staple in every Repossessors truck for decades to come. While homemade versions and variations may have existed as far back as the 1950's, this was the first mass manufactured and trademarked.

Cousin Kevin, Teen Sleuth

Sweeping floors and moving cars, a skinny sixteen-year-old Kevin McGivern was working in his cousin the cop's side-business, "Evanston Enterprises", a repossession agency in 1968. Kevin did the dirty work for almost two years while the repo agents, who worked in teams of two without a tow truck, made $10 a car ($77 in 2021) and their drivers $8 ($61) per repossession. Through professional osmosis and some mentoring by the agents, Kevin learned to break into cars, make keys and hot wire ignitions before even learning to shave. Having a "hardship" driver's license since fourteen-years of age, at sixteen, Kevin's first trip into the field came when a driver called in sick on a Thursday night.

Leaving the garage late at night, Kevin travelled two hours to Aurora, Illinois with a seasoned and experienced agent. Their target, a delinquent nineteen-year-old kid who'd taken advantage of a Chrysler Credit "first time buyer" loan program and bought a 68' Dodge Superbee. Dropping by the police station to state their business, they proceeded to the residence only to come up empty with the car not showing. Looking at the assignment papers, Kevin realized the agent he was with had already run this account seven times.

Unwilling to lose out on his first $8 driver commission, Kevin talked the agent into stopping at a phone booth. Unable to talk Kevin down, he called the residence at about 3 a.m. When the startled woman on the other end answered, Kevin asked for the borrower only to be told that he was no longer living there. Thinking quick, Kevin spotted a name written on the phone booth wall and assumed the name.

Pretending to be an old friend from high school sent to Vietnam that had promised to call the minute he got back to town, the borrower's mother opened up. Thankful for his safe return to the states, she disclosed his location across the street from a school supply building, but no phone or address adding, "*you'll know it, his bright yellow Superbee sits in the front yard.*" Thanking the woman, Kevin hung up with the agent over his shoulder not having heard her response.

After another stop at the police station for directions, they arrived at the residence and as described, the bright yellow muscle car was in the yard. The agent pulled the ignition, drifted it out of the yard and fired up the 426 Hemi with glass packed mufflers waking the entire neighborhood in the process. Regardless, they got away clean, and most important, Kevin got his $8!

Kevin found his talent in skip tracing and within a few years, made friends with a client at Chrysler who offered to send all his repossession assignments his way if he opened his own company. A thousand dollars and two agents later, Kevin founded Equitable Services, a company he built into one of the nation's largest repossession empires in its history. His accomplishments and influence made him a major industry leader in many ways that we will discuss later.

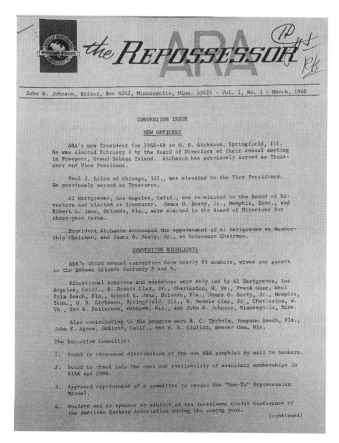

1968 ARA "The Repossessor" Newsletter

The Banana War Repo

Anyone with exposure to the mob will tell you, despite their wealth, they are some of the worst people in the world when it comes to paying bills. That includes Salvatore "Bill" Bonanno, son of notorious mob Boss Joe "Bananas" Bonanno. "Bill" quit making lease payments on a black on gold 67' Cadillac when he fled New York during a mob war. The car was last seen in early 1968 being driven by Bill's bodyguard Sam Perrone in Tucson, Arizona, but Perrone was later gunned down in a New York mob hit earlier that March.

Later in August, the lender, who preferred to remain unnamed for good reason, received a tip that the car was back in Tucson. On Wednesday night of August 21, 1968, an agent from "Phil's Receiving" arrived at the Tidelands Motor Inn and found the vehicle. Accompanied by a pair of police officers, the agent recovered the vehicle without incident. - Tucson Citizen - (Tucson, Arizona) – August 23, 1968

Salvatore "Bill" Bonanno's history with Arizona goes way back to his childhood when he attended a catholic boarding school there. Following his father Joe's heart attack in 68', they ended the "Banana War", as it was known. As terms of the peace agreement with warring rival Gaspar de Giorgio, he retired and moved with his sons, Bill and Joe Jr. to Tucson. It was somewhere during these years that Bill gave birth to "Charles", one of four children.

Bill and Joe Jr. soon moved to the San Francisco Bay Area where in 1970, Bill was convicted of fifty-two counts of mail fraud and sentenced to four years in prison. In 1971, both brothers were convicted of extortion and conspiracy and in 1977 were trapped by an undercover informant, "Lou Peters", an undercover informant for the FBI, as they tried to buy his Cadillac dealerships to launder money. They may have left the mob, but the mob hadn't quite left them and their name, as you will later see, became a hard one to live down in the state of California.

While the newspaper was kind enough to not post the lenders name, they seem to have purposefully and conspicuously added the Tucson address to "Phil's Receiving" at the bottom of the article. Setting bait for a later story perhaps? As early as the 1925 "Car=Snatcher" article with George D. Wright and again in the 1949 interview with Ray Barnes' run in with "Murder Inc.", accounts of repossessions from mobsters have been perversely common throughout the industry, perhaps as bragging rights or perhaps it was just that common.

A Hollywood Bomb

Twenty-five-year-old Mike Allen was out repossessing cars with his twenty-three-year-old hairdresser girlfriend Sue McKay when he picked up a Chevrolet Impala without incident. Driving it back to the lot of his employer, The Ray Wilson Company on N. Cahuenga in Hollywood, he parked it and opened the trunk. Inside was a pint bottle of buckshot and a green plastic explosive packed with sand and a blasting cap. Police soon arrived and dismantled the bomb stating that the bomb could have caused injury to someone if it has exploded. - The Los Angeles Times - (Los Angeles, California) October 28, 1969

Seven years later, Mike opened his own agency in San Bernardino. Michael P. Allen & Associates operates to this day under the management of his son Michael P. "Rocky" Allen Jr. who has been working there since 1998.

Holidays in the Sun

As the 60's concluded, the repossession industry prospered as did the association's membership rolls. Member agency families continued to travel all over the nation with their families in tow. Spending their days on trips to amusement parks and local tourist attractions as their husbands tended to stay inside for conferences. To illustrate the industries prosperity of the era, in 1968, the ARA held its annual convention in the Bahamas where sixty-five members, their wives, guests and children enjoyed what had become a very normal part of their lives in the industry.

One of many anti-war protests of the 1960's- (photo by the National Archives)

1973 Oregon Gas Station. Odd and even number plate systems used to dispense gas during OPEC oil embargo – (photo by the EPA)

CHAPTER 7 – THE 1970'S – RUNNING ON FUMES

"Rich people plan for four generations. Poor people plan for Saturday night."
— **Gloria Steinem**

The 70's began with Richard M. Nixon as President to a population of over $205 million. The economy was in a recession with a 6.1 percent unemployment rate and a stalled GDP of 0.2 percent. The nation and society were still embroiled in, and at odds with, the war in Vietnam. American society, as we knew it, was at a major crossroads.

The average annual income now stood at $9,870 and the average price of a new car was still very affordable at $3,542. Detroit pumped out almost 8 million automobiles this year, but imports were beginning to take a bite out of the market share. Driven by the need for fuel efficiency and the 1973 OPEC created fuel crisis, by 1977 foreign vehicles had eclipsed the 2 million sold mark.

To the booming repossession industry, these imports were inconsequential, a car is a car and a repo a repo. But to Detroit, their growth in market share took a hit on production. By 1975, America was in another recession and unemployment had risen to 8.2 percent. Lending was down, but repossessions were up!

A Shooting of Minor Mention

Ronald D. Clark laid motionless on the ground by his truck near the intersection of 67th Avenue and Van Buren north of Phoenix, Arizona. A single bullet wound to the left side of his head left him in critical condition and hospitalized as police searched for a suspect. Four days later, on January 10, 1970, a 22-year-old Sylvester Keith was arrested for the shooting. It is unknown if Keith was convicted or if Clark survived, but even if he did, he likely suffered chronic issues from the injury. - Arizona Republic (Phoenix, Arizona) - January 10, 1970, Page 12

Shootings and killings of adjusters have historically been minor news stories. I could find no follow up to this story which was buried way back on page 12.

The Real get Out of Jail Card

Back on the block and on leave from an eighteen-month tour of Vietnam in 1970, a young Ron stepped out of an Oklahoma City theater into the late-night air after a late showing of "Cinderella." Enjoying a break from military fatigues, he walked to his Harley in his cowboy boots, shirt and jeans ignoring the condescending "cowboy" remarks from a trio of smarmy college boys and their girlfriends in passing. With a kick, his motorcycle roared to life, and he sped away with thoughts of singing birds and fairies dancing in his head when, suddenly, a Cadillac pulled out in front of him, cutting him off and nearly causing him to crash.

Leaving the area, he noticed a car speeding up from behind. It was the Cadillac that had cut him off and it was being driven by the same college boys from the theater and their girlfriends. Kindly slowing to let them pass, they persisted with their tail until pulling up alongside him. With their thrown beer bottle whizzing past his head, Ron thought, "That wasn't very neighborly" so he sped up and passed them, slowing to a stop as they obliged to meet him in this secluded part of town.

Stepping off the bike, a friendly smile crossed Ron's face as he sauntered toward the driver's door and it opened with a leg stepping down to the ground.

The pop of a fractured bone and a scream of agony filled the air as Ron Slammed the door on the driver's leg. Coming to their buddy's aid, his friends poured out of the car only to be greeted by a warning shot from Ron's always handy Colt .45, which they now stared down the hot barrel of. "Uh-uh boys." kindly suggested Ron as the smell of fresh underwear loads of preppy poop wafted through the air in the seconds before they fled for their lives. Just another night for Ron, he remounted and went on his merry way.

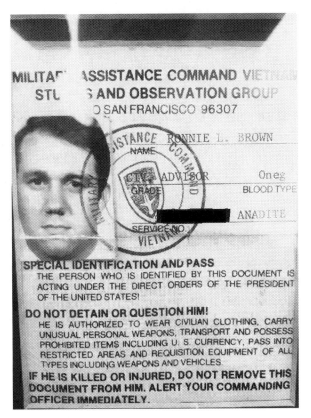

Ron Brown's "Get Out of Jail Free" military ID card – (photo by Ron Brown)

Passing back through town, he was greeted by a flashing red light. Pulling over, Ron was politely asked to dismount, place his hands on his head and come back to the police car by the nice young man in the clean pressed uniform pointing his service revolver at him. Doing as requested, they soon had company as three other carloads of friendly policemen arrived and proudly displayed their guns to Ron just as those fine outstanding college boys from down the road arrived at the scene to gloat, probably stopping to wipe their soiled posteriors on the way. Finding Ron's Colt 45 in his saddle bag, they preferred not to believe Ron's account of things and offered him a ride to the police station in handcuffs. Just as Ron was about to get his chauffeured ride to the station, the shift sergeant arrived.

Thumbing through Ron's wallet, they shared pleasantries of their common experiences in Southeast Asia when Ron's "Get Out of Jail Free Card" fell from his wallet. Picking it up, the sergeant shook his head and he ordered the officers to uncuff Ron and then walked over to the nice college boys in the Cadillac and spoke to them briefly. Returning to Ron as the poopy pants preppies drove away, Ron asked what he told them. The sergeant replied, "I told them that they were dealing with a crazy son of a bitch, and they were probably lucky to be alive. The sergeant then winked at Ron and said, "Stay sane and safe, get out of here and always remember "Airborne... All the Way!"

Ron Brown holds the distinction of being one of the few men you would ever meet to hold a military ID card that literally identified him as acting under the direct orders of the President of the United

States. This "Get Out of Jail Free Card" authorized him to carry any type of weapon in civilian clothes and requisition weapons and vehicles of all types and reads, *"Do not detain or question him!"* Ron returned to Vietnam for one more tour as an interrogator and security specialist for the infamous MAC SVOG.

Ron Brown would be back, and the repossession and skip tracing world would never be the same. Ron went on to train the Texas Rangers, US Marshals FIST units and many other law enforcement agencies in "manhunting" and went on to become one of the industry's most colorful and influential leaders. Setting aside my facetious description of Ron's escapades in "charm school", Ron is actually one of the nicest and kindest men you would ever want to meet. Just don't be unneighborly.

Another Loss for GMAC

Frank Passingham, Field Agent for General Motors Acceptance Corp. (GMAC), had arrived at the Detroit residence of an unnamed borrower at 8 mile and Wyoming on January 15th of 1971. Spotting his vehicle, he went to work unaware of his witness. Believing Passingham was a car thief, the borrowers fifteen-year-old son grabbed a rifle and fired a single round striking Frank in the shoulder. Twenty-eight-year-old Passingham was pronounced dead on arrival at Mt. Carmel Hospital and the boy was incarcerated in juvenile hall. - Detroit Free Press - (Detroit, Michigan) January 16, 1971

GMAC had maintained field agents clear into the 2000's when their local branch offices finished closing and consolidation ended the practice. Killings like Frank's likely weighed heavy on their minds, as well as other lenders still engaged in handling their own repossessions. Detroit's reputation for deadly repossession encounters was just beginning. For GMAC, this was a dark day, but their darkest day was yet to come.

The Rise of the TFA

In 1971, Harvey Altes published his first association book for his reformed Time Finance Adjusters. Most TFA members were members of other associations as well and this was encouraged. Harvey's influence of his members extended into the other three associations through the "TFA Block" of votes as it became known. The TFA would go on to have a tremendous following and a lasting impact on the repossession industry for decades to come.

It was also in the 1970's, before the passage of the Fair Debt Collections Practices Act (FDCPA), that, according to daughter Nicki Merthe-Altes, Harvey founded a company known as "Florida Auto Theft Mutual." This company, really just a shell letterhead going to a PO box, was a cover company used to intimidate borrowers in hiding and enticing them to respond. It was reported as having been very effective in its time.

But it wasn't until 1975 that Harvey made one of his greatest entrepreneurial ventures when he bought a hamburger joint down the street from his Miami office and founded "Cousin Kevin's Hot Dogs." According to both Kevin McGivern and daughter Nicki, it was named after Kevin McGivern. Unfortunately, Miami wasn't ready for quality Chicago hot dogs and went with the cheap beachfront hot dog stands instead. "It was fun while it lasted." said Nicki.

Be Careful What You Ask For

California repossession agency owners, James Austin, Richard H. Egley, William Maloy and A.J. Rushford filed a Federal class action lawsuit against eighty-three California banks in the name of all other licensed California Repossessors. Named in the lawsuit were Bank of America, Wells Fargo, and United California Bank to name a few. At issue were the banks, also licensed to conduct repossession in the name of their businesses also being members of a national directory of interstate repossessors published by the American Bankers Association (ABA). The lawsuit alleged that the defendants had been in agreement since 1967 to the exclusive use of members in the ABA's directory for repossession services.

Included in the allegations was that the defendants fixed prices for repossession services and diminished interstate repossession assignment volume to the licensed state repossession business plaintiffs. Also claimed was that their complaint of the inequity that repossession agencies were regulated by section 7522 of California's Business and Professions Code, but banks were not. - The San Francisco Examiner (San Francisco, California) - July 27, 1971

The exact details of this settlement are lost, but in the end, the ABA ceased these directories and the repossession industries long practice of price fixing was becoming common knowledge. A major issue that would arise ten years later.

So Long Sucker

Victory laps are for later, learned thirty-year-old adjuster John Robinson III of Austin, Texas. And learned the hard way when repossessing a car from Bill Peterson on the night of November 18, 1971. Awaken from his sleep by noises in the parking lot, Peterson looked outside to see a man in his car with the motor running. Grabbing his .38 revolver, Peterson ran outside demanding Robinson get out of the car.

"So Long Sucker!" Robinson allegedly shouted as he laughed aloud and put the car into gear. Peterson again shouted for Robinson to get out of the vehicle. Watching his car begin to pull away, Peterson fired two rounds at Robinson. "I've been shot!" screamed Robinson through his shattered face as he scurried out the car's passenger side door and ran to his getaway driver's car.

Robinson arrived at the Brackenridge Hospital Emergency room soon after and was treated for a gunshot wound to the right side of his jaw. The bullet had broken his jaw, fractured several teeth and split his tongue. Robinson was listed in stable condition.

No charges were filed against Peterson. The District Attorney claimed that since the repossession was being conducted without a court order and the vehicle was not on a public roadway, Peterson had done nothing wrong in the eyes of Texas law. The Austin American (Austin, Texas) November 20, 1971

This attitude toward adjusters and self-help repossession in the state of Texas has long shielded many murders through the decades and would eventually become a source of national outcry after one tragic night in Houston many years later.

The Cost of Doing Business

In an April of 1972 newspaper interview, fifty-one-year-old, Johnny Gordon claimed to have been repossessing cars since 1945. He alleged at that in 1945 he was earning $12.50 ($189.59 in 2021) a car commission in town and $25 ($379.17) for out of town plus mileage. At the time of the interview, Gordon claimed to be making $40 ($293.90) plus mileage and a driver fee for local recoveries and $100 ($653.12) for out of state lenders. The Daily Oklahoman - (Oklahoma City, Oklahoma) April 9, 1972

Meet Millard

Planning to work his way through law school, Millard Land never envisioned himself in the repossession industry. Regardless, he ended up taking a job as an adjuster/collector with Ford Motor Credit in the early 70's. By 1973 he purchased Adjusters Inc. of Houston, Texas. During his long and storied career, Millard repossessed everything from an 1873 stagecoach to singer Tony Bennett's limousine to Las Vegas showman Wayne Newton's jet.

Relentless, creative and detail oriented, Millard climbed the ranks as one of the industries most respected figures. Despite these tenacious characteristics, Millard remained humble, humane, and generous. He was even known on occasion, to pay out of his own pocket to set families up in hotels after repossessing their mobile homes.

Of Minor Mention or Consequence

On Saturday night of March 24th, 1973, William Elmer Russell of Dallas was shot to death during a repossession. Officers held an unnamed twenty-one-year-old man for questioning. The man claimed that he thought Russell was trying to steal his car. Corsicana Daily Sun - (Corsicana, Texas) March 26, 1973

This four column Associated Press story was about a weekend of murders and vehicular deaths occurring in Texas over the previous weekend. No further news of charges for this murder could be found. While covered in numerous Texas newspapers, this snippet of Russell's murder was buried deep on page 7.

Another Down in Detroit

Early in the morning of April 23rd, 1973, Gary Lee Sutton, his twenty-six-year-old wife Diane, and a third man were pushing a repossessed Pontiac Catalina down the street from the Detroit residence of James Alvin Watts. Emerging from his house with a .30 caliber carbine rifle, Watts fired several shots at them. One struck twenty-six-year-old Gary in the neck. Watts was charged with assault with intent to commit murder.

On May 11th, Sutton died of the wounds at Mt. Carmel Mercy Hospital. In February of 1974, Watts was convicted of manslaughter. Sutton was employed by Allied Finance Adjusters member, Al Michel's Midwest Recovery and Adjustment Service. - Detroit Free Press (Detroit, MI) - May 12, 1973

The following year before Watt's sentencing, consumer advocates came to Watt's defense in an article in the Detroit Free Press on February 28th, claiming that the death was the fault of the self-help repossession process. The Secretary of State's off ice was quoted as stating that there were on average, eighty-five repossession conducted in the state daily. It also stated that there was legislation pending in Michigan that would require legal process before an attempt at self-help repossession. As you will soon see, this legislation went nowhere.

More Murder in the Motor City

It was 3:50 a.m, on a warm summer night on Detroit's Burlingame Street when the four men arrived. Douglas Haskins, twenty-one-years-old and another employee of Al Michel's Midwest Recovery and Adjustment Service left the safety of their car, repo order and wire coat hanger in hand. Following him, a non-employee, seventeen-year-old Terry Miller, stood at his side as Haskins checked the vin number and slipped the wire coat hanger into the window of the two-tone 1970 Ford Thunderbird. All the while, thirty-year-old borrower, Edward Cranford was watching from his apartment window in the brick building above.

Cranford fired. seventeen-year-old Terry Miller was hit with the bullet passing through him and striking Haskins in the shoulder. Miller died soon after and Haskins recovered in Detroit General Hospital. Cranford claimed that there had been three previous attempts to steal his car and he thought this was a fourth. No immediate charges were filed, but the District Attorney later filed charges of second-degree murder.

On August 7th, Cranford was brought before Judge George W. Crockett Jr. to face the charges. Miller's father, Everett Miller was charged with contempt of court during the hearing after shouting that "a white man could not expect a fair hearing by a black judge." Judge Crockett ruled that "the action of the defendant was reasonable. There was no way to differentiate between the boy and a burglar." Miller's father was released from arrest ninety minutes after the hearing. - Detroit Free Press - (Detroit, Michigan) August 2, 1973, and The Times Herald - (Port Huron, Michigan) August 8, 1973

Al Michel's Midwest Recovery and Adjustment Service had been around for over fourteen years at this point and there were allegedly additional deaths before these two occurring so close together, according to George Badeen, current owner and executive Director of the Allied Finance Adjusters. Detroit was the cradle of the auto industry and probably the repo industry but was also earning the deadly distinction for murder, one that would carry on for years to come.

A Short Retirement

Robert C. Blackwell was fifty-nine-years old and a recently retired California Highway Patrolman working as a repossessor for Bank of America when he arrived at the address of 1304 E. Lorena Ave. in Fresno, California. After he had gone missing for two days, this empty apartment is where they found him with a small caliber bullet wound in the back of the head and lying dead in a black pool of drying blood. Erwin Curtis Rogers was identified as the suspect but later released.

Days later on the 8th, a twenty-three-year-old Sandy Lynn Brown was arrested for the same crime and also later released. Also being sought for investigation was Roger's cousin Allen James Garland. A $2,500 reward was offered for information leading to the murder. The Fresno Bee - (Fresno, California) June 5, 1974

The investigation on the murder went cold until October of 1988 when Allen James Garland, aka; thirty-eight-year-old Allen James Vercher, was arrested and charged with the murder. According to the prosecuting attorney, Vercher had ambushed Blackwell in the known empty apartment with the intention of killing and robbing him. In June of 1990, Vercher was convicted and sentenced to life in prison plus five years. The Fresno Bee - (Fresno, California) June 8, 1990

Another Down in Houston

Thirty-year-old Tom Lewandowski was running a small repo company out of his La Porte, Texas home when he received an assignment on a 1974 Cadillac that led him to a parking lot in Houston. It was there that he encountered the lot attendant and borrower, Raymond E. Banks. Lewandowski was shot in the head with a single bullet. As is the custom, Banks claimed he thought Lewandowski was a car thief. Longview News-Journal - (Longview, Texas) October 8, 1974

This two-sentence story was buried in section B, page 4 of the newspaper. I could find no news to suggest that he was charged with anything. Just another day in Texas I suppose.

Golden Rule

Jim Golden had climbed from being an Adjuster to an agency owner when he bought Frosty Thomas's Lubbock, Texas repo office. By 1975, Jim had ascended to being the President of the Allied Finance Adjusters when he saw an opportunity to branch out using a business model more commonly reserved for the then booming fast food industry. Franchising. That was when he created the Business Investment and Development Corp. (BIDCO), the parent company of American Lenders Service Company (ALSCO.)

Jim Golden, 1981 – (photo permission of the AFA)

Repossession companies were not always the best at marketing their services. Aside from dropping off donuts and business cards to local clients, most relied upon the association directories for their marketing. Jim saw this as an opportunity to create a unique company with a national focus on marketing and a franchise structure gave investors territorial market exclusivity from other franchise owners, much like the associations.

ALSCO supported their franchisees through marketing. In 1979, they expanded with a crew of three national marketers focused on not only the big national lenders, but in gathering as many smaller lenders as possible. ALSCO established 7 national districts and obliged franchisees by contract to market the national company and its franchises locally. Each franchise served a region based upon population density.

This structure ensured ALSCO a strong market presence without its franchisees experiencing territorial conflicts. ALSCO's network also "forwarded" repossession assignments solely to one another. Had this structure and strategy maintained, ALSCO, would have created the first and largest account forwarding company in the nation.

ALSCO differed greatly from the traditional repossession association in their exclusivity. While the associations also maintained exclusivity, they were not enforced as tightly. ALSCO standardized all forms, processes and procedures and conducted lot inspections, much like are done today, but I'll cover that topic later. Jim kept such a tight hand on the company owner, Ron Adams, complained that he could buy a pencil for his office, but the lead had to come from ALSCO.

But alas, as the repossession industry was prone to do, they attacked ALSCO with accusations of restraining trade. This led to a series of lawsuits which ALSCO ultimately defeated. Eventually, a complaint was filed against them by a then unnamed agency owner from New Mexico who had been shut out of numerous associations as well as ALSCO. This complaint, however, was filed with the Federal Trade Commission (FTC), which illuminated both ALSCO and the associations to the FTC with dramatic repercussions to follow in the coming years.

In this era, it was the lenders who maintained the repossession insurance. Repossession agencies, if they were association members, maintained bonds, which across the associations was almost identical in value and worth. Looking to further the companies market appeal to the lenders, Jim reached out to an insurance broker, Ernie Powell from Phoenix in 1982. Ernie was in the business of writing policies for ambulance companies and tow companies and was taken back when approached with insuring the wild world of the repossession industry.

The first repossession insurance carrier, according to Mike Howk of RSIG, was Fireman's insurance, who cancelled it despite its strong profits and low losses, so they went to a smaller company. For better and worse, Jim can be credited, or blamed, for the advent of repossession agency insurance. Prior to this era, lenders carried their own repossession insurance as part of their lending bond.

By 1988, ALSCO had grown to up to 130 offices nationwide when they created their National Assignment Center (NAC). The NAC took a cut of every assignment forwarded to an ALSCO office to support their operational expenses and expand marketing. This, for all intents and purposes, was the industries first repossession forwarding company. In years to come, bids came in from outside parties attempting to buy it, some from forwarding companies in operation today.

Ron's Back, and Hooked

Back in the states again, in 1972, Ron Brown took a job with a local collection agency, CSI, during a ninety-day leave between government tours in Southeast Asia. His fascination with skip tracing began with a fraudster that used a fake check to buy a Porsche in California. Already a monkey brained adrenaline junkie, without thinking it through, Ron leapt at the opportunity to assist in repossessing it. In no time, Ron was in California staking out the suspect's sister's house when around midnight the fraudster and the car showed up.

Parking the Porsche under a window on the side of the house, the fraudster locked it and entered the dwelling. Briefly peeking out the window and assuring its safety, the thief turned out the lights and called it a night. "It's all yours. Go and get it." said Ron's boss as he slapped the keys into his hand. Snatching the keys, Ron left the safety of the car.

Creeping like a cat around the back of the house, Ron stayed on the window's blindside until coming up on the car. Slipping the key into the door lock, he opened the door triggering the dome lights and illuminating him to the entire neighborhood. Slipping into the driver's seat, Ron eased the door shut and extinguished the dome lights rude glare before inserting the key into the ignition and placing the transmission in neutral. With a twist of the key, the German engine rumbled to life.

Ramming the gears in neutral, Ron backed down the driveway, across the yard and off the curb into the street. Gaining speed, Ron stole away in reverse until reaching the street corner where he cranked out a "bootlegger turn" and kicked it into first gear and ascended gears on his way to completing his first repossession. Adrenaline pulsing through his veins, Ron was hooked. He'd found the profession that he wanted to spend his future in, he wanted to be a "Repo-Man."

Photo by Efe Yağız Soysal on Unsplash

Oh, The Things You See

Running accounts at 4:30 a.m. on a Saturday morning isn't for everyone. Call it dedication to the job or nothing better to do, but one unnamed adjuster was at an address in Fontana, California when he left the comfort of his car to peek into the garage of a borrower's address in hopes of spotting his unit. Peering through the mail slot with his flashlight, he lost thought of the car when he found a pair of eyes staring right back at him. The eyes of a 300-pound Bengal Tiger.

Needless to say, the adjuster called the police. Upon arrival, he reminded officers of a news story he'd heard of a tiger recently stolen from a small San Diego zoo. Police verified with the San Diego Sheriffs Department that indeed a two-year-old female tiger named "Ada" had been stolen from an inland zoo. Officers were advised that Ada had been declawed, was missing most of her teeth and had been used primarily in commercials and promotional events. Bravely, the officers removed the big cat and transported her in the back of their patrol car to Holter's Animal Farm until the owners could claim her.

Happy ending, right? Wrong. From there, the story takes a sad twist.

Jocelyn Hampton, age twenty-six and Sanderson Smith, twenty-five, were arrested for grand theft. As it turns out, Hampton's ex-husband, William, was living at the home of the tiger's owner in Lakeside. Having quickly made bail, Hampton returned to the scene of the crime the next day at 2 a.m. with twenty-two-year-old Michael Wood, allegedly intent on serving him divorce papers. Creeping around the house, Wood was mistaken for a prowler and police were called.

When police arrived, they heard a shotgun blast. Officers found Wood outside the house with twenty-one bird-shot pellets in his chest fired by Mr. Hampton. Officers entered the residence to find the weapon when they encountered the tiger. Frightened, the tiger ran into a bedroom with five sleeping children, ages six-months to five-years-old, three of them Hampton's and two from the homeowner.

Officers claimed the tiger lunged at the children and began wrestling with one. The officers beat it away, but it attacked another before turning on a dog only to be restrained once again. Breaking free, the tiger reared up on its hind legs and lunged at another child. Both officers opened fire on the tiger and killed it. San Bernardino - (San Bernardino, California) August 7 and 8, 1973

Five kids sleeping in one room with a tiger running free through the house, what could go wrong? It is unknown if officers allowed the agent to recover the unit or if it was even there, but that's kind of petty in relation to everything else that went down. Peeking through garage door windows and mail slots was standard agent practice well into the twenty-first century and in many cases is still done today.

The Bible or the Tow Boom

Picking change out from under the back seats of cars, Les was always the richest kid in grade school and always willing to drop his pennies, nickels, and dimes down to buy my friends candy at Scooter's store. Born of auto blood, the son of a used car dealer with a repo business in Waco, Texas, he earned his repo stripes sweeping floors and working on the lot like so many others in the business. His first repo assist was with his father when he was twelve, dragging a Hudson with a chain from the back of his father's pickup truck.

Growing up in the repossession industry, Les had his driver's license by the age of fifteen and with it, a "Blue Bar" tow bar for his birthday. License in hand and Blue Bar in the back, he was running his own repossession assignments before he left high school. Leaving home every Thursday night or Friday morning, Les travelled to auto auctions from San Antonio, Dallas, Abilene, Phoenix all the way to the Los Angeles Auto Auction and saw a lot of our country and had the opportunity for unique experiences on a weekly basis before joining the Army.

Les McCook, 1980s – (photo courtesy of Les McCook)

While the Vietnam war came to an end as Les was in basic training, that didn't stop Les from getting in a little action at Fort Hood. His Dad still needed cars repo'd, and there were plenty to drag off base through the back gates. Even when transferred to Germany, Les found side jobs in the repossession world and took his adventures to the German countryside.

Leaving the service, Les was soon back in Waco, TX and returned to school. Never one to only do one thing at a time, he opened a small car lot and began helping his mother run the family repossession company. Studying theology in college, one day Les's religion professor called him from class to make him a deal, check out of his class and get an incomplete or flunk. Les chose the world of repossessions and has never looked back.

Les McCook eventually went to work for Jack Schwan of Central Texas Auto Recovery. There, he was afforded the privilege of attending many TFA, NFA, AFA and ARA meetings and events where he was provided the opportunity to listen and learn from the leaders of these associations and the many other people willing to help a youngster learn the business. Les finally settled down with Preferred Adjusters, Inc. in Austin where he is the company President. Briefly an AFA Executive Committee member, he eventually settled in at the ARA, where he climbed through the ranks and finally settled in as Executive Director of the ARA.

Les McCook is the consummate repossession industry evangelist. The passion for the industry running through his veins has sparked generations of new repossession industry blood running through the ARA ranks to this day.

A Friendly Revolt

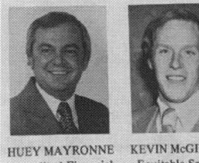

HUEY MAYRONNE
Accredited Financial
Adjusters
New Orleans, La.

KEVIN McGIVERN
Equitable Services
Chicago, Ill.

In 1976, the American Recovery Association (ARA), was still a part of the American Collectors Association (ACA). ACA President John Johnson was too busy for it and its near absolute control was in the hands of one of the ACA's secretaries, remembered only as "Dorothy". To its members, the ACA seemed somewhat ambivalent to the ARA and its direction. Frustration boiled over that called for action.

Seeking to maintain the associations momentum, Kevin McGivern of Equitable Services of Chicago and Huey Mayronne of Accredited Financial Adjusters of New Orleans offered to assume control of the ARA. To everyone's surprise, the ACA handed over the association, lock-stock, and barrel for free, no strings attached and within a few days, McGivern and Mayronne arrived at the ACA's Minnesota headquarters. Wasting no time for fear they might change their minds, they loaded a truck with all the ARA's records, files, and materials. After a long drive to New Orleans, the modern American Recovery Association was born.

On His Own

In June of 1975, the TFA held its annual convention in San Francisco. In the audience were the owners of AOC Adjusters, Bud Krohn, Tony Tomasello, Walt Burleson and Derrell Biddy along with Bud's son Ken Krohn. As nominations for new association Presidents were taken, Bud's name was brought forth. "Over my dead body!" shouted Bud's partner Tony Tomasello.

BUD KROHN
National Auto Recovery
Oakland, Calif.

Insulted, Bud and Ken walked out of the room. Partner Walt Burleson walked out right behind him. On July 15th, Bud bought Oakland, California based "National Auto Recovery Bureau" (NARB) from long time owner Charles Clark. In the following years, Bud, his sons Ken, David and daughter Deborah were running offices from the Northern California border city of Eureka all the way down to the south-central coastal town of Santa Maria.

Innovation Overseas

In 1976, America was thumping its chests over the nation's bicentennial. In the meanwhile, our former oppressors were launching a revolution of their own, a technological one. Facing an epidemic of auto theft, The British Police Scientific Development Branch (PSDB) began dabbling with a crude prototype of a camera that could read license plate numbers. Their early prototypes were of low accuracy and only worked under restrictive laboratory conditions, making their implementation unfeasible at that time.

Eventually, workable prototypes were created by EMI Electronics and then at Computer Recognition Systems (CRS.) These were implemented at the Dartford Tunnel in Kent, UK in 1979. By 1981, they were attributed to the first LPR arrest for auto theft in the world. Unfortunately, this technology, still in its infancy and was expensive and difficult to use.

A Deadly Pursuit

William Nespor and Mary Weatherbee of US Recovery of Huntington Beach, California found their unit at the given address in Lynwood but needed a tow truck. Arriving with the truck was Clarence E. Clark. "Hook and book", Clark had it and drove away with Nespor and Weatherbee following him back to the lot. Hot on their tail was the twenty-three-year-old borrower, Charles F. Shelton in a panel truck.

Shelton opened fire on the agents as he chased them around Lynwood. Firing several shots at Nespor and Weatherbee, he fired several more at Clark, hitting him in his side. Running his tow truck up and over the curb, he slumped over the wheel as Shelton continued the pursuit on the other adjusters. Nespor and Weatherbee managed to elude him unharmed and made a frantic call to police.

Officers arrived at Sanborn Street and Long Beach Boulevard to find Shelton trying to unhitch his car from the tow truck. In the front seat and hunched over the steering wheel sat forty-five-year-old father of two, Clark, shot dead. Independent - (Long Beach, California) July 10, 1974

The Price is Right

One of the added values of association membership was access to the establishment of industry best practices. This included the establishment of suggested fees, stated as not mandated, but strongly suggested. Although not publicly stated, the consequences of not abiding by these suggestions could result in an error in a company's association directory listing phone number resulting in a complete loss of value in their association membership or worse losing their membership completely.

1978 ARA Service Fees Schedule

These tables included, tow, storage, forwarding and fees of all types. To the casual observer, the repossession industry made its income from the repossession. On a deeper review of invoices of the era, it becomes obvious that the repossession is a "vehicle" for other fee incomes.

All four of the associations were in the practice of posting suggested fee tables at this time. Illustrated from a 1978 ARA association book, we can see what Service Fee industry best practices looked like during the era.

Just to put these fees in perspective, their 2021 equivalents are in parenthesis.

Fifteen cents per mile. (Don't laugh, that's $0.78 in 2021 value)

$20 for developing a new address that results in a recovery. ($79.87)

$10 for making a demand for collateral. ($41.29)

$45 for a Voluntary Repossession ($179.72)

$50 for a truck repossession ($206.20)

$75 for a tractor trailer ($309.66)

$10 for selling repossessed collateral. ($41.29)

Keep in mind, these prices were a la carte and added to the recovery fee for the full aggregated bill. While not mentioned in the schedule, in this, and earlier eras, assignments were assigned and worked to its "Resolution", which was the industry standard of the time. Closing fees varied, but "contingent" (no recovery, no fees) assignments were rarely accepted. Contingent assignments were severely frowned upon and rare for many years to come.

The associations were noticeably clear in their preface to these fees in stating that; *"Fees are a matter of contract between authorized users of the directory or forwarders and members, or forwarders of the association, does not presume to establish any fixed policy that is intended to be binding upon its members."*

While it may appear that competition between the associations would sway prices, with the majority of agency owners being members of anywhere from two to three associations, these fees were almost identical from one association to another. These Service Fee schedules, as well as association guaranteed exclusivity to territory that barred other companies from membership were soon to face a day of reckoning.

The Recession of the Mid 70's

In the midst of the mid-70's recession of 1973 to 1975, Dr. William Ford, Economist for the American Bankers Association, reported that the repossession rate for indirect auto loans was at 5.13 percent of every 1,000 auto loans granted and 1.76 percent for direct auto loans. This did not include the number of loans affected so no estimate of actual volume is known.

But in a 1976 article, the American Bankers Association was quoted as stating that the repossession rate was at 1.25 percent of every 1,000 auto loans granted. This was quoted as an annual estimate of 190,000 repossession per year. Missing that needed numerator, one can only assume that auto repossession volume was considerable and well in excess of 200,00 units per year or perhaps as high as 300,000.

The Repo Queen

According to Allied Finance Adjusters Executive Director George Badeen, In 1970 and again in 1974, Lorna Lou Barnes was elected President of the very same association she co-founded, the Allied Finance Adjusters. By all known records, this makes her the first woman to hold presidency of a national repossession association. She opened the door to change from the "good ol' boy" industry to the one it is now. One in which many women have risen to lead and one in which women make up some of its strongest leaders.

Lorna Lou Barnes - The Miami News, 18 Apr. 1977 - © Bill Reinke — USA TODAY NETWORK

It had been over forty years since the foundation of the Allied Finance Adjusters when Lorna gave this newspaper interview from the back of "a desolate office above a tire shop and across from a junkyard" and the Miami River. Hardly the glamorous backdrop expected of the founding first lady of the first repossession association. Regardless, this was only her Florida office, and from her accounts, and she also ran two more "Barnes Detective Agency, Inc." offices in New York state, including the one she and Ray opened in Flushing.

Lorna Lou Barnes would have been about sixty-seven-years-old and in her forty-seventh year in the industry during this interview, which was one of several during the 70's, but this was her last from what I could find. Still sporting her signature bright red hair, Lorna Lou was described as *"a short vivacious woman"* by the reporter. While most women of this age would be slowing down, retiring or already retired, Lorna Lou had reported to have just returned from a repo convention in New Orleans and was soon to head to another on the West Coast.

Lorna Lou reminisced of her early years with Ray; *"My husband and I used to make a game of repossessing"* she said, *"We'd have some friends over and we'd be sitting around and then one of us would say 'Let's go out and get a car.'* And they would. *"I used to do a lot of repos myself"* she said, *"I used to be out on the street."*

In an earlier 1971 article, she had filled in for AFA Treasurer Michael Grady at a New Jersey Banks Association Conference at the Cherry Hill Inn. During this event, she claimed to co-founding the Barnes Detective Agency in 1931, when they were still in Los Angeles and just a year after meeting. She also stated that so far as she knows "*she is the only woman in this type of business*." While not an accurate statement, Lorna was a pioneer and paved the way for growing numbers of women in the industry as agency owners and field adjusters in the decades to come. The Miami News - (Miami, Florida) – April 18, 1977, and Courier Post - (Camden, New Jersey) October 7, 1971

Lorna Lou Barnes operates out of an office over a tire shop: 'But I'm known nationwide'

Lorna Lou Barnes. The man in the background is Louis Platt - The Miami News, 18 Apr. 1977 - © Bill Reinke — USA TODAY NETWORK

It was not too long after this last interview of Lorna that she approached Ken Krohn of NARB in Oakland, California asking him to come to Florida and take over her office. She was ready to retire. Ken declined the offer and stayed in the family business. Louis Platt and Sam Corolla were working for Lorna at this time. Sam recalls Louis's face having been disfigured by a borrower's blow with a tire iron.

President Jimmy Carter – (photo from the National Archives)

Reining in the Wild West

Debt collections was, as Senator Elizabeth Warren put it years later, the "*Wild West.*" It was a wide-open, lightly, if at all, regulated industry notorious for aggressive tactics, and to be fair, the repossession industry wasn't much, if any better. The days of legal harassment, late-night calls and overt threats was about to come to an end. On September 20, 1977, President Jimmy Carter signed into law the Fair Debt Collections Practices Act (FDCPA).

The FDCPA established the first federal laws for protection against abusive collections practices. This included the use of threatening language, communication with third parties, and more. The Act extended rights to debtors, including verification of debt and notification of a consumer's right to dispute a debt. While other civil remedies were available prior to this, the FDCPA was the first national effort to reign in the "*Cowboy*" tactics of old.

With these new federal regulations in place, a new question arose, does this apply to the repossession industry? The Act left the distinction between what is a "Debt Collector" and what is a "Repossessor" silent. Absent binding legal clarification, the issue became a litigation "puppy mill" for decades to come.

Historically, repossession agencies had routinely collected payments, it was part of the positive resolution desired. In the absence of clarity, most agencies became one dimensional and just went after the vehicle. "Door Knocking", a longtime offered service, soon fell from the menu of offered services. Who knows how many borrowers lost their vehicles because agents weren't allowed to discuss or accept payments?

Likewise fed up with the antics of the repossession industry, states began to follow California and adopted their own repossession related legislation. Most of these laws passed in the 1970's remain in place with little change. To date, there is no sole federal regulatory body or action governing the repossession industry. That is not to say that other legal actions wouldn't be taken or attempted in the future.

Art Meets Technology

This was the decade that technology and its expenses began creeping into the repossession industry. In 1977, computers were still a far cry in speed, memory, price and functionality of the PC's and smart phones that we enjoy today. Regardless, Art Christiansen saw the potential technological advantages and hired three software and network developers. Soon after, the repossession industries very first repossession management software, "CADO" was born.

Art Christiansen, years later, sans guitar

Art, already a longtime ARA member, first approached ARA co-founder, Kevin McGivern of Equitable Services and made his first sale. Soon to follow were Dave Wright, Bud Krohn of NARB Oakland, the Dunleavy's at TCAR in New York and more to follow. Soon after, Art helped introduced both the ARA and the AFA to computer automation and soon the repossession industry was bit by the technology bug. Other software programs would enter the market through the years, but this was the first step away from manual ledgers.

Art remembered this from 1980, but Kevin McGivern of Equitable Services found his receipt from his purchase dated 1977.

GM in the Groove

Prior to 1978, repossessing GM vehicles with column mounted ignitions was relatively easy. Using a slide hammer, an agent would pry off the ignition "fly wings" and insert a sheet metal screw with the slide hammer grommet into the keyway. They would then screw in the rod of the slide hammer into the grommet and with a few hard tugs back on the weighted hammer handle, the ignition lock would pop right out.

This engineering deficiency was also exploited on other vehicles. But it was GM who first put a halt to it by incorporating a groove in the lock cylinder. The groove hosted a screw that was only accessible by pulling the steering wheel removing the lock ring. In the years to come, repossessors became quite adept at steering wheel removal, some even doing it without a steering wheel puller!

First in the Parthenon or Second in Rome

Art Lamoureux at a
1977 NFA conference

Over the 1970's, the friendship and business relationship between Equitable Services Kevin McGivern and Frank Mauro grew. Early in the decade, Kevin had dated Frank's daughter Roxane and Kevin was actually doing Frank's repossessions. The problem was, Frank notoriously hated paying his bills and was not a man anyone intimidated. In 1979, Frank's bill with Kevin had grown substantially and Frank had been avoiding Kevin for a few days until responding to him, ignoring the billing issue, and instead "telling" Kevin to give him a ride to the airport.

Being a family friend, Kevin saw no problem with this and arrived at the Mauro home, picking up Frank and waving goodbye to Frank's wife Rita as they left. All but silent the entire way, they arrived at the airport and waited for Art Lamoureux before going inside and settling down at a coffee shop to talk about Kevin's bill. Silk suit and dressed to kill, Frank took the seat across the booth as the likewise well-dressed Art, took a seat at Kevin's side. Lighting a cigarette as they waited for coffee, Frank broke the ice.

"I like you, Kevin. You need to come work for me. I can get you all of the biggest clients." Frank stated as he leaned in between puffs from the cigarette. Not being a man that you said "no" to, Kevin squirmed under Frank's glare as Art leered on from the side. Kevin knew what this meant and knew it would be the end of his company if he agreed. *"I'm sorry Frank, I just can't work for anyone else."* Kevin replied, most likely with a bead of sweat forming on his brow and quite a lump in his throat.

Frank snuffed out the cigarette in the ashtray as the coffee arrived as sat back for a moment before replying. *"Would you rather be number one at the Parthenon or number two or three in Rome?"* he asked. Frank was notorious for having a statement like this for any occasion and Kevin, having little idea what he was talking about, replied, *"Sorry Frank, I just can't."* To Kevin's relief, Frank shrugged it off and promised to pay the past due invoices when he returned.

Although Frank's interest in the repossession industry was, at this time, waning, Frank never ceased to desire control of all that he could. As intimidating as Frank was and as much a stereotype as he posed, you will find no evidence of Frank or Art's involvement in any nefarious activities. Kevin's friendship with the Mauro family maintains to this day.

In 1977, Frank was threatened with state legal action over campaign irregularities for providing then Governor Thompson a dealer plated vehicle to use during his gubernatorial run. Dodging the allegations, the Governor appointed him a seat on the Illinois State Toll Highway Authority, a position he had also served as interim Chair of from 1978-1991. Art maintained the role of Secretary of the NFA well into the 1990's while Frank maintained Presidency and complete dominance until the mid-70's before relinquishing control and being made an Honorary Chairman of the Board, a position he held for decades.

One Shot

Just old enough to drink, twenty-one-year-old William McGuigan of Egg Harbor Township, New Jersey had taken a part-time job as a repossessor for Louis Miller, the owner of "Capt. Hook's Tow Service." At about 2 a.m. they arrived at a debtors residence to repossess a 1974 Chevrolet Malibu for an unnamed finance company. Hooking it up to the tow truck, they began to leave. Stepping out from a neighboring small corner store where he worked part-time, was the borrower, thirty-one-year-old Arthur Pearl Jr.

Pearl ran back inside, emerging seconds later with the store owner's .32 caliber revolver kept under the counter. Pearl fired one shot and struck McGuigan in the head. Five hours later, William McGuigan was pronounced dead in the Atlantic City Medical Center. Pearl was charged with murder. - Asbury Park Press (Asbury Park, New Jersey) – June 30, 1978

At twenty-one, McGuigan left behind a young wife and a daughter. The McGuigan family suffered even more tragedy the next year, when William's father Hugh, six-year-old brother, two uncles and two cousins drowned at sea after their fishing boat capsized.

Battle Born

In 1979, a young Field Adjuster named George Badeen came to work for Al Michel at Midwest Recovery and Adjustment Service just outside of Detroit in Redford, Michigan. Through the years, he would rise through the ranks to manager, VP of Operations and eventually President. George's tenacity, conviction and passion for the repossession industry would eventually carry him on to lead the nation's oldest association, the AFA. Not content with his roles in the industry, George would go on to wage a war on behalf of the industry that would carry on for over ten years!

A Hostage Lender

Billing lenders was always a sore point in the industry. The blatant hypocrisy of a lender hiring a repossession agency to recover their collateral and then not pay them has always been an issue. To solve this, many agencies would not release the collateral to a transporter, borrower, or lender without being paid in full. One humorous and possibly true story of how this was resolved in the 70's was provided by Wes Carico of Nostalgic Towing.

"My first experience with wreckers was in the 1970's. My dad owned a service station with a full-service garage and wreckers in Wise County, VA (Appalachian Mountains.) When I opened a Repo company, he became very nostalgic about it and relayed the story of our families first repo around the mid to late 70's."

"Two "bankers" came by the station and inquired if he knew "so and so", and dad told them he did. They ask where he lived, and he told them. They then asked if dad would take them to repossess the car and he agreed but they had to pay his past due bill at the shop. Agreement reached, dad told them to get in the truck and wait for him. He grabbed his .357 and off the went through the hills of Southwest Virginia."

"They pulled up and dad broke straight for the front door, knocked, and put the gun in the customers face and demanded the keys. The customer handed them over and dad threw them to one of the bankers. The other banker had to stay with him until he got paid. Guess they held the bankers for payment then. No such thing as a garage filing a lien back in those days."

"He said I was crazy for releasing cars to the bank without getting paid first. True or not, can't say. Mom says, very likely true, as he didn't put up with much."

Shot in the Back

On October 20, 1979, at 2:30a.m. on a Saturday morning, Michael Manno, twenty-five, and his fellow repossession agent, Terrance Jarrus, located a vehicle assigned for repossession registered to thirty-year-old Carl West parked against the curb in front of the given address in Signal Hill, California. Hearing the men out front, West emerged with an automatic pistol. West opened fire as the duo were preparing to tow it away.

West fired fifteen rounds. Manno was shot in the back and died on the scene. West claimed that he thought they were thieves. West was booked for investigation of murder and attempted murder. - Los Angeles Times - (Los Angeles, California) October 21, 1979

Department of Justice

FOR IMMEDIATE RELEASE
TUESDAY, JANUARY 6, 1981

AT
202-633-2007

The Department of Justice today filed a civil antitrust
suit against Time Finance Adjusters, a national association of
repossessors located in Daytona Beach, Florida, alleging a
conspiracy to restrain competition in the independent repossession
service market, in violation of Section 1 of the Sherman Act.

Repossessors, or adjusters as they are sometimes called,
provide services for banks, credit unions and other lenders
that seek to recover merchandise sold under a security agreement.

Attorney General Benjamin R. Civiletti said that the suit
was filed in United States District Court in Orlando, Florida.

Sanford M. Litvack, Assistant Attorney General in charge
of the Antitrust Division, said the complaint alleges
that, beginning sometime prior to 1975 and continuing to the
present, Time Finance Adjusters agreed to, published, and
disseminated fee schedules for various repossession services.

CHAPTER 8 – THE 1980'S – THE END OF THE INNOCENCE

Bud: "An ordinary person spends his life avoiding tense situations. A repo man spends his life getting into tense situations."
"The Repo Man" Alex Cox - 1984

The decade began in President Jimmy Carter's final year. America was in the midst of another recession, economic growth was sluggish, inflation high, and the unemployment rate was at 7.2 percent. The American embassy in Iran had been overrun and fifty-two American were being held hostage by Iranian revolutionaries. On October 4th of this year, Ronald Reagan was elected president to the US population of now 226 million.

With high fuel prices, the market share of import autos had climbed to 35 percent of all auto sales. Detroit had its worst production year since 1961. With only 6.4 of the 8.9 million vehicles sold made in American, Detroit laid off over a quarter of a million workers. This environment was fertile ground for the repossession industry, but what happened in this decade would change the repossession industry forever.

Trust and the DOJ

As shown the previous chapter, associations published non-mandatory minimum price lists in their adjuster directories. In these lists, were almost every type of ancillary service from storage to keys and mileage. Depending upon association bylaws, these were voted for by the board of directors or through democratic vote. Perhaps most important, these fees usually increased on an annual basis to accommodate for inflation.

Prior to this period, the associations were free to deny any new agency membership. Associations also had the right to refuse a member agencies expansion into additional territories. Any effort to expand into a territory without the association's approval was done at the peril of expulsion. In 1981 the era of competitive advantage through a guaranteed territorial marketing monopoly came to an end.

As mentioned in the last chapter, internal squabbling had already shined a spotlight on industry practices with the Federal Trade Commission. On January 5, 1981, this unwanted attention came to a boil when the NFA, TFA, ARA And AFA were served papers by the Antitrust Division of the Department of Justice. The charges against them were, conspiracy to fix prices, restrict territories and limit membership in violation of the Sherman Act, 15 USC.

The TFA, still owned and run by Harvey Altes, was unfazed by the accusations. His response to the DOJ, although reasonable, was the equivalent of giving them the middle finger. Harvey stated that they sold ad spaces and were a marketing association and not a trade association and that the allegations against them were not applicable. Although they paid and complied like everyone else, Harvey's response, illustrated a vastly different perspective of the role of the associations than his peers.

Without an admission of guilt, the NFA and AFA and TFA settled without court trial. Reportedly, all of the associations except the ARA paid a fine of about $25,000. The agreed upon terms of the settlements were sweeping.

Prohibited Conduct

Under Section IV of the proposed Final Judgment the defendant is restrained from (l) fixing any price schedule or list for repossession services; (2) advertising any price schedule or list for repossession services; (3) publishing any price schedule or list for repossession services: (4) participating in any communications with representatives of other repossessor associations that relate to any price schedule or list for repossession services; or (5) engaging in any conduct the effect of which is to influence the formulation of any price schedule or list for repossession services.

Numbers (4) and (5) utterly neutered the associations. After a three-year fight until the last association settled, the associations lost the opportunity to even discuss what a best practice in pricing looked like.

Hamstrung by these agreements, life went on for the associations. But the ramifications of their agreements, left the industry out of control of its own destiny and in an "every man for himself" posture with consequences that resonates to this day. Technology, which made leaps and bounds in the 80's, would eventually assist in exploiting this vulnerability. The 80's were what could probably be marked as the end of the "*Golden Age of the Repossession Industry*,"

The race to the bottom had begun.

Golden Drags Down the AFA

Jim Golden's 1979 reign as Chairman of the Board of the Allied Finance Adjusters (AFA) compromised the association when in November 16, 1981, a $14.5 million antitrust lawsuit was filed against ALSCO, it's officers and himself. Edward M. Stoll, the owner of Western States Auto Recovery in New Mexico, an AFA member since 1947 filed the lawsuit with claims that the AFA, through BIDCO and ALSCO, were attempting to monopolize the repossession industry in his state. Named in the suit were, Jim Golden, Robert Matthews of Texas, E.R. and Verne Engdahl of California, Ruthnan Bigelow of Nevada, David Schwebe of Wisconsin, and Thomas Vietz of Ohio. The defendants were all elected to the AFA Board in July of 1979.

Stoll's attorney claimed that, at this time, 60 to 70 percent of agencies received their out of state repossession referrals through the association directories and that they were essential to the agencies business survial. The lawsuit claimed that ALSCO was created by the AFA to compete on a nationwide scale with their own association members. He alleged that the AFA officers actively contacted association members trying to induce them into buying ALSCO franchises. Stoll's probable final straw was when ALSCO opened a franchise in his business hometown of Albuquerque run by Max Forney.

At this time, ALSCO allegedly had 60 owner operators in 25 states. - Albuquerque Journal (Albuquerque, New Mexico) - November 17, 1981

No newspaper record of the results of this lawsuit could be found, but ALSCO continued on unhindered. Regardless, his standing in the AFA was somewhat diminished. It is a belief by many that Stoll was the one who brought the associations practices to the attention of the DOJ that led to the earlier 1981 antitrust suit.

Too Young to Die

On the afternoon of February 5, 1981, in Burbank, California, a six-foot seven and 480 pound, twenty-two-year-old Bernard Reardon of Glendale went to the home of fifty-year-old Epworth Croft to repossess a station wagon. In the process, Croft emerged from the home armed with a hunting rifle. After an exchange of words, Croft shot Reardon in the chest and killed him. Croft fled but was captured within 30 minutes. The Signal - (Santa Clarita, California) February 6, 1981

According to a 1987 interview with The Morning Call (Allentown, Pennsylvania) June 29, 1987, Joseph Sharlin, Reardon's employer at Key Auto Recovery in Van Nuys, California was especially upset that that the lender did not advise them that the borrower, Croft, was at the time of the murdrer out on bail.

No Justice in Ohio

It was about 2:15 a.m. in Mount Airy, Ohio when Gary Pitzer and Floyd "Rich" Barber of Tri-State Recovery spotted the 1978 pick-up truck on the repossession assignment. Nosed into the carport of the two-story brick apartment building, Barber got out of the truck and approached it. Breaking into it, he quickly had it started and either didn't hear, or ignored the shouting from behind. Two shots from a .357 magnum revolver later, twenty-six-year-old Floyd Barber was dead.

His shooter was twenty-three-year-old laid off autoworker, Cecil John Partin who was charged with murder and released on bond under the representation of his attorney Will Outlaw. Partin, facing fifteen years to life, went on trial on August 22nd claiming that he was only trying to shoot the tires and thought it was being stolen. Judge Donald L. Schott declared him not guilty of the charge of murder and reduced the charge to negligent homicide, a first-degree misdemeanor with a maximum six-month sentence and a $1,000 fine. The courtroom, packed with Partin's family and friends, erupted in applause, celebration and tears of joy, but not everyone was happy.

Reporters reaching out to local Repossessors felt quite the opposite. "It's not very much, is it? Six months jail time isn't enough." Complained one unnamed adjuster. "It stinks. At least he didn't get off scot-free, otherwise it'd be open season on repossessors" grumbled another. - The Cincinnati Enquirer - (Cincinnati, Ohio) August 22, 1981, and March 28, 1981

The Dunleavy Brothers at Edward's retirement party in 1980 - (L-R) Craig 15, Brian 20, Brad 22, Chris 27 – (photo courtesy of Chris Dunleavy)

From Father to Sons

In 1980 Edward "Ed" Dunleavy sold his credit reporting service and essentially retired, leaving his two oldest sons, Chris and Brad to take over and run the repossession company, then, called Tri City Auto Recovery, Inc., Later known as TCAR. At that time, there were three employees operating out of a location in Schenectady New York. Chris and Brad began expanding the company, opening locations in Syracuse, New Windsor and Plattsburgh (all New York State). By the early 90's, they had gotten very busy, and their two younger brothers Brian and Craig had also joined the family business.

Over the next decade they expanded the company further, to a total of 15 locations, 125 employees, operating in five different states. In the early 2000's the third generation of family joined the family business, Patrick, Brad's son, Ryan Alverson, Chris's son-in-law, and Kyle, Craig's son.

The Dunleavy's attribute their success to the hard work and dedication of their staff and the core principles instilled by the Patriarch of the family, Ed Dunleavy. "Professional Service, provided with personal relationships, in an ethical and fair manner."

The Dunleavys at a 2006 SBA Award Ceremony – second from left, Chris, Father Edward and Mother Beverly (center) with brothers Craig, Brian and Brad along with a representative from 1st National Bank and a couple reps from the SBA. – (photo courtesy of Chris Dunleavy)

Infighting

On November 5, 1981, counsel for Jim Golden and American Lenders Service Co. (ALSCO) filed for a temporary restraining order against the NFA, case No. 81-74201. Golden, a member of NFA, claimed that the NFA had restricted the manner in which that he could advertise his service area in the 1982 NFA Directory in violation of the DOJ consent decree. The Court granted Goldens petition for a TRO and on December 16, 1981, a default judgment was granted in his favor, only to be later dismissed over procedural issues.

Just the Fax

In 1843, Scottish engineer and inventor Alexander Bain invented the first telefax machine. After a century and a half of improvements, this device would become a staple in the American office space.

(L-R) Kevin McGivern, Harvey Altes, Art Christensen, 1984 – (photo Courtesy of the ARA)

By 1981, repossession orders began creeping into agency offices. "Facsimile Machines" as they were first known, were soon to replace the phone calls and mail by which assignments used to come in. Pouring assignments in at all hours, "fax machines" spewed chemically treated paper into baskets that once full left them scattered on the floor waiting for office staff in the morning. The luxury of this transformational device then came at a staggering price of about $20,000 ($59,282 in 2021 value)!

Kevin McGivern recalls an ARA convention in about 1981 that Millard Land invited a fax machine salesman. He sold six on the spot, unfortunately, the rest of the industry wasn't quite up to speed yet. For months, Kevin, Millard and others could only fax notes back and forth amongst each other to assure they still worked. Eager to see this technology come into play, they soon began buying fax machines for their larger clients and soon assignments began to pour in and taking assignments by phone and mail was a thing of the past.

Weighing in at about a hundred and forty pounds and costing over $20,000, Ken Krohn of NARB recalls their first fax machine in 1983. It was at the urging of a client, Security Pacific National Bank, that they purchased it. One led to two and two to three, before long, they had one in every office. An expensive but necessary piece of technology, but at that time, fee structures were still reasonable, which years later became issues that would suck the industry's profitability dry.

The Long-Lost ARA Blimp - Just Joking! Kind of…

The ARA Repo Blimp

In October 1981, the ARA held its annual convention in New York City at the Statler Hotel's Grand Ballroom. Being in the "Big Apple" ARA cofounder Huey Mayronne chose to do something big enough to suit the city. He bought a blimp (a 4 ft x 6 ft balloon) described as "*It is white with red, white and blue fins, has a large ARA logo and a banner saying, 'Repossession Specialists.*" according to Art Christiansen in an October 9th newspaper article. The balloon valued as worth $1,300 disappeared from the ballroom after the end of the convention.

"It's a little embarrassing, not only for us but for the Statler as well," Christensen said. *"After all we're Repossessors and any of the 10,000 or so people from whom we monthly repossess cars, trucks, tractors mobile homes, whatever, must be having a laugh.*

"It was taken from under our noses, so to speak, so someone has to know about it. That's why we're offering a reward," he said. Art filed a police report with the NYPD.

Allegedly, years later, during an evening of drinks, ARA member Don Blanchett confessed to its theft being a practical joke and that once Art filed the police report, he didn't want to face the consequences. The balloon was allegedly never recovered, and Blanchett never showed it to anyone. Its whereabouts remain a mystery to this day.

Alleged Blimp Pirate,
Don Blanchette

The Lowest Rung in the Ladder

The Stumph family lived on a poultry farm in rural Pierz, Minnesota. John was one of 11 children and shared a room with his bothers until he got married. John graduated near the bottom of his high school class, so with bad grades and a lack of family income, he ended up working in a local bakery. After about a year, he enrolled in St. Cloud University on a provisional basis and in 1982 graduated with a bachelor's degree in finance. After all that hard work and tenacity, at the age of twenty-nine, he landed his first financial service industry job for Minneapolis-based Norwest Corp., as a Repo Man.

John's work schedule started at 10 a.m. and the first shift ended at 5 p.m. These were the suit and tie hours that he spent collecting payments and tracking down skipped borrowers. After a quick dinner, he'd change out of his banker suit and suit up for his second shift repossessing cars until often after midnight.

In a 2016 Walls Street Journal interview, he remarked on his years in the field. *"When you collect bad loans…. you sure learn a lot about making good ones,"* Stumpf told Institutional Investors. *You also learn a lot about the power of persuasion, persistence, and desperation.*

"You'd have these cars memorized. You would know there was a '69 Buick of a certain color and the person was 90 days past due and wasn't answer your telephone calls. You would track him down, call the tow truck and just as the car started to lift off the ground, out of the bar would walk a giant of a guy with two six-packs of confidence in him and he wants to know what you are doing with his car. Now that is exciting! You learned the power of persuasion,"

Through the years, John climbed the corporate ladder until in 2005 he was elected to the position of CEO of Wells Fargo Bank. While his eleven-year term was marred with the "fake account opening" scandal, he retired in 2016 worth an alleged $41 million and a compensation package valued at $130 million. This more than made the lifetime ban from the banking industry and combined 2020 fines of about $20 million. Say what you will of John Stumph, but he rose higher up the corporate ladder than any Repo Man in history.

Another Dead in Houston

It was a cold Saturday night in Houston when Edward S. Garcia, thirty-two had arrived at the residence of Ronald E. Moore. Garcia spotted Moore's car and hooked it up the tow truck. He hadn't made it more than few blocks when twenty-seven-year-old Moore caught up to him and opened fire. Garcia was hit and sped to safety, making it to the Gulf Freeway before losing control and crashing.

Moore was charged with murder and held on a $10,000 bond. This charge is in stark contrast to so many of these murders at night that went unpunished in Texas. This story circulated nationally through the Associated Press but no follow up stories could be found. In Tyler, Texas, this story warranted a page 27 story buried in the classified section. Tyler Morning Telegraph - (Tyler, Texas) January 1983, Page 27

At Buzz Greenwoods Lake House, R-L - Rusty Ansell and Jack Barnes – photo courtesy of Steve Summs

A Family Affair

The association conventions had become multi-generational affairs, and began to resemble an extended family reunion with many of the future generations of repossession industry leaders in attendance with their families. As in the past, bonds developed between these children as had happened with their parents and sometimes grandparents.

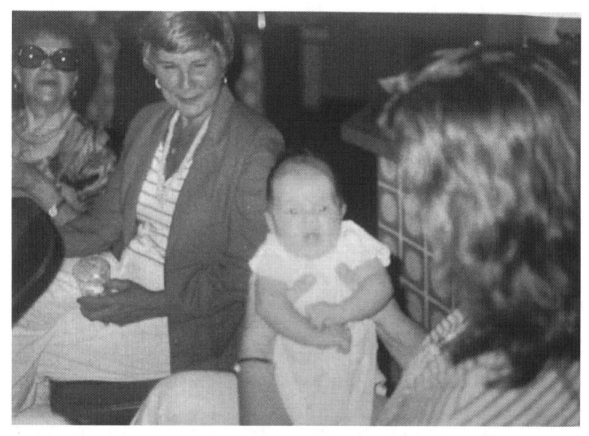

1st Repo Generation repossession pioneer meets the 4th - 1984 NFA Conference, Charolette, NC – L-R – "Auntie" Lorna Lou Barnes, Grandmother Agnes Summs, one-month-old Steven Summs, and Mother Cindy Summs – (photo courtesy of Steve Summs)

In August of 1984, the National Finance Adjusters (NFA) held their 48th annual convention in Charlotte, North Carolina. In attendance was co-founder and first lady of the repossession industry, Lorna Lou Barnes. Lorna, seen on the far left with her signature red hair. Lorna Lou is credited with the development of many repossession industry owners such as Sam Corolla, Rusty Ansell, and Henri "Hank" Leleu, who reportedly referred to her as "Auntie" Lorna Lou.

In 1981, the Allied Finance Adjusters held their annual convention in Hawaii. While suits were obviously not practical, nor comfortable in the humid tropics, the wearing of suits to these events was on the decline.

Repo Blood

Janice "Repo Rita" Krohn and son Ken
Krohn, NFA Conference 1988

1981 AFA Conference, Hawaii

Ken & Dave Krohn.

Mike Baldwin, Barbara Blanchette and Bruce Schneider.

Pat Cornett, Emily Murphy — Bank of America, Los Angeles and Connie S. Andrews.

Ntil Ekalheimer.

Harry & Karen Forest.

Paul & Susan Lamoureux.

Addison Kelly and Marjorie Bennett.

Derrell Biddy and John Musico.

Ernie & Katherine Horton.

Ernest & Sue Mitchell and Wayne Tannery.

Kathryn, Barbara Biddy and Shirley Burleson.

Ray DuBoise.

David & Linda Volpe and Marcia Musico.

Fred & Sheri Barnes.

Peggy Musico.

Derrell & Barbara Biddy and Burton Greenwood.

1986 NFA Conference, Los Angeles, California – (photo Courtesy of Les McCook and the ARA)

119

ARA Conference 1988 - Hawaii – (photo courtesy of Les McCook and the ARA)

Tradition

Also shown in the forefront of the photo, taken in August 1984, is a one-month-old Steven Summs, Jr. at his first National Finance Adjusters, Inc convention. Steven, along with his siblings Matthew and Kelsey went on to become the fourth generation of the Summs family operation.

Steve grew up in the repossession industry recalls with fondness the convention experience.

The Summs - L-R - Brock, Fred Jr., Mark

Steve Summs, Fourth Generation
in the Summs Family Business

"Between Jack Barnes, Buzz Greenwood, Jerry Wilson, and Brad Webb they all watched me grow up. This industry is a tight group of individuals that have always been willing to offer help and support at a moment's notice. The overwhelming majority of our family vacations were planned around the NFA/ARA conventions. I always remember my dad being in the seminars and board meetings while my mom took us around the city and then in the evenings attended the receptions.

This experience is shared by many others. These agencies often belonged to two or more associations and would often attend multiple conventions a year. These association were fierce competitors. Regardless, amongst the owners and their families, there were and still are strong bonds of unity.

A State of Order

For more than twenty years, the state of California's politicians had been railing on against their allegations of nefarious activity and "thugs and muscle men" of the repossession industry. In 1981, they took action and made major changes to the state Business and Professions Code with the establishment of Chapter 11. The "Repossessors Act" established new legal requirements to both agencies and agents that operate in the state. These include background checks and licensing.

This was the nation's first governmental repossession licensing requirement and to date, although not perfect, still one of the best in the nation. Florida instituted their own in 1998 Title XXXII

Regulation of Professions and Occupations, Chapter 493. In 2012, the State of Illinois adopted the Collateral Recovery Act, 225 ILCS 422/1 et seq., also establishing similar licensing requirements.

Typically, most states consolidate the licensing of repossession agencies and repossessors with that of collection agencies or collectors. This obviously creates confusion when dealng with matters involving the 1977 Federal Fair Debt Collections Practices Act. To date, many states have no state licensing requirements at all and there is no Federal law governing the industry.

What's in a Name?

It was also in 1981 when a man named Chuck came to work for Ken and Bud Krohn at their NARB office in San Jose, California. The then, three-year-old licensing requirements for repossession agents allowed him a 30-day temporary permit until his background was checked and a final license granted. So, when Bud and Ken were advised by the state that Chuck's application had been denied, they reached out to the state for an explanation. Little did they know, who they were about to employ.

Bud Krohn (L) and Jack Barnes (R) 1986
– (photo Courtesy of Ed Marcum)

As early as the late 1950's, the state of California had a very negative view of the repossession industry when they claimed that the repossession industry was "a hunting ground for petty racketeers, thugs, wildcatters, e-Convicts and muscle men." Charles "Chuck" Bonanno was the son of Salvatore "Bill" Bonanno and the grandson of former New York mob boss Joe "Bananas" Bonanno. As mentioned earlier in the 1968 story, Bill Bonanno and his brother Joe Jr. had been running amuck engaging in everything from extortion to money laundering since moving to California in 1970.

According to Ken Krohn, Chuck was a really genuine and straight guy that said, "wanted nothing to do with the family business." Having full faith in Chuck's credibility, Bud and Ken appealed to the State Department of Consumer Affairs, but they refused to budge.

On November 18, 1982, Charles was arrested trying to sell stolen truck parts which led to twenty-five other charges that he was conducting a "salvage-and-switch" scheme. In 1983, Charles was convicted of seventeen counts and sentenced to four years in prison. - Oroville Mercury Register - (Oroville, California) July 15, 1983

While many scoff at the state's licensing and enforcement, they certainly may have helped the Krohn's dodge a bullet.

Scirocco

I was a long-haired nineteen-year-old lot attendant at Bay Cities Auto Auction in Fremont, California back in 82'. Washing, parking and driving cars through the auction block on auction days were the majority of the duties, but one day, Operations Manager Don Nelson called me into his office. I thought I was going to make a special delivery to a dealer, detail his Ferrari, or get fired, but that wasn't it at all. In fact, it was an unbeknownst warm up for a job I'd never considered.

Don handed me an auction invoice and explained that the dealer's check bounced, and we needed to pick it up and bring it back. But there was one catch, I couldn't let them know what I was doing. I don't even remember the word "repossess" even being used. His instructions were pretty simple, look around at a few cars and keep your eyes open for the 79', VW Scirocco on the invoice and then just drive off with it when the salesman was out of the vehicle.

So, on that sunny day, the delivery transit driver dropped me off at the Fremont Blvd. dealership, I followed his instructions and shopped the lot. Before the salesman could even catch up to me, I'd spotted the Scirocco but stepped over to a Camaro instead. Asking if he could help me, I told him I wanted to hear the engine on the Camaro. Running off to get the keys, he soon returned and started the engine for me.

Asking him to pop the hood, I asked him to rev the engine, which he did. Twisting my lip with disinterest, I closed the hood and approached another car and repeated the routine with the same response. Stepping up to the Scirocco, we repeated the process until he revved the engine. "That doesn't sound good." I stated as his foot eased off the gas pedal.

Curious, the salesman climbed out from the driver's seat and stood next to the open hood by my side. Not hearing anything wrong, the salesman listened with intent as I suggested that I rev the engine. Climbing behind the wheel with the door open, I revved the engine, and the salesman shook his head, still hearing nothing wrong. "Close the hood and listen." I shouted over the revving engine as I checked the fuel gauge.

As suggested, he closed it. Then I closed the car door. Then he walked to my side and then I sped away. That was my first repo.

It wasn't for another eight years that I would do another, but that tactic became one I was pretty good at. A tactic that led me to the incident I spoke of in the book's introduction. But that's a whole different story for some other time.

Repo Goes Hollywood

In 1984, Director and writer, Alex Cox, released his iconic 1984 cult film classic "The Repo Man", Hollywood's first portrayal of the auto repossession industry. This satirical comedy takes place in Los Angeles where depressed, broke, and unemployed nihilistic young punk rocker "Otto", played by Emilio Estevez, encounters a shady man named "Bud" played Harry Dean Stanton, in a car who offers him $25 to drive his car back to his office. While a fun film, it is clearly an unrealistic view of the repossession industry at that time, but not by too much. Cox, an English film student at UCLA, actually worked with a Los Angeles repossessor named Mark Lewis and his experiences were the basis for this story.

While not portraying the repossession industry in a positive light, it is forgivable. This fun film made actor Harry Dean Stanton forever to be lovingly known as "The Repo Man" by many. One line of dialogue from this film, quoted by veteran repo man Bud, stands the test of time. "The life of a repo man is always intense."

GM Ignitions Go High-Tech

Ever since GM added the retaining screw to their ignitions, adjusters endured countless hours pulling steering wheels in driveways in the middle of the night. Sometime during the mid-1980's the GM Magnum Ignition force tool made its way into the field. This socket, fit on the inside cylinder of the GM ignition years 1984-1996 and when tapped firmly into place allowed the user to insert a ratchet and snap the lock sidebar and force the six wafers under the sheer line. While reasonably functional, it destroyed the lock and on occasion, snapped the ignition post and would just spin with no function.

In 1986 the Allied Finance Adjusters Celebrated their 50th Anniversary

Not done creating hurdles for adjusters and thieves alike, General Motors introduced an even bigger "time vampire." In 1986, the Chevrolet Corvette had become a huge target for car thieves. To address this, GM employed a new technology. The Vehicle Anti-Theft System, aka; VATS, (*not very creative, I know*) brought chip technology into play as the newest form of theft deterrence.

VATS employed a resistor pellet embedded on the blade of the key that required the resistor value to match that of a multimeter inside the ignition before allowing the ignition to engage. If the resistor value was wrong, the module would shut down for four minutes. For the agent in the field, even if they had the ignition key codes, there were fifteen different resistor chips. Overcoming this required a functional standard key blank, a nine-volt VATS decoder box with fifteen resistor settings and a mountain of patience.

In the years to come, this chip found it's way into most GM vehicles. With the later introduction of airbags complicating this, workaround bypasses of the multimeter spread through the underground.

Insurance Issues

Ed Marcum remembers a different era when "...the client assumed the risk and liability for the actions of the repossessor: therefore, the repossessor didn't need liability insurance." But around 1985, all that changed as lenders began to experience firsthand the problems that overanxious and inexperienced repossession agencies could cause. In addition, court rulings started to invade the safe harbor of the lender's legal defense of no responsibility for the actions of independent contractors. As a result, lenders began to demand that repossession agencies be responsible for their own activities.

Confronted with the problem of these new demands, Ed resolved it by purchasing a franchise of Jim Golden's American Lenders Service Company (ALSCO) in 1985. ALSCO had started marketing a program that included the first viable group insurance program for repossession agencies in 1983.

In a matter of a few years, the insurance market softened, and the federal government passed legislation that created the opportunity for other insurance options. At a 1987 ALSCO meeting, a group of unhappy American Lenders franchisees began discussing the idea of organizing a group of recovery companies to approach insurance carriers to purchase insurance in bulk. This idea led to approximately seven ALSCO franchisees leaving ALSCO and establishing American Locators and Recovery Association (ALRA) to purchase insurance as a group.

Another Falls in Detroit

By the age of twenty-three, Paul Sydney Taylor of Detroit had already been fired from the Wayne County Sheriffs Department and was pending trial for the death of a prisoner dropped down an elevator shaft. His poor judgement carried on when he was awakened by the sound of his car alarm in the early morning hours of December the 19th of 1987. Leaping from bed, he grabbed a small caliber rifle and ran out onto the front porch where he saw a man standing over the hood of his car. Taylor later claimed that he shouted at the man asking what he was doing but received no response.

Taylor denied that he purposefully fired the gun and claimed that the rifle just went off. Either way, yet another unarmed employee of Al Michel's Midwest Recovery and Adjustment Service had been shot. Forty-seven-year-old William Paul Sharp was shot in the right side of his back with the round passing through his second left rib and through his chest going through the right lung, aorta and esophagus before exiting through the front of his chest. Sharp was pronounced dead on arrival at St. John Hospital in Detroit that morning.

In 1988, Taylor was found guilty of careless and reckless use of a firearm. His sentence, sixteen months to two years in prison. A slap on the wrist for a cold-blooded murder. Newspaper clippings and medical data supporting this story were provided by current Midwest Recovery and Adjustment Service owner, George Badeen.

For Al Michel, these tragedies came far too often. Michel was reportedly a friendly and warm man and how he stayed in the repossession industry this long is a wonder. These losses no doubt weighed heavily on his mind over the years.

Deadly Heroics

It happened at about 3:30 a.m. on Wednesday, August 17, 1988, in Dallas, Texas. Allen Thompson, a part time adjuster for Dallas Auto Adjusters and his driver, twenty-one-year-old Marty Patrick, arrived at a residence with a tow truck to recover a 1988 Hyundai. An alert neighbor spotted them, and believing them to be prowlers, called police and fellow neighbors. With delusions of heroism running through his head forty-two-year-old neighbor William Knowles grabbed his M-14 automatic rifle and ran off into the street.

Thompson's driver, Patrick, spotted the neighbor coming at the two truck and started yelling *"wait, hey no, you got it all wrong! Repo men, repo men!"* Patrick's pleas went unheard or ignored. Knowles claimed that he had yelled for the men to identify themselves to which they didn't respond. Patrick alleged that Knowles almost immediately opened fire. The first shot went into the tow truck's radiator, the second through the windshield and the last fatal shot hit and killed Thompson.

On October 1, 1988, a grand jury declined to indict Knowles on the charge of involuntary manslaughter. Abilene Reporter-News - (Abilene, Texas) October 1, 1988

A Craze Idea

Almost as soon as Ernest Holmes invented the tow truck in 1918, they had become an often-used necessity for repossessions. But because of fuel prices and truck expenses, prior to the late 1980's, manual methods of recovery were still the primary means of recovery. With steering wheel locks now mandatory and vehicle ignition technology improving, the need for towing increased in necessity. The expense barrier to this was broken by a series of new inventions that transformed the industry.

The below story of a groundbreaking pioneer of the tow industry was provided by industry expert and publisher of Professional Repossessor Magazine, Mark Lacek.

"In 1986, Dave Craze working for his father-in-law at the family Texaco station near Norfolk Virginia. Dave had recently purchased a Holmes 440 tow truck and began towing cars for area dealers. Dave also found himself towing for local Repossessors. One day while towing a car off a local interstate, a car passed within inches of running over his extended leg while hooking a chain. Dave realized how dangerous it was for towers and Repossessors to lie on their backs to hook up to a car. Dave set out to find a way to design and build his own creation, a device to help make hooking up to a car a not only safer but faster."

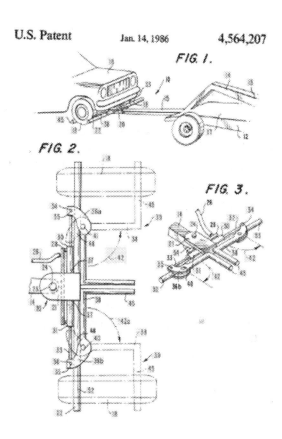

Patent Illustration to Dave Craze's 1986 Self-Loading Wheel Lift – US Patent Office

"The idea was to design something to swing from the inside outward to lift the vehicle by cradling the tires. Resolute in his efforts Dave labored day and night, he struggled through bloody knuckles, exploding hydraulic hoses and cylinders. Dave welded and sheared tons of metal and finally the project was completed. Dave had created the self-loading wheel lift. Towing has never been the same."

During the late 80's and early 90's repossession companies focused on becoming more professional, separating themselves from the public perception that repossessors were car thieves and state associations had begun being formed. Dave Craze changed the way cars would be hooked, lifted, and towed for many years to come. In time, after the twenty-year time restriction of the US Patent office, every manufacturer of towing equipment started its own version of the self-loading wheel lift.

Repossessors and towing professionals have a lot to be thankful for. Starting the day early and finishing the day at the dinner table with your family should never be taken for granted. Sometimes you never know when someone has saved your life. One day Dave Craze turned right, and the repossession and towing industry followed. Thanks Dave.

Sold under various names, such as "Illusionist" and "Transformer", slide-in hydraulic tow booms became a reasonable economic option to any medium to heavy grade pick-up truck. These tow booms folded up via hydraulics into the bed of the truck making their purpose hidden until the repossession agent was ready to spring on his unsuspecting debtor. In addition, these booms had the quick and stealthy functionality of "Pinning" bumpers. By inserting two long steel pins to the lower tow boom, repossessors could pin the subject vehicle by the bumper and lift it into the air while remaining in the truck manipulating the boom by joystick.

Of course, this nifty trick did have perils. Bumpers would often be damaged, gas tanks punctured and, if the pin caught under a rear mounted spare tire, the pin could puncture it. The resulting "pop" resembled that of gunfire, which would provide the agent a sudden boost of adrenaline until the reality of the situation settled in. Regardless of causing insurmountable damage, they very well may have saved more than a handful of lives by reducing agent exposure at the point of recovery.

Recovery during this era could still at times be considered a little aggressive by today's standards. Agents would, at times, hook and drag vehicles out of driveways by their locked rear or front wheels. This would result in a blood curdling scream of dragged rubber on concrete waking the entire neighborhood as the agent left a black snail trail of burnt rubber into the street. To ease the friction, agents would at times soak the tire and ground below with liquid detergent for lubrication.

This process, aside from causing potential damage to the collateral, left a mess and woke the entire neighborhood. In time, tow damage increased as metal bumpers became less common and front or all-wheel drive vehicles increased in numbers. While damage made these tactics obsolete, a solution to the problem soon emerged from an unlikely source.

Transformer Tow Boom demonstrated at a 1983 NFA Conference – Steel pins shown on lower tow boom arm – (photo courtesy of Ed Marcum)

Go Jack

In 1984, the Zendex Tool Corp. of Danbury, Connecticut invented the "GoJak" self-loading wheel dolly, patent# US4690605A. Founder, Al Coccaro, drew his inspiration from his auto body roots and developed this quick and efficient method for moving disabled cars in his shop and paint booths. Using four casters on a horizontally ratcheted hydraulic jack and two rollers to pinch and slide under the tires as the jack was tightened by foot levers, the "GoJak" was born. Since its invention, it has become an industry standard on tow and repossession trucks across the nation and has saved an immeasurable amount of damage and time for the repossession industry alone.

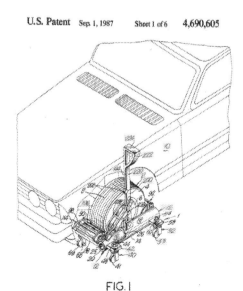

U.S. Patent   Sep. 1, 1987   Sheet 1 of 6   4,690,605

FIG. 1

GoJack Patent Diagram from US Patent Office

Art's Yellow Rag

It was during the latter part of this decade that Art Christiansen created "*The Hard Times News*", referred to as "The Yellow Rag" by Jim Golden and others. Long before the internet, this inside industry magazine illuminated and editorialized on current industry issues. It was one of these editorials that crossed Art with TFA owner Harvey Altes.

Harvey had created an 800 number on the TFA directory for lenders to call where he would tell them who the best agency was anywhere in the nation, with some TFA member agencies left out, this angered many members. Art had travelled to Sacramento, California to attend the California Association of Licensed Repossessors convention and had handed copies of "The Hard Times" out to the attendees. On its cover was a scathing editorial on Harvey's new 800 number titled "*Rug Pulled Out from Under TFA Members*." Harvey arrived to find this magazine in the hands of his fellow conventioneers with the editorial on the cover and all hell broke loose.

Some Voluntary...

It was a sunny day in 1988 when Ed got the assignment. Easy money, a voluntary repossession and the collectors from Chrysler Credit, who he'd been working with for the past eight years, were at the address to hand him the assignment paper, what could go wrong? So, Ed drives across town in his shiny new tow truck and meets the collectors to verify it was a voluntary, which the reps did verify. The NO KEYS should have been the tip-off, but Ed was in a hurry that Friday afternoon at 4:30 p.m. and had promised to take his wife out to dinner. Backing his tow truck up to the car, everything was going fine until the front door flew open.

Charging across the front yard, the bear of a man was spitting fire and pissing vinegar. "*Get your damn hands off of my car!*" he shouted as Ed's head poked up from setting the tow chains to the rear of the car. Before Ed could say a word, the man raised a pistol and opened fire.

Five rounds pierced Ed's shiny new tow truck. Uninjured, Ed looked back across the street to the collectors, only to see their tail lights as they sped away. Neighbors called the police as Ed talked the man down and explained the error. Ed got the car, the borrower was arrested, but Ed's truck was a bullet riddled mess.

When Ed sent Chrysler the invoice for the recovery, he included the cost of repair to his truck. Refusing to pay the damages, Chrysler cut him off from any future business. Lender credibility and loyalty are fleeting characteristics in the repossession industry. A fact that Ed learned the hard way.

When Ed Marcum left law enforcement to start Tri-State Recovery Bureau in 1978, he'd never been shot at. It was in the repossession industry that he was first exposed to this, let me say, unique experience shared by many of its veterans.

Double Murder

On an early San Bernardino, California morning, a pair of adjusters arrived at the offices of Commercial Security Alliance. Spotting their assignment, they backed their tow truck up to the blue 1976 Toyota pickup. Unknown to them, fifty-nine-year-old, off-duty security guard Jerald Groninger the debtor was sleeping inside. Awakened, Groninger emerged with a .22 rifle in hand and opened fire.

Both men fell to the ground with his first shots but were still alive. Groninger then walked over to them and fired one round into the head of one of the men and three into the head of the other. Murdered, were twenty-six-year-old father of two, Mark Brian Ridder, who had only just opened his new agency "Rhino Recovery" earlier that April. Also killed was his twenty-nine-year-old employee Rick Tallon, a father of four.

At 6:20 a.m., police arrived and questioned Groninger who claimed it was self-defense. Neither of the two repossessors were armed and both were wearing visible California state agent licenses. Regardless, Groninger was adamant in the justification of his actions. He was later charged with two counts of murder.

Belinda Tallon, Rick's widow, expressed her emotions at his sentencing in November of 1990. She reported that her children still had nightmares that their fathers' killer would come after them. "*What you did, was really devastated six little kids. You have destroyed not only two men, but families that will never, ever get over this.*" she said, voice cracking as she fought back her tears. "*Mister, if I could, I would strangle you myself.*"

The District Attorney recommended the maximum sentence due to Groninger's "*complete lack of remorse and almost jocular attitude concerning these crimes.*" Superior Court Judge Art McKinister stated that Groninger demonstrated unusually callous attitudes and "*an extraordinary lack of value for human life.*"

Groninger was found guilty and due to his age, the prosecutor did not seek the death penalty. Instead, he received two life sentences that would have made him ninety-seven years old before he would have been eligible for parole, essentially a slow death sentence. San Bernardino - (San Bernardino, California) September 1 and 3, 1989, November 6, 1990

A Society of Silence

Newspaper interviews with Repossessors and agency owners have been going on since at least 1925. An essential element of these stories are stories of being shot at, which is an obvious occupational hazard and one experienced by most repossessors at some point in the careers. While everyone talks about being shot at, rarely were the murders discussed, as evidenced by a 1982 interview with veteran California agency owner Jack Whaley.

The reporter quoted Jack as saying that "he knows of only four Repossessors killed in the nation on the job in the last 25 years." Standard-Speaker (Hazleton, Pennsylvania) - November 15, 1982

Let that sink in, he knew of only four in 25 years and long before the internet and long before twenty-four-hour news. Unless you could find it buried deep in a newspaper, word of mouth was the only way you would hear about these things. As tragic as these killings are, the industry preferred not to talk about them, it wasn't good for business and in most cases, agency owners carry a lot of guilt over these deaths. Clients didn't want blood on their hands and might shy away from using an agency with a bad history, agency owners didn't want agents getting squeamish in the field and there was nothing to gain from discussing it.

Even to this day, it's just one of those things you don't easily bring up. No one feels good about it. This is and always has been a small industry of men and women who harbor secrets. It has only been since the advent of the internet, social media and repo industry websites like CUCollector, CURepossession, Repoman.com and RepoBuzz that these secrets have become of common industry knowledge. But before that was the story of Tommy Deen Morris.

Photo by National Archives

CHAPTER 9 – THE 1990'S – PEACE, PROSPERITY AND THE INTERNET

"The only man who sticks closer to you in adversity than a friend is a creditor."
- Unknown

George H. Bush was president to a population of 250 million Americans with an unemployment rate of 5.6 percent. The median annual household income was $35,353 and the average cost of a car was $15,472. American auto manufacturers had built 4.7 million automobiles this year, but the line between foreign and domestic had become blurry. Foreign auto manufacturers began some production in the United States and American Manufacturers had begun moving production into Canada and Mexico with parts supply networks growing in Asia.

1990 Jacksonville GMAC Massacre — Photo © M. Jack Luedke — USA TODAY NETWORK

Collections Deadliest Day

On the morning of June 17, 1990, at approximately 10:45 a.m., forty-two-year-old James Edward Pough casually walked into the suburban Jacksonville, Florida offices of General Motors Acceptance. Earlier in the year, Pough's 1988 Pontiac had been repossessed without incident or threat. Inside the busy office, about eighty-five people were going about their day-to-day business unaware of what was about to unfold.

Without uttering a word, Pough's assault began. Rapid fire bursts from the .30-caliber carbine rifle cut through his first innocent victims waiting in the lobby who had merely come to make car payments. Pausing, calm and methodical, Pough moved from the lobby and into the office area where he took deliberate and cruel aim firing on the GMAC workers taking cover under their desks or behind filing cabinets. The final police reports stated that he had fired 28 rounds in total.

One employee, Richard Langille, said: *"And then we realized the guy was pointing his gun underneath people's desks and killing them one by one. I just saw the bottom of the carpet and just prayed."*

The scene was pandemonium as the survivors scrambled from the office to the streets outside, leaving the dead and wounded littering the office. Having wounded four and killed nine, Pough had run out of victims. He then turned the gun on himself.

What set Pough off almost half a year after the repossession is unknown. Neighbors later recounted that Pough, whose terminally ill mother he cared for had recently died, had been acting erratic in the weeks leading up to the incident. Whether one of GMAC's collectors, who also conducted some of their own repossessions was involved is also unknown. GMAC, as well as many other lenders, soon curtailed and eventually ceased do conduct their own repossessions as they had been doing since at least 1918 and left the deadly duty to the repossession industry.

The Recession of 1990

In 1989, repossession volume was climbing even though the next recession didn't hit until July of 1990. In a June of 1989 article by the Associated Press, the American Bankers Association was quoted as stating that the repossession rate of banks that lend directly to borrowers was 0.12 percent of all outstanding loans. This was a 2-basis point increase from 1988 when it was .010 percent.

Bruce Scheinder of Oregon based Allied Recovery Inc. was quoted as saying that they used to receive one or two voluntary repossessions a week and that they were now getting that many a day, a five-fold increase. Equitable's Kevin McGivern stated that voluntary repossession volume was double what was considered normal at the same time. - Associated Press - The Times-News (Twin Falls, Idaho) - June 15, 1989

A Failed Experiment

In the late 1980's, Anglo American Auctions, an English/American corporation owned by the alarm company, ADT who was owned by Tyco Intl., saw an opportunity in the repo agent/auction relationship and jumped into the repossession business. Since the dawn of the industry, agents had worked on a contingent basis where if the account did not conclude in a positive resolution (payment or recovery), they did not get paid. Anglo American recruited managers and agents in key markets and offered higher salaries, benefits, and even hourly wages to attract repossession agents.

While breaking the agent pay model, rumor has it that their recovery ratios were too low to satisfy their client base. Within a couple of short years, they terminated operations. According to Kevin McGivern, TYCO was unaware of ADT's auction operations and once they came to light, chose to sell them to ADESA in the early 90's.

With ADESA years later acquiring some of their auctions, the concept of an all-in-one relationship later bloomed. ADESA, a KAR Global corporation, later launched PAR North America, the nation's largest repossession forwarding company.

Training Day

It was just before 3 a.m. on a cold December Monday morning when Steve Morgan of Credit Casualty Recovery and his partner arrived at the Lakewood, Colorado residence of Robert F. Willner. Twenty-four-year-old Steve was still in training and on his third week on the job when they spotted the 83' Chevrolet pick-up in the driveway. Under the experienced supervision of a senior adjuster, Steve approached the vehicle, entered and started the engine. Backing out of the driveway, the front door of the house burst open.

Bare foot, in his underwear and pistol in hand, Willner chased Steve two doors down. Unfortunate for Morgan, the truck's transmission was broken and Willner caught up to him with ease when he fired four rounds at close range through the windshield. Steve Morgan, a married father of two, was killed on the spot as his supervisor watched from across the street in horror. Limp and lifeless, the truck rolled back into a neighbor's front yard as Willner ran back to the house, got dressed and fled.

Willner later surrendered and went on trial in 1991. As is the disingenuous custom, Willner claimed he thought it was being stolen. The District Attorney argued that Willner had been working on the truck and knew it wouldn't run. Willner was convicted of murder and sentenced to life in prison without parole.

"Over a $6,500 truck, he chooses to take a human life. This is murder." Stated Dave Wright, Morgan's employer, owner of Credit Casualty Recovery and head of the Colorado Association of Professional Repossessors.

This was not Willner's first shooting encounter. A year earlier he was arrested for chasing and firing at three men he accused of stealing a Christmas tree on his lot. "*He was just waiting to kill somebody and I believe he's the kind of person who would do it again. Because he's the kind of guy who says you mess with me and I'll kill you,*" later stated Colorado repossession veteran "Cadillac Repo Man" Bill Bowser.

"*I have bits and pieces of memories,*" said Chris Harris, Morgan's son, who said all the years have not eased the pain of only knowing his father through photos. "*The hardest part for me was not having a dad to help me through life, to teach what his dad taught him.*"

In 2011, Governor Bill Ritter issued several last-minute pardons and commuted Willner's sentence, making him eligible for parole in December 2015, after serving twenty-five years. Despite pleases from Morgan's family, in 2021, at the age of seventy, Willner was granted parole. - The Daily Sentinel - (Grand Junction, CO) December 11, 1990, and CUCollector, October 7, 2014

A Day in the 90's Repo Life

2 a.m. and face numb from the cold, I'd pull my motorcycle up to the gates and leave the engine running as I unlocked the chain and greeted the lot guard dog RD. It was a small, rented lot and office whose former tenant's sign "El Camino Paving" still hung on the awnings hiding the actual company, A1 Adjustment Service. Riding inside and locking the gate behind, I'd shut off the motor welcoming the warming to my face as the wind chill subsided before stepping into the office. Like most Adjusters of the era, this was how my average work night started in 91'.

Warming to the inside of the office with dog behind me, I'd grab a package of Pop Tarts from the honor box which I shared with the dog as I thumbed through my clipboard reviewing new assignments. With only two Adjusters, we rarely ran into each other but would chat from time to time on the two-way radios, when within range. Grabbing the key gun, code books, Thomas Brothers map books and my toolboxes, I'd hit the streets in the company owned Ford F-250 diesel with an Illusionist collapsible tow boom concealed in its bed.

Tape deck blaring Jerry Lee Lewis, Van Halen or whatever loud music fit my mood to pump me up, I could hook up a car and have it gone before they had the chance to get their robe on. Regardless, I always chained the residence door side axle first so that I had the truck for frontal cover from any awakend unpleasantries coming out to greet me. On older vehicles with sturdy bumpers, I'd just "Pin" them by snagging the vehicle with a pair of steel pins in the lower tow boom arm and never even leave the vehicle until a safe distance away. Of course, those were on the easy ones.

Breaking into cars was a breeze and once inside, key codes were often easily found on a sales contract or manufacturer sticker in the glove box or easy to find on a glovebox or door lock. Penlight in mouth, I'd spent many an hour reading the faint pin or wafer marks on the edges of smoothed or knife edged key blanks until the ignition turned. And of course, some ignitions just had to be destroyed to get around and GM vehicles were a prime for slamming over. Living the credo that "nothing is illegal unless you get caught", garage doors and gates were only minor barriers when living contingent on a $75 commission per car.

It was a simpler time and the process was more mechanical. The cops and borrowers were basically clueless to the repossession laws or tactics, lock and security systems were pretty simple, no cell phones and without cameras everywhere, we got away with murder. I'll spare you the repo war stories, but sometimes a little fear is a good thing and I kept this up for three years until my adrenal glands dried up and I started getting sloppy.

Fast forward twenty-five years and just about the only things that haven't changed are the risks or low commission. Modern repossessions are almost all conducted by wheel lifts in tow trucks with internet access to one or more laptops loaded with mapping software and repossession assignment databases. Locks and ignitions have advanced so much that picking, slamming or impressioning keys is virtually impossible. The days of going to the door and demanding the vehicle are essentially over since lenders deemed any form of agent contact to be too great a risk for lawsuits.

Of course, another thing that didn't change was the repossession fees. Most repossession fees in the 90's were between $300 to $350, not much less than now. But back then, agencies were paid a closing fee of about $75 if the borrower paid current or the lender chose to assign it elsewhere or employ a skip tracer. Currently, most assignments have no close fee or any other fee, but we'll get to that later.

Those Things Happen

Christopher Edwin Creech of Rowan County, North Carolina, a roofer, had been talking to Lonnie Britt about a possible job and left soon after. Unbeknownst to Creech, twenty-one-year-old Britt was a freelance repossessor scouting out his 87' Nissan for an unnamed finance company. Britt's fiancé Patricia Simmons later brought him back later with a set of keys, entered the car and began to leave when twenty-six-year-old Creech stepped outside, shotgun in hand. Creech fired one round through the rear window striking Britt in the head.

Britt died later on that Thursday night of January 27, 1994, at Rowan memorial Hospital. Of course, Creech claimed that he thought the car was being stolen. Rowan's County Sheriff's Department Captain Rick Thibodeau stated that investigators did not feel the shooting was premeditated and only charging him with voluntary manslaughter. Creech was later released on a $3,000 bond.

"It's scary, those things happen." Thibodeau said. *"People are concerned. They are concerned about crime."*

A Grand Jury convened but did not indict Creech. In March, Britt's family and friends gathered at the Rowan County Courthouse carrying pickets and passing out fliers demanding justice.

On April 4, 1994, the Grand Jury reconsidered and resurrected the manslaughter charge. - The Charlotte Observer (Charlotte, NC) - January 29, 1994, and March 8, 1994

1994 would prove to be an especially deadly year for the industry.

The Shot Heard Across the Nation

On February the 24th of 1994, a murder took place that, unlike the many buried deep in local newspapers through the decades, made national news. It is a tragedy that was all too common and well remembered in the repossession industry to this day.

Tommy Deen Morris – (photo provided by Donna Morris)

It was a cold Houston, Texas morning at almost 3:00 a.m. when a tow truck idled backwards up a driveway intending to repossess a Ford truck. Without warning, the lights in the house came on and a man ran outside. The repo driver, fearing for his life, drove away and left the truck intended for repossession behind.

The story should have ended here, but about 15 minutes later, a second repossession agent named Tommy Deen Morris, from yet another company, backs up into the same driveway. This time the debtor, Jerry Casey Jr., is waiting on his porch with a 30-30 telescopic rifle. Casey shot Morris through the neck and both lungs, killing him on the spot.

Responding police refused to arrest Casey. Their reasoning referred to a frontier-era law. Texas Penal Code 9.41, an 1800's frontier era "stand your ground" law created to deal with cattle thieves. This archaic law gives Texans considerable leeway to kill suspected thieves and intruders after dark.

Tommy Deen Morris left behind his wife, Donna, and four children.

Harris County District Attorney, Johnny B. Holmes Jr., said that the matter simply boiled down to whether a grand jury believed that Mr. Casey believed Morris was the repo man or an auto thief. Holmes defended the Texas law and showed no interest in prosecuting Mr. Casey. Holmes instead chose to lay the blame on Morris and questioned why he didn't call or give warning that he was coming.

"Do you have to sit still when a guy's driving off with your car?" Mr. Holmes said in an interview. *"No, I don't think so. I think you ought to be able to use deadly force. That's an additional risk that the thief is exposed to and that's an additional deterrent."* Furthermore, Texas Legislature has still refused to overturn this law.

"If Tommy Deen would have been a police officer or a firefighter, they'd have a parade. But everybody thinks, 'Oh, he was just a repo man.' Nobody cares." Texas Repo Man Jim Douglass," – "The New York Times" 1994.

Repossession agents get killed every year and as you've seen in earlier stories, the sentences for shooting one tend to be on the soft side if charges are even filed at all. The District Attorneys adamant refusal to charge the shooter sent the story nationwide and created a national outcry over the injustice from all corners of the public as well as the repossession industry. Regardless, the District Attorney cleared Jerry Casey Jr. of any wrongdoing. Casey committed suicide eight months later.

Donna Morris recalls the press's reaction to Casey's suicide. *When Jerry Casey was found dead in his house, I was swarmed again at my residence by the media and asked the DUMBEST questions! The answer back to the media was; "There is no VICTORY in Mr. Casey's death! Now there is a young daughter and another wife WITHOUT HER HUSBAND and another child WITHOUT HER Dad!" I was asked by one reporter if THAT WAS THE ONLY COMMENT I COULD GIVE THEM........I simply shook my head in disgust and walked back inside! my home. News folks are "cold hearted individuals simply doing their JOBS!"*

Three years after the shooting, in a civil lawsuit initiated by Tommy's widow, Donna, a jury ruled that the assigning lender, Steeplechase Motors, was mostly liable for Morris' death. Evidence disclosed in trial proved that Steeplechase Motors maintained a policy of double assigning repossessions (assigning repossessions to more than one agent at a time.) A $2.3 million judgment was awarded against Steeplechase. Ultimately, the judge disregarded the jury award and reduced it to a mere $750,000.

Donna, who even after all these years, still came to tears when speaking of this incident, refers to Tommy Deen as "TD", describes him as; *"A loving, hardworking, Christian, family man who loved his family and worked hard to, as he said, "make bread to buy beans". A very gentle individual who helped everyone. Loved his work and always had a smile for everyone. He was such a sweetie! We were married 23 yrs. and had 4 children: his two boys, my daughter, and our daughter! He always had that smile on his face and was called "preacher" cause he worn starched blue jeans, tennis shoes and a shirt while working. He always greeted you with that contagious smile!"*

Tommy Deen Morris is buried at Klein Memorial ark, Decker Prairie, Montgomery County, Texas.

Donna and her family have never gotten over this tragedy. *Per Donna; Mine and Toms four kids have all grown up, 3 with college degrees and one a Masters. Melissa (Missy) Toms pride and joy being his ONLY little girl has a wonderful husband and a son 8 yrs. They have a thriving business, but Missy has*

NEVER FORGOTTEN HER DADDY. She still seeks counseling from time to time and she makes every birthday and Father's Day out to the grave and we sit on the bench and share thoughts of Tom. Tyler Deen is my grandsons name and he KNOWS all about the Grandpa he never met!

The tragic part of this story is that this senseless killing could have been avoided. If the dealership did not engage in the dangerous practice of "double assignment", Tommy might still be alive today. Double assignment of an account is: assigning an account out for repossession to two or more repossession agents in the same geographical area at the same time.

Following the Tommy Deen Morris murder, the practice of double assigning repossessions had all but completely vanished in Texas and most other states. For years, the auto finance industry took note and ceased this practice. Unfortunately, with the later explosion of forwarding companies and contingent (no repossession, no fee) fee contracts, this practice resumed, further exasperating the already dangerous nature of the industry.

A Tragic Reminder

It was just after 4 a.m. when John Henry Peters, his wife Veronica and John's partner Joseph Holland arrived at the address of thirty-one-year-old Roberto Pagan at 211 W. Alva St. in Tampa Heights, FL. In the open side yard of the small house Pagan lived in with his mother on the corner, they spotted Pagan's 84' Ford Bronco. With Peter's wife at the wheel, he and Holland left the safety of the car and approached the SUV. A dog barked from the backyard as Peters entered the Bronco and started the engine when they heard someone inside shout: "Get out of my yard!"

A shot was fired from inside the house and Holland ducked for cover, yelling *"Repo!"* repeatedly. Pagan stepped out of the house and into the yard leaving his mother in the doorway as he fired round after round at Peters backing out of the driveway all the way to the street and speeding away. Veronica and Holland realized he'd been shot as they saw him slumped to the right side of the seat driving past them and heading south. Fearing more gunfire, Holland told Veronica to drive east and they lost sight of Peters.

Recorded 911 calls painted two different pictures of the event. Pagan called 911, breathing heavy, but calm as he told the operator, *"I've just had my vehicle stolen. I'm at 211 W Alva."* He never mentioned the nine .45-caliber rounds he'd fired.

Shortly after, Joseph Holland, called 911. His tone was far more agitated and panicked than Pagan's. *"We've got gunshots,"* Holland shouted. *"My buddy here's been shot."*

"*We repo'd a car and the guy shot him,*" Holland shouts through his cell phone to the 911 dispatcher as Veronica can be heard sobbing in the background repeatedly stating to herself aloud, "*Oh, my God.*" Getting a description of the Bronco from Holland, the dispatcher suddenly realizes that the description matches the one given earlier by Pagan as well as officers up the road.

"*Listen to me, Listen to me, or I can't help you.*" Urged the dispatcher. "*Go to Tampa and Indiana.*" Almost at the same time, Holland and Peters spot the flashing lights of police cruisers at the intersection ahead. "*We see the cops,*" Holland says. "*We're going to them.*"

As they neared, they spotted the Bronco parked by the police cruisers. Closing in, they saw a lifeless body in a pool of blood on the ground next to the bullet riddled Bronco. "*Aw, man,*" Holland muttered over the phone as Veronica Peters begins to wail in the background: "*Oh, my God! Oh, my God! John! John*!" she bawled in a chilling surge of grief.

Peters had been shot twice in the left arm, severing an artery. He was rushed to Tampa General Hospital, but emergency room staff were unable to stop the bleeding. John Henry Peters, thirty-two-year-old husband and father of two, died two hours later.

On November 6, 1995, charged with second-degree murder, Pagan went to trial. As has traditionally been the disingenuous defense for murdering repossession agents, Pagan's attorney, Nicholas Matisini, claimed the shooting was in self-defense and that Peters had pointed something silver and shiny at him. Pagan claimed that he pushed his mother aside and fired through the window as Peters began backing out of the driveway. He claimed that Peters again pointed the silver and shiny object at him when he fired again.

When Pagan was arrested, his attorney said that Pagan feared for his property, his life and the life of his mother and that he thought he was being burglarized and that the intruder had pointed a gun at him. "*Mr. Pagan's actions were justified that night. He fired in self-defense and used deadly force.*" Defense attorney Matisini urged the jury and Hillsborough Circuit Judge Cynthia Holloway.

Contrary to Pagan's testimony, police found spent bullet casings littered around the yard, disproving his claim of shooting from inside. No weapons were found on Peters by police who responded before Holland and Veronica Peters, also discrediting Pagan's claims.

John Peters Family – John Henry Peters (top), John David and Theresa Marie Peters (photo provided by Veronica Kardamis)

Almost as damning was a video tape of Pagan during a daytime repossession of his Jeep at a gas station in July of 1993 by "Repoman.com" Publisher Dan Meeks and another agent. "*Where I come from, you get shot or hurt for doing something like this. If you had come over to my house at night, I would have blown you away.*" Pagan boasted to them when he found out that they were not allowed to carry firearms.

During the 1993 repossession by Dan Meeks, Pagan was delinquent five payments for $2,022. Soon after, Pagan, bought the Bronco from Gulfcoast Auto Mart in St. Petersburg and soon after defaulted. He was three months' delinquent and about $700 in arrears at the time of the Peters murder.

"*Perhaps it was to remind himself of the dangers of his job, perhaps it was a premonition*" remarked the prosecuting attorney as he described Peters blood-soaked belongings at the time of the murder. Along with a "World's Greatest Dad" baseball hat, Peters kept a newspaper story clipping of Tommy Deen Morris's murder in his wallet.

On November 8, 1994, Pagan was convicted of second-degree murder and sentenced to twenty years in prison. In sentencing, Judge Holloway told Pagan that she strongly believes in the right to own a gun and to protect yourself and your family. "*But not in my wildest dreams do I think it's appropriate to defend a vehicle,*"

Peter's ten-year-old daughter Theresa read her statement to Pagan. "*You can always buy a new truck, but nothing on earth will bring my Daddy back. I just want you to know that you killed someone's Dad.*"

"*I hope he spends as many sleepless nights filled with pain as we have,*" said Peters' widow Veronica as she hugged her daughter and her twelve-year-old son John. "*I hope everybody has learned from this,*" Mrs. Peters said. "*You pull a gun, you shoot somebody, you go to jail. We know that Daddy didn't die for nothing, don't we?*"

When Donna Morris recently discovered that John Peters carried Tommy Deens story in his wallet, Donna responded: *What an HONOR it gives me to know that John had Tom's article in his wallet...lets me know someone else cares remembered/cares!*

With so little justice having been served for the senseless murders of Repossessors over the decades, at least the Peters family, unlike Donna Morris and so many others, had a taste of it. Regardless, none of this can take away all that they've lost. According to Veronica Kardamis (formerly Peters) who reached out to me just before publication;

We would like for everyone to know the John Peters that we all love and knew. He had a great love for life and making sure everyone around him enjoyed life. He always had a smile for someone who he didn't know. He had many friends but few that he truly called family. If he did call you family, he would protect you with everything he had. His children were his pride and joy. They were his greatest love! When he was killed, he was still carrying the ribbons he received from the hospital for both announcing he was a father. See when he was so selfishly taken away over a car, the world didn't just lose another man or a person that "we could just get over" like we were told. We lost a Husband, a Father, a Son, a Grandson, a Brother, and just a great human being that was never given the chance to live and grow old and get to know the wonders of watching our 8 grandchildren grow. You also stole the greatest Grandfather my grandchildren would have ever known. We have moved on and life has changed, but the wound has never completely healed. We all still love and miss you greatly Tow-a-way Johnny! Until we meet again!!!!

RSIG

Years passed and the American Locators and Recovery Association (ALRA) struggled to maintain insurance until the early nineties, when it became entangled in litigation, during which it changed its name to Recovery Specialists Insurance Group, Inc. In May of 1995 Ed Marcum formed IG., Inc. to purchase the assets of Recovery Specialist Insurance Group, Inc., including the use of the name, Recovery Specialist Insurance Group (RSIG.)

Operating as a purchasing group has advantages for both the insurer and the insureds. For the insurer, the underwriting process, pricing, state filings, and deductible issues are simplified. For the insured, the group environment allows a broader negotiating field with regard to coverages and rates. In addition, the insured receive the economic advantage of pooled premiums and the protection for individual members by having losses weighed against the larger premium pool of the group.

RSIG's mission is to locate, secure and maintain insurance for its members. Its not-for-profit corporate capacity acts as a client liaison and lends credibility as a guarantor of deductibles while maintaining high standards and bonding for its members. Since its inception, RSIG has demonstrated its ability by becoming the largest national repossession insurance group in the industry, with a reputation for reliability, support, and coverage accepted by lenders nationwide.

Recovery Specialists Insurance Group is a not-for-profit corporation that operates for the benefit of its members and recognizes and supports the trade associations that promote the professionals in the repossession industry. RSIG encourages its members to become active in any trade association, local, state, or national. Memberships in such groups provide individual agencies with a channel to network with people who experience common problems and have common goals.

Ed Marcum says: "*Our group is everybody. We are the family run business, the partnership, and the larger corporation. We are members of Allied, and ARA. We belong to CFA, CALR, GAPRA, MARA, MAPRA and Texas ARP. We are dedicated professionals and have great respect for an industry that has evolved over the years and recognizes that change is facilitated through education and the common bond between its members.*" To date, and for many years, RSIG has held their annual conference with the Allied Finance Adjusters.

Al Michael, Early NFA, AFA member and Founder of Midwest Recovery & Adjustment

Ed's statement about association membership is very accurate, which is odd considering that in many ways they are a lot like the other associations which is why they are included in this book. RSIG offers Compliance Certification and Continuing Education to its members and others in the industry through their RSIG University (www.rsiguniversity.com) which they established in 2008. Their information and training resources are the benchmarks of RSIG's risk management philosophy which they continually update and train to reduce loss and keep premiums stable and affordable.

A Changing of the Guard

In 1996, after more than forty years in the repossession industry, long time AFA member, Al Michel retired. By this time, Al had been the longtime owner operator of Midwest Recovery and Adjustment Service for twenty-nine years. Midwest was one of the first repossession companies in the United States to offer 'Dealer Only' asset liquidation sales to the banking industry. Taking the helm was George Badeen. Al had mentored George since his beginning as a Field Adjuster to President when he sold it to him upon his retirement. George would go on to modernize the auction and recovery ends of the business while expanding it to add three new divisions.

George Badeen, as is the sad legacy at Midwest Recovery & Adjustment, has been shot twice

The First Lady Passes

On March 18, 1996, industry legend and mentor to so many generations of the repossession industry, Lorna Lou Critchfield Barnes passed away at the age of eighty-six in Dade, Florida. Lorna Lou's memory and legacy endures in the AFA's "Lorna Lou Barnes Award." This is the Allied Finance Adjusters Achievement Award for the recognition of trailblazers in their association. Lorna certainly fit that bill and it may be a long time until anyone in the industry comes even close.

Lorna Lou Barnes (L) and her sister Lee, 1986

The Railway Rollup

In March of 1997, Advanced International, a venture capital firm from Boston, Massachussets, reached out to a select dozen repossession agency owners with $100 million idea. Consolidate the nation's largest and most profitable repossession agencies into a coast-to-coast agency. Roll-Up strategies were nothing new to business, but this had never been attempted on a large scale in the repossession industry.

A unique technology for its time, the handheld PC was in the sole proprietary ownership of a man who had developed it for Railway Express, a company recently acquired by Advanced International. Brought to the attention of attorney, Todd Hodnett of later RDN fame, The early intention of this company was to place these handheld devices in each truck for improved communications between the office to the field, truly an idea ahead of its time.

Engaged in the initial conversations were, Kevin McGivern of Chicago, Bud Krohn of Oakland, California, Chad Latvaaho of Minnesota, Bob Wilson of UAR and the Dunleavy's of TCAR in Upstate New York, just to name a few. Somewhere during the process, Bud Krohn called me to ask if I would come back to work with him in this. I probably would have too.

Contingent to this acquisition and consolidation was the financial viability of the chosen agencies, with each being required to demonstrate at least $3 million a year in gross revenues. After this, the list of agencies dwindled to eight. Further examination forced two more out of the pool, after which Advanced International advised that this could not be done with less than the six remaining. By this time, it was June 98' and the deal was days from closing.

Financial auditors from Ernst & Young were brought in to conduct thorough onsite examinations of every facet of operations and financial management. During their examination of the very last of the to be acquired companies, one company fell just short of meeting the exam requirements. Ernst and Young notified Advanced International of their findings. On a Thursday night, a mere two business days short of closing the deal, Advanced International killed it.

What this could have meant to the industry is unknown, but this was not the last the industry would see of roll-up strategies.

Another Okie Enters the Biz

Ray Barnes, Jack Barnes, Ron Brown, a lot of big names in the repossession industry came from Oklahoma. Corey Cox was born there too. But as an army brat, his childhood was spent in Europe and all across the US until his parents' divorce landed him and his mother in Phoenix. It was from there that Corey and his mother would visit family back in Oklahoma and that's when he began spending time with his uncle.

Fourteen-year-old, Corey tagged along with his uncle on repossessions across the vast rural Oklahoma farmlands. As Corey explains it, "It was different out there. We would drive up to the house or farm and simply knock on the door. Everything started with a conversation. You looked people in the eye and listened to them. We didn't just go dragging cars away from people."

This is how Corey spent many a summer and this is how he would later approach borrowers down on their luck. Something he himself would later learn all too well.

Manhunt

In July of 1998, "Manhunt: The Book" was published. In its time, it was like a skip tracers bible. Authored by repo industry legends Harvey Altes, Millard Land, Ron Brown, and international private investigator Joseph Culligan, they shared decades of experience that they had already been sharing through their award-winning seminar for skip tracers of people and assets. Never before, and never since, has such an eclectic culmination of experience and techniques been available to the public.

Pandora's Box

Not quite done with the 90's, the ever-present Harvey Altes launched Transnet, the industry's first "Forwarding Company". While forwarding repossession assignments from one agency to another, this was the first attempt to standardize pricing and assignments through a single entity. While revolutionary, it did draw the ire of some TFA members who were being paid higher than Transnet's negotiated prices. Transnet never really took off like most forwarders, but the company survives to this day and the model carried on into the next century, forever changing the industry, and not for the better.

The New Standard

In early 1999, industry veteran Joe Taylor was tapped with an unusual request by the Empire Fire & Marine Insurance Company and AEON Insurance Groups. Create a nationally accepted repossession compliance certification program that meets the strict requirements of the insurance industry. After spending about 500 hours researching both the state and federal self-help repossessions laws, Joe was finished. By the end of the year, the Certified Asset Recovery Specialist program was born, known more commonly as CARS.

CARS was the first agent compliance program in the industries long history. As desired, it became the first nationally accepted repossession compliance certification program and is still the industry standard. Joe went on to speak and hold compliance classes to agents, lenders, law enforcement and politicians over the years to come. CARS is run and managed by Recovery Industry Services Company (RISC.)

By the end of the 1990's, technology was coming on in full force. Fading and gone were the days of telephone spoofing, lock picking and slamming ignitions. Recoveries began to more resemble simple tow jobs than the sleuth and stealth tactics of old. The very relationships

Joe Taylor in 2020

between lenders and the agencies themselves were soon to be interrupted by outside forces who'd never even gotten grease under their fingernails.

One Last for the Millinium

It was just before 2 a.m. in rural Gregg County when four agents from East Texas Auto Recovery of Longview arrived at the home of forty-one-year-old Michael David Mason. Mason's Ford Taurus had been repossessed recently, but he stole it back from the dealer and was hiding it. Agents found the car hidden in the open backyard and pinned it by the bumper dragging it out north on Road 2207. Stopping to hook it up to the more secure tow chains, they were returning southbound and passing Mason's residence when one of the agents saw Mason in the front yard of the house, with a shotgun in hand.

Two of the agents then heard the shotgun blast and shattering glass as the fired round tore through the driver side of the truck. They quickly realized that twenty-six-year-old agent, Kevin Pierce Sr. had been hit. The shotgun blast tore a hole through his upper torso.

Frantic, the men sped Kevin to the hospital when they encountered a Kilgore, Texas policeman on his way to respond to the reports of gunfire from the incident. Pierce was first transported to a Kilgore hospital before being airlifted to the East Texas Medical Center in Tyler. At 4:48 a.m. on Tuesday, May 11, 1999, Pierce passed away. Pierce left behind his wife, Janet and three children.

Unlike so many Texas repossession murders at night, Mason was arrested for murder and held in the Gregg County Jail with a bond set at $75,000. Twice convicted of drug offenses in the past, he failed to make bail and was later indicted for the murder on July 22nd.

Defense Attorney Odis Hill claimed that Pierce and the other agents had left a local bar before going to Mason's home and were "Highly intoxicated" before arriving there. District Attorney William Jennings confessed that they had been drinking but would not go as far to say that they were drunk.

On February 8, 2000, Mason pleaded guilty to federal charges of being a felon in possession of a firearm and then pleaded guilty to the state's lesser charge of manslaughter. For the manslaughter charge, he was sentenced to 12 years in prison without the possibility of parole for 6 years. On the firearms possession charge, he was sentenced to an additional 10 years.

After the trial, Defense attorney Hill provided Gregg County law enforcement a video tape that identified a wrecker truck backing into a mobile home on the Mason property in August of the following year. The mobile home was pushed into the Mason home causing some damage.

Following Pierce's death, DA Jennings commented that there was a drive by shooting on Mason's home and that the occupants had received death threats. While no arrests were made, Jennings said that he couldn't be sure that these incidents were connected to the killing and felt that "innocent persons have been the victim of vigilante justice.

Following decades of recovery agents being murdered and killers being released with little or no charges, it should come of little surprise that some level of vigilante justice was going on here. Pierce's murder closed out the twentieth centuries last known repossession murder. Unfortunately, the twenty-first century would prove no safer.

9/11 World Trade Center - National Archives

CHAPTER 10 – 2K –
AN INDUSTRY IN DECLINE

The Y2K scare of the new millennium was a big "*nothing-burger*" and the world went on as normal. In an election marred by disputed "hanging chad votes" decided by the Supreme Court, George W. Bush had just been sworn in as President of the United States. For the American population of 282 million, the average median annual income was $42,148 and the unemployment rate was only 4 percent. The average car cost $21,850 and 17.6 million were manufactured.

Nine months into this decade came a day that irreparably change America forever, 9/11. The drums of war sounded and aside from the swell of new military enlistees that became newly covered under the SCRA, the repossession industry was, for the most, unaffected. However, the largest threat to the industry since World War II took root in this decade, the Forwarding Companies. Growing in numbers and acquiring larger market shares of repossession assignments, their dominance increased in the coming years.

A Miami Shootout

It was just after midnight in Miami on Monday, February the 14, 2000 when a neighbor began beating on the apartment door of Kendria Vann's shared apartment on NE 80th Street. "I think someone is stealing your car!" they shouted. Startled, he and his stepfather, David Black, ran down the stairs and hopped into Black's mini truck and took chase. With Vann at the wheel, they turned a bend on Bayshore Drive where they spotted the tow truck at a stop with Vann's car facing the opposite direction with a wheel having fallen off.

Recovery agent Roberto Ortega had unhooked Vann's 87' Chevy Caprice and was maneuvering his tow truck to pick it up by the rear end when Vann brought his stepfather's truck to a stop in the middle of the road. "Hey man, why are you stealing my car?" Vann shouted as he and Black jumped from the mini truck. "Next thing I knew, as soon as my foot touched the pavement, guns went off" recalled Black.

Both Ortega and Vann had fired multiple shots at each other. Vann, nineteen, was hit in the chest and staggered about twenty yards back toward home before falling to the ground and dying. Ortega managed to get back into his truck and sped away only to wreck his truck into a 10-inch-thick wall. Ortega had been shot in the head and died on a stranger's front porch. - The Miami Herald (Miami, Florida) - February 15, 2000

In the same story, John Kilpatrick, executive of the Florida Association of Licensed Recovery Agents, was quoted as saying that he only knew of one other fatal shooting during a repossession and that was in Tampa in 1996. In the era before the explosion of the internet, either the repossession industry was horribly informed, or was living in a state of denial. Either way, the new decade was off to a bad start.

A Founder and a Friend Passes

On April 8, 2000, an NFA co-founder, Honorary Member of the Board and its longest standing Secretary, Art Lamoureux passed away at the age of 78 in Hancock, Michigan. Art and his wife Allie had retired to Rabbit Bay, Michigan in 87' leaving the Auto City Auto Auction in the capable hands of son Paul. Art was seventy-eight, a World War II Army veteran and for almost fifty years, his family and the Mauro family were as one, travelling everywhere together. The NFA had lost a founder, wife Allie had lost a husband of fifty-one years and Frank and the Mauro family, a best friend and their beloved "Uncle Art."

Art's son, Paul had taken over Art's Auto City Auto Auction in 1985 and sold it to Insurance Auto Auctions (IAA) in 2000. Paul stayed on with IAA until joining ADESA auto auctions in 2006.

The First Crack

According to forty-eight-year industry legend and retired agency owner Millard Land, 2001 marked the downfall of the repossession industry. Prior to this period, lenders assigned repossessions on a one-on-one basis. While they may have had favorites, there was some variance in pricing and terms from year to year and agent to agent. These terms allowed for adjustments for inflation and the growing new operational expenses created by the technology boom.

It was during this year that Chrysler Credit and Federal Assurance decided to offer agencies contracts. Seeing the danger of allowing the lenders to call the shots by contract, Millard called for a meeting of the Time Finance Adjusters board of directors. At the meeting later held in Orlando, Florida, he made an impassioned plea for them to not sign the lender contracts before the board and attending members. Providing a new industry standard contract, he hoped to counter and avert the dangers he foresaw.

Upon the meetings conclusion, Millard's efforts appeared fruitful with the members leaving in agreement not to sign the lender contracts and to stand behind the new industry standard contracts. Unfortunately, greed intervened. Many of the agency owners believed that a contracted client would be a loyal client. And that a loyal client meant higher assignment volume and thus greater income. In essence, making up for lower wages with higher volume, a "race to the bottom" strategy that plagues the industry to this day.

This, coupled with the association's inability to help manage, let alone discuss fees, set most of the industry into a dog-eat-dog competition ready for exploitation. This spurred a flurry of other lender and forwarder contracts that further splintered and fractured the industry beyond repair. With the lenders and forwarders now in control of all terms, the industry had to either comply with their terms or lose the bulk of their assignment volume and income. To this day, most agencies blindly chase this strategy down the rabbit hole in ignorance of sustainability or survival.

"Buzzy" Passes

The second generation of one of the repossession industries oldest repossession companies and patriarch of two after, Fred G. "Buzzy" Summs, passed away in his hometown of Norfolk, Virginia on February 19, 2001, at the age of seventy-four. Buzzy was a World War II Navy veteran and attended The College of William and Mary's Norfolk Campus (Later being renamed Old Dominion University) before joining his father, Fred Sr.'s Summs Skip and Collection Service Inc., established in 1932. A founding member of the NFA, he maintained a lifelong work ethic of honesty, integrity, and professionalism.

Two of his five children, Mark and Brock followed in the repossession business. Brock took over Summs Recovery, Inc the company Fred "Buzzy Summs founded in 1959. Mark took over Summs

Skip and Collection Service, Inc., now dba Summs Skip and Collateral Solutions. Mark and Cindy's children Steven, Matthew and Kelsey became the fourth generation to carry on the Summs family business, and long family legacy in the repossession industry to this day.

The Summs family credit their success for all these years to the strong work ethic established from our forefathers along with the dedicated employees, including Patricia Bivens who retired from the company in 2020 after fifty-five years of dedicated service.

Unsolved

Early morning in the morning of March 19th, 2002, forty-three-year-old repossessor Gary McCracken was found dead in an alley in South Bend, Indiana. Shot in the head execution style, detectives speculated that he was forced to his knees beforehand. Police found McCracken's car still running. His wallet and briefcase were still sitting on the front seat.

Police received tips right away, but a mass shooting three days later diverted their attentions. McCracken's wife, Deanna and his children were devastated. As of now, this crime remains unsolved, and the McCracken family is left with an open wound that continues to bleed.

The RABF

Death and injury have been sad risks that Adjusters have been suffering since the industries inception. With low pay and little or no insurance, they have all too often been left to fend for themselves for hospital bills and worse, funerals. Long before the internet and GoFundMe websites, Ed Marcum of the RSIG saw an industry in need and took action.

In 2002, Ed made a request to the Board of Directors of Recovery Specialist Insurance Group (RSIG) to donate funds to open a bank account at The Fauquier Bank to establish the Recovery Agents Benefit Fund (RABF). Soon after, they started the lengthy process of becoming a non-profit 501c3 charitable organization. Ever since, in times of need, the RABF has been there to support agents who have fallen on exceptionally hard times due to debilitating injury, illness or death. This includes times when the fund was called upon because families did not have the money required to pay the expenses to complete their loved one's burial.

The RABF is available to anyone in the industry regardless of their trade group affiliation or insurance provider, whether they are an owner or an employee. Requests for disbursements are reviewed on a case-by-case basis. Accounting services for the RABF are donated by an independent certified public accountant; and no one involved with the fund draws any sort of financial compensation for their time and efforts. With donations from fundraisers, agency owners, forwarding companies and lenders, the RABF has been there for been there for dozens of families a year.

Still in the Blood

In 2003, Frank Mauro's forty-nine-year-old daughter Roxane Malo died of cardiac arrhythmia. Kevin McGivern, long-time family friend attended her funeral with his wife. Coming to the front to pay their respects, Kevin and his wife turned to Frank and Rita to offer their condolences. According to Kevin, Frank appeared lost and lonely. Pulling Kevin to his side, they talked.

Kevin McGivern 2020

As dozens of family and friends passed by, Kevin and Frank spent over half-an-hour talking about the repossession business, past and present. With his daughter's coffin a mere ten feet in front of him and her body in repose, Frank became reanimated and engaged as they carried on their conversation, almost ambivalent to the procession of mourners that passed. Frank had already made a fortune in the auto business, but the repossession industry was still in his blood.

Eagle Lee and the Little League President

Lee began as a Field Adjuster for "Total Recovery" in Los Angeles in the early 1980's. Slamming ignitions, impressioning locks, tryout keys and Curtis Key Guns were the Tricks of the trade. Ten year later, Lee left his employer to strike out on his own and founded Eagle Adjusters in Norco, California in 1992. In a business rife with confrontation and conflict, it was in little league baseball where a battle erupted that would change his life forever.

Lee McDaniel's Favorite Team, he's in the white hat

There was really only room for one baseball little league in Corona. Cindy, President of the Corona American Little League was having issues with the, often brash, President of the Corona American National Little League, Lee. Tensions rose as conflicts in field schedules and recruitment territories escalated, so Cindy confronted this lifelong Cleveland Indians fan. Once confronted, Lee was on a more familiar and honest playing field and softened enough for them to resolve their conflicts.

Finding common ground in their shared love for little league baseball and their children, they met for coffee. Coffee led to dinner and dinner led to dates. Which with Lee McDaniel, often meant running accounts in his repo truck. That was 2004 and by 2005, Cindy had quickly found her way from her job in medical billing to working with Lee in the front office. With her now firmly in the business, they married In 2008.

Lee and Cindy McDaniel

Together they raised Lee's two young sons, Brandon and Cody with Cindy's sons James and Trevor and daughter Courtnee while Lee's adult sons followed him into the field. Robert started in a truck at the age of nineteen working tirelessly through thick and thin while brother Danny joined after two tours with the Marines in Afghanistan, eventually joining law enforcement in 2015. Like so many repo families before them, their children were raised in the trucks, lots, and garage of their small family-owned repossession company. That is, when they weren't playing little league baseball.

Renovo

In 2005, Chicago businessman, Kevin Flynn launched Renovo. After some legal quarrels with original investors, Flynn wrestled control of Renovo and grew it to a repossession forwarding network of over 300 employees, a core of 100 sole proprietors and over 1,000 agencies. This was at the time, the largest repossession forwarding network in the nation. What made Renovo unique was its agency ownership and operational tactics.

Kevin Flynn, Renovo
Founder and CEO

Decades earlier, Flynn's family had built their fortune consolidating the numerous garbage companies around the Chicago area. According to Kevin McGivern, Flynn was buying and "rolling-up" junk yards into a venture called LKQ Quick Part when he discovered the repossession industry through agencies renting lots from his new acquisitions when he saw another opportunity. Ready to make a move on the repossession industry, he'd discussed his new venture with McGivern, who warned him "*they will dig in deeper than a World War II foxhole."*

Undaunted, Flynn found out Kevin's advice to be more than prophetic. According to McGivern, Flynn had later admitted to underestimating the pioneer like tenacity of these family businesses. Regardless, Flynn purchased numerous companies around the nation and launched Renovo. Flynn, a shrewd businessman, was quick to recognize the weaknesses in the industry and wasted no time exploiting them.

According to McGivern, when Flynn bought Memphis based forwarder ADT, they had a practice of providing a two-day turnaround on recovery fees to their agent partners. In an industry where the turnaround on repossession fees was anywhere from 30 to 120 days, this was attractive. For cash strapped agency owners, this payment option provided the opportunity to catch up on or maintain other bills and payroll. This of course came with a catch, a 2 percent of payment fee, both of which, Flynn ended.

During a social run in, McGivern recalls chiding Flynn on this practice, equating it to "removing the needle from the addicted agency arms." Renovo may have ended this for the acquired ADT, but other unnamed forwarding companies, soon picked up on the practice. Flynn's seeming ambivalence to the survival of the industry as whole is one that was and is still shared by many, if not most of the repossession forwarding industry to this day.

The Writing on the Wall

In 2005, almost thirty years to the day that A.M. "Bud" Krohn bought National Auto Recovery Bureau of Oakland, California, both he and his son, Ken called it quits. Bud, then eighty years old, had spent over fifty years in the business and Ken was raised in it having swept floors and learning his skills until old enough to join his Dad in the field at the age of sixteen. NARB was still a staple repossession company in the industry, but lender demands for free storage and no closing fees showed them the writing on the wall. NARB was sold to a man inexperienced in the repossession industry who promptly ran it into the ground and fled the country with hundreds of thousands of dollars in unpaid payroll taxes and over $200,000 still owed to Ken.

I left my prior agency in 93' to work at NARB for "Bud" and Ken Krohn at their San Jose, California office. Comfy and warm in a daytime office job, my adrenaline addiction gnawed at me daily for months. Impatient, I had a hard time staying in the office and found myself frequently in the field checking my own skip relocates. It helped ween me off of my addiction.

Bud Krohn was the greatest boss I ever had and one of the nicest men you would ever meet. His wife, Janice, known industry wide as "Repo Rita", would drop by once or twice a year with a cake or cookies. By 97', I was done with the repo industry. My new wife was pregnant, and a shave, a haircut, my wedding suit and a lot of BS'ing with a VP and I was hired as a Regional Collections Manager at a subprime lender. I swore I would never go back to the repo business, but some things just die hard.

I learned a lot there under Bud and Ken and made long-time friends of my coworkers Jimmy Hunt out of the Oakland Office and Werner Silber in Salinas. Warner eventually bought Bud's daughter's company "Golden State Recovery" in Santa Maria and Jimmy and his sister Mary later founded "New Era Recovery" in Martinez.

The Definition of Insanity

In 2000, after three years in the army, Corey Cox had tired of his MOS in artillery and wanted something new, 00B, Army Diver. The wait list was two years long for the rigorous eighteen-month course with a high washout rate. That would mean reenlisting just to wait, so instead, he switched to the infantry, just before 9/11. Two and a half tours of Iraq later, he was back on the block.

Tribal police were strict in their voluntary repossession only laws. Cold faced receptions to Corey's visits warmed after a couple of beers and with a belly full of burgers, "no" often turned into a "yes" when it came to surrendering their vehicles. Laid back with a gift of gab, this variation of the face-to-face old school Oklahoma repo tactics he'd learned from his uncle came in handy. By 2006, Corey had partnered with a friend and opened his own repossession agency. But as partnerships often go, it was not going well.

Ink sleeved with a fire red hair to match her brash and opinionated personality; Corey's new girlfriend, a veterinarian technician named Bryanna, was tiring of his complaints. Corey was sick of the repo industry and his partner alike. Coaxing him to quit, she asked "What's on your bucket list?" And just like that, it began.

So, in 2008, with a career in commercial diving in mind, they quit. Packing up the old Mustang and a U-Haul trailer with all they owned, they headed to Houston. With only Corey's GI Bill for the school and $6,000 to their names, they landed in an apartment in a crime-ridden neighborhood littered with tire and rim shops serenaded by the wailing of police sirens. While Corey's arduous diver training was going well, they were struggling financially, so Corey sprang into action.

Using their apartment kitchen table as an office, he opened Asset Resolutions, Inc. Having left her job and following him a thousand miles to get away from the repo business and start over, Bryanna was not happy, and that's putting it kindly. She refused to talk to him for months.

Graduating at the top of his class, Corey was one of only four to land job offers. Employing his less fortunate classmates in his newly founded business, it grew, as did the length of his overseas assignments. A Nigerian oil rig is an odd place to take client calls for a repo company from, but that's what he often did. Knowing he couldn't keep it up, he did it again, and again. It took two more failed business partners for him to realize the solution was right in front of him, but she still wasn't talking to him.

Dragged kicking and screaming from the calm comforts of her art gallery job, Bryanna entered the repossession world, but not without shedding some blood. By 2015 she'd already fired the entire original staff and started things over, her own way. Soon, business was booming, and they moved from the land of tires, rims, and sirens into their dream home in Kingwood, but that's another story.

The Great Recession

The year 2008 kicked off with "The Great Recession" as it would later be coined. It wasn't all that great but it was a recession like none before it. Traditional auto loan underwriting philosophy had always maintained that homeowners presented a lesser risk than renters, but this recession threw that out on its ear. The prior hierarchy of payment importance beginning with the home loan, then auto, then credit card was reversed.

Emboldened by press driven hysteria, people walked away from their home loans in record numbers and real estate values took massive hits. Encouraged by the Federal Reserve, FDIC, FFIEC and NCUA, lenders became liberal with loan modifications hoping to stave off further losses. Caught in this melee were auto loans, which managed to fare better, but were still robust. Rod Bowser, then President of the Rocky Mountain Repossession Association was quoted in a newspaper article as stating that he was seeing double the assignment level from a year earlier and "*We're seeing people who have $400,000 homes and higher units like Lexus or Mercedes,*"

James Chessen, chief economist for the Washington, D.C.-based bankers association reported that the auto loan delinquency rate in 2007 was 2.86 percent and that this represented the highest level since 1991. Expert industry analyst, Tom Kontos of Adesa Analytical Services estimated that auto repossessions went up 10 percent from 2006 to 2007. Kontos, using auction sales data, was quoted as saying that "the industry sells about 9.5 million cars at auction each year and that of those, 1 million to 1.5 million are repossessed vehicles." - The Cincinnati Enquirer (Cincinnati, OH) - January 11, 2009, and the Denver Post - February 6, 2008

LPR

On a rainy Fort Worth, Texas night in 2008, attorney Cort DeHart flew in several repossession agency owners and picked them up in a limousine from the airport. Bringing them back to his office, he commenced to discuss with them a new invention, license plate recognition cameras (LPR). Piling them into trucks, they were then taken into the field and shown how these cameras could recognize, capture, and process license plate numbers fed into a database for possible matches

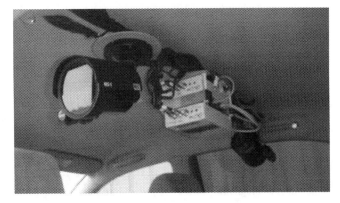

2008 Palantir Associates Group LPR
Camera – (photo by Dick Frame)

to target vehicles. This early model could process 1,100 plates an hour and accounted for 13 hits in its first 13 hours.

This successful demonstration launched a company known as the "Palantir Associates Group." Seven pioneering agencies took part in this revolutionary new concept. Mounting cameras in the backs of vehicles, they applied and improved upon the English technology that began in the 70's. Jim Hall, of Texas based Hall Recovery, was the first to purchase these cameras and leased six sets on the spot.

The cameras and laptops were leased to the agencies for $6,400 to $8,000 depending upon the configuration. By this time, Cort DeHart's camera system was already on its way to its two-hundredth repossession.

These cameras were created by Vigilant of Livermore, California. Todd Hodnett of Recovery Database Network (RDN) was first to market these to the industry. This later grew into the national leader in LPR, Digital Recognition Network (DRN.) With association discounts offered to members of the ARA, DRN quickly to become the cornerstone of the license plate recognition world and changed the repossession industry forever, for better and worse.

Over the next ten years, LPR cameras had flooded the repossession industry with newer and smaller versions equipped to tow trucks and scanner vehicles, usually hybrids or electrics. Millions of plates are scanned a day and "hot lists" of open assignments are in the hundreds of thousands. Hot listed accounts that can also be on active and open assignment with other agencies. This has caused issues.

Double assignments, like the one Tommy Deen Morris died on in 94' have become a rarity, but over the years, LPR equipped tow trucks and camera cars have found themselves in confrontations with agents already assigned the same vehicle for recovery. This has resulted in fist fights, guns drawn and on at least one occasion in Texas in 2020, the vehicle in contention became the center of a tow truck tug of war with the car lifted completely in the air by wheel lifts on both ends. While this technology is remarkable, many in the industry do not feel that the relationship between the LPR providers and the agents is equitable.

Enter the Forwarders

The repossession industry was, and still is so fractured, that an attitude persists that "*If I don't do it someone else will.*" This defeatist attitude coupled with associations, that dare not out of fear of the FTC and DOJ, utter a word of "proper fees", allowed the forwarders to exploit their weaknesses.

Over the next decade, the direct relationship between the lender and the agency owner faded as the forwarders took control over near 80 percent of the assignment market.

For executives in the nation's largest banks and lenders, repossession forwarding companies replaced their need for large repossession management departments which equated to large reductions in staff expense. Despite paying more per repossession, about $400-$475 and lower recovery rates of about 35 percent vs 75 percent, the net savings were still considerable. The days of direct agency and lender relations were eroding and with it, any level of price control beyond the power to say "No".

Agents no longer received closing fees and were forced to work contingent for $250-$325. Note the comparative price to earlier eras where recoveries were closer to $370 plus other fees. As of the writing of this book in 2021, this erosion of fees has hit rock bottom and other fees are rarely paid, even in the event of the use of dollies or a flatbed. In the meanwhile, consumers are charged $450-$475 for a repossession that only costs the forwarding company $325-$350.

In all fairness to the forwarding companies, they are in competition with one another. It is the nation's largest lenders, Santander, Chase, Wells Fargo, Bank of America, etc., who hold control over fees. The forwarders are along for the ride, just like everyone else. No one in their right mind would expect the lenders to wake up one morning and say "Hey, I want to spend more company money and I think we should pay more in repo fees."

If any fault lies in the relationship or the state of fees, it lies with the agency owners who over the years have given in to one exception after another. Now, there are little fees left to waive.

Jimmy Tanks Meets Renovo

It was about 2:30 a.m. in Halsell, Alabama on June 26, 2008, when Jimmy Tanks, a retired railroad worker, heard a commotion outside his bedroom window. Believing there might be a thief in his driveway, Tanks grabbed his gun and went outside. But outside, Tanks didn't find a thief, he encountered a repossessor and two helpers. Shots were fired and Tanks was hit in the chest and died. - The Montgomery Advertiser (Montgomery, AL) – February 28, 2009

The shooter, Kenneth Alvin Smith, was an employee of Kevin Flynn's Renaissance Recovery. Smith and witnesses claim that Tanks fired a shot at them. Smith claimed to have shot back in self-defense. Smith was charged with murder. The trial ended in a hung jury.

Jimmy Tanks died over a Chrysler Sebring. It only took a couple of years for one of Flynn's repossession agents to be involved in a fatal shooting. While the charges in this death were dismissed, it made national news and brought unwanted attention to Renovo's operations. This attention only worsened less than a year later.

Clowns Worthy No Mention

No legislation or litigation has done more damage to the repossession industry image than the plethora of "Reality TV" shows that flourished between 2006 and 2014. These programs set a tone for public expectation of what occurs during repossessions that has endangered repossession agents nationwide ever since. These were actors and not repossession professionals and have no place in the history of the industry.

The Debt Collector Threat

Historically, lenders and debt collectors prefer non-judicial foreclosure proceedings. It accelerates the timeframe of the process on defaults where in most cases judgement enforcement is unavailable. By requiring the application of the FDCPA to non-judicial foreclosures, lenders and their entities performing these actions would be bound by the FDCPA on all future and past non-judicial actions.

This would create a bank crushing avalanche of FDCPA lawsuits and stifle the entire foreclosure and their supporting industries. The glaring similarity between a non-judicial foreclosure and a self-help repossession are obvious. Disruption to this process would have brought the American credit machine to a screeching halt.

In about 2009, Political activist and homeowner, Dennis Obduskey went into default on his Colorado home. Wells Fargo Bank hired the law firm of McCarthy & Holthus after they attempting to enforce a nonjudicial foreclosure on his Obduskey's home. Attorney, McCarthy sent pre-foreclosure letters to Obduskey regarding the impending foreclosure, to which Obduskey responded by accusing the law firm was in violation of the FDCPA,15 USC §1692g(b) in regard to its mandated disputed debt verification procedure requirements.

Lower courts disagreed as to whether the FDCPA applied to non-judicial foreclosure proceedings, and this case climbed its way to the nation's highest court, the Supreme Court.

On March 20, 2019, the US Supreme Court came to a unanimous decision. *"A business conducting nothing more than a security interest enforcement action, is not a "debtor collector" under the Fair Debt Collection Practices Act (FDCPA), except in enforcing security interest under actions covered under 15 USC §1692f(6)."* While the repossession industry dodged a huge bullet, future conditions and political climates would make other attempts to place the shock collar of the FDCPA around its neck.

A Fatal Honeymoon

Sixty-four-year-old Lidie "Joe" Clements was an underemployed painting contractor who had fallen behind on his payments. Clements had made arrangements with Nuvell Auto Finance, a GMAC subsidiary, to voluntarily surrender his vehicle. Renovo received the assignment and assigned it to a Renaissance Recovery employee, newlywed twenty-seven-year-old Michael Faron Brown. Brown, accompanied by his pregnant wife, arrived at Clements' Martinez, Georgia home on April 9, 2009, a day earlier than scheduled.

The situation became heated when Clements refused to surrender the vehicle until the next day, as was previously agreed. Now that Clements had refused to surrender the vehicle, the assignment status changed to being involuntary, which increased Brown's commission from $30 for the voluntary to $70. Under the repossession dispatcher's instructions, Brown refused to leave despite the truck he was attempting to repossess being blocked in by a neighbor's van owned by Bill Jacobs. Undaunted, Brown attempted to maneuver the truck past the van, clipping it in the process.

Brown and his wife were confronted by Jacobs and as things heated up, Jacobs was knocked to the ground. Brown ran over Jacobs, crushing his ribs and internal organs and killing him on the spot. Whether Brown knew he had killed Jacobs was in dispute, but Brown and his wife went on the run. Posting their side of the story and regrets on social media, they surrendered five days later.

Brown was sentenced to twenty years in prison while his wife Victoria received two years. Mr. Jacobs' widow received $2.5 million in a wrongful death lawsuit in 2011. As of the time of this writing, Brown is still in custody of the Georgia DOC with a scheduled release date of April 13, 2029.

This, and other deaths, taught two different lessons to two different parties. To lenders, this illustrated the importance of training and compliance, and to the larger repossession industry, this also demonstrated the dangers of contingency assignments. With no pay when there was no recovery, the additional pressure to recover, was partly to blame for Brown's actions. Unfortunately, this practice endures to this day, maintained by the forwarding industry and driven by the nation's largest lenders and their relentless demand for lower expenses.

A Solemn Tradition

At around 1:00 a.m. on November 13, 2009, in Fulton County, Georgia, Willie Thackston, thirty-six and Brandon Thomas, twenty-seven, still on his first week on the job, went to the home of a Justin Moore to repossess a Mustang. Thomas knocked on Moore's door and spoke with him briefly before Moore slammed the door in his face. Thackston then secured the Mustang to the back of his tow truck and Moore emerged from his house with a sawed-off shotgun and fired a shot in the air before aiming at the tow truck. Safe inside the tow truck, Thackston and Thomas began to leave with the Mustang in tow as Moore ran behind them and fired at them twice.

Moore then ran to the front of the tow truck and shot out the front passenger side tire. Afraid for his life, Thackston sped away from Moore's house with the Mustang still in tow. Stopping his truck, a short distance down the street, he assessed the damage to the truck and called 911. Moore, now driving a van, arrived pointing his shotgun out of the window while speeding directly towards the men. Thackston and Thomas ran back into the truck and fled with Thackston weaving the truck across the road to prevent Moore from pulling alongside and shooting them inside.

Moore then crashed his van into the tow truck, and the two vehicles came to a stop, window-to-window. Moore then fired his shotgun directly into the cab of the tow truck, hitting Thackston in the leg and Thomas in the arm and chest, killing him on the spot. *"The guts of [Thomas'] arm blew on me,"* Thackston later testified in the trial. After Moore drove off, Thackston checked on his associate, still in his first week on the job. *"Brandon's eyes had rolled back in his head,"* he said. *"I knew he was gone."*

The Repossessors Funeral Procession for murdered Repossession Agent Brandon Thomas in Georgia, November 15, 2009

Moore, still armed, returned, and ordered him to *"put the car down,"* Thackston testified. *"I thought he had every intention … to finish what he started,".* Because of that, Thackston said he told Moore to get into the Mustang as he lowered it. As soon as the wheels hit the pavement, Thackston ran. He said he watched from a distance as Moore got out of the car and approached the tow truck, gun cocked.

"If I hadn't run, he would've killed me," said Thackston. Moore went on the run and was eventually captured, convicted of felony murder, and sentenced to life in prison.

Thomas left behind a wife and two small children. On November 15th, in a show of unity, repossession agents and tow drivers from all over Georgia and beyond, escorted Brandon's body to his final resting place. These tow truck processions, where trucks have their wheel lifts raised in the sign of a cross, have become a solemn repo industry tradition through the years. One repeated many times a year over the next decade.

In 2011, the AFA Celebrated Their 75th Anniversary

CHAPTER 11 – THE 2010'S – THE FORWARDER ERA

Barack Obama was in his second year as 44th President of the United States of America this year. The nation of 309 million was still reeling from the effects of the housing meltdown that caused "The Great Recession." The unemployment rate stood at a staggering 9.6 percent and the national average annual income was $44,495 a year. The average car cost $29,217, of which 12.6 million were produced domestically, an improvement over 2009 by almost 4 million units.

These should have been profitable times for the repossession industry. But ever rising operating expenses and stagnant fees sucked the wind out of this opportunity. The Forwarding industry, at the mercy of the nation's largest lenders, kept fee income flat and had begun to erode at other incomes such as storage, delivery, keys, and personal property. On the horizon sat the consequences of a new liberal political agenda that appeared to threaten all, the Consumer Financial Protection Bureau (CFPB).

NARS

In 2009, Art Christiansen and Les McCook of the ARA looked across the industry landscape and saw division. Drawn across four different association lines, the opportunities for the sharing of ideas and collaboration were limited. Desiring to bridge that gap, they decided to  develop an association neutral event where professionals in the recovery and remarketing industry from across the country could come together to discuss the many key issues impacting the industry and their businesses. Receiving approval from the ARA Board of Directors, in 2010, they launched the North American Repossessors Summit (NARS.)

Held annually at the Omni Hotel in Las Colinas, TX, this two-day event has been running strong since year one. Its attendees range from agency owners to lenders and features representatives from every major repossession vendor company in the nation. Its speakers include former astronauts, athletes as well as many industry experts. In the years to come, this event could very well be attributed to some of the industries major changes that were to come.

Repo Madness and the CFPB

In March of 2010, the nation was still recovering from the "Great Recession" when the National Consumer Law Center (NCLC) issued a publication entitled "Repo Madness: How Automobile Repossessions Endanger Owners, Agents and the Public." In this publication they touted their proposals for massive legal changes to the self-help repossession process that seemed far-fetched. In July of the same year the "Dodd-Frank Wall Street Reform and Consumer Protection Act" was signed into law. This bill was created with Then Harvard Professor Elizabeth Warren's idea of a Consumer Financial Protection Bureau (CFPB) and the threat of these proposals no longer seemed so wild.

Amongst the NCLC's proposal were:

· Federal mandates of "Right to Cure" letters.

· A provision to require a repossession that is opposed "in any way" by the consumer, to immediately cease.

· Requirements that repossessions only be allowed with a court order and include specific dates and times for it to occur.

· Repossessions could only be performed by law enforcement personnel.

To dramatize their "Agenda for Reform", they published a map titled "Locations of Violent or Traumatic Repossession Incidents Since 2007 That Resulted in Deaths, Injuries or The Taking of Small Children." This overly descriptive titled map was littered with tombstones, guns, knives, fists, and red crosses to pinpoint the location of incidents. However, if you read the details of these incidents, repossessors were the victims in the vast majority.

George's Ten-Year War – Opie vs. Godzilla

George Badeen is anything but Opie Taylor, but in comparative scale to the monster sized corporations he chose battle with, the analogy is fairly accurate. Two years into his role as President of the AFA and only four since acquiring Midwest Recovery and Adjustment Service, George had watched the repossession forwarding industry overwhelm and dominate the repossession industry with an equal amount of frustration as his industry peers. While others sat back and did nothing or just griped about it while at the same time accepting the low wage work conditions for the sake of volume, George picked a fight.

George Badeen

In April of 2010, George, filed a proposed class action lawsuit against PAR, Inc. ("PAR"), Remarketing Solutions, LLC, and Renovo Services, LLC. In his lawsuit, he alleged that the named defendants had been actively soliciting accounts that the Plaintiffs (Badeen and class) historically managed. This competition itself was not the issue, the lawsuit was based upon the Forwarder Defendants not being licensed to collect debt in the state of Michigan.

The class represented, "*every automobile repossession agency or owner who held a license as a debt collector in the State of Michigan during the last 6 years [– i.e., April 2004 to April 2010].*" This is estimated to represent approximately 150 agencies. At risk was treble damages of $175 for every vehicle repossessed under their direction. The number of vehicles repossessed at this time was 1.8 million and it is still growing!

In the amended complaint it was stated; *Considering Plaintiffs' allegation of 1.8 million repossessions together with their request for treble damages under Mich. Comp. Laws § 339.916, it is unambiguously ascertainable that the amount in controversy exceeds $5,000,000. In fact, multiplying the trebled damages available under § 339.916 by the alleged 1.8 million repossessions/violations, the amount in controversy is at least $270,000,000 (i.e., 1.8 million * $150). See Mich. Comp. Laws § 339.916(2) (if it is a willful violation, the Court "may award a civil penalty of not less than 3 times the actual damages, or $150.00, whichever is greater . . ." (emphasis added)).*

The first line of defense for the Defendants was to assert that they were not "Debt Collectors" and not subject to Michigan's collection agency licensing laws. On Friday the 13th, 2014, the Michigan Supreme Court ruled that the action of forwarding is a collection activity and as such is required to be licensed and regulated by the state.

The court ruled that forwarding companies acted as collection agencies under Michigan law and had been doing so without a license, in violation of MCL 339.904(1), and that defendant lenders, who hired the forwarding companies, violated Michigan law by hiring unlicensed collection agencies, in violation of MCL 445.252(s). Round 1, Badeen.

On November 18, 2015, Circuit Judge, Clinton Canady III, listened to arguments by PARS Attorney, Larry Saylor, on the case of PAR North America vs. Michigan Department of Licensing and Regulatory Affairs which revolved around PAR'S contention that they are not a collection agency and as such not required licensing in order to conduct repossession forwarding activity in the state of Michigan.

Saylor argued that they were not a collection agency at the time of the class action ruling against them, but they were not required to be licensed as a collection agency but regardless, applied for licensing after the ruling but should have the previous ruling against them dismissed since they did not consider that they should be defined as a collection agency.

Judge Canady shot down PAR's arguments.

"They contract with the lender. They hire the independent contractor to get the car. The car goes to the place they contracted for the auction house. The auction house sells the car. They give the money back to PAR. So, under that scenario it would seem to me that they are acting in the capacity as a collection agent."

In closing, the Judge stated.

"The court concludes that's inconsistent with the fact situation that the Court's has been presented with, which shows that the Lenders are working directly with PAR who in turn is the collection agency."

Round 2, Badeen, and he wasn't even in this fight.

PAR continued their appeals on every conceivable legal ground they could, venue, procedures, etc. but failed to have their judgement reversed. This legal tennis match has been going on ever since, and to the date of this writing, PAR continues to fight back. George has spent countless hours, days, and dollars in this war, largely forgotten by most. Regardless, George has vowed to fight this to the end, a testament to his conviction, resolve and love for the future of the mostly family owned and operated repossession industry.

Rise of the Eagles

In a hotel room on a balmy Daytona Beach summer night in 2010, Ron Brown, Rusty Ansell, and Millard Land met to discuss the failures of the Time Finance Adjuster's (TFA) "20 Groups". These group concepts go all the way back to Benjamin Franklin who established the Junto Society in 1727 with the goal of assembling twenty close friends to meet weekly to discuss topics of the day, politics, business ideas and ideas for mutual improvement. This concept was already used successfully in the auto industry but had failed to garner the desired enthusiasm and understanding desired in the TFA. Brown had been a regular speaker at many of these auto industry "20 Groups" over the previous year and had gathered a lot of information regarding the formation and internal workings that made this type of group function and remain successful.

Ron L. Brown

Eagles - L-R - Ron Brown, Millard Land, Jerry Farese

Brown explained that there were three things which seemed to be constant in the successful groups, a 12-month commitment, a monetary commitment in form of pre-paid twelve-month dues, and an extremely strong commitment to assist each other in any and every way possible to ensure each members success.

Ron suggested Rusty should start a true "20 Group", to which, Rusty complained that he just did not have the time to devote to such a project. Ron then suggested Millard start one, to which Millard replied that he just was so disappointed in the first attempt he did not have the enthusiasm needed to make such an endeavor successful. Turning the finger back at Ron, Rusty and Millard said in unison, "You need to start a 20 Group". And with that comment, Ron launched the first 20 Group in the Asset Recovery Industry.

The goals set for the group were discussed and Rusty mentioned that they were *"very lofty"*. *"Very lofty"* struck a chord and to get *"very lofty"* one must fly high and the one creature that flew higher than anything else was the Eagle. That was it, a group of twenty Eagles, and that was the birth of "Eagle Group XX".

Invitations went out to the entire TFA membership with the caveat that only the first twenty applicants would be accepted. Millard Land wrote his check on the spot and became EGXX01, Chad Latvaaho was next and became EGXX02, then Curtis Nelson joined and became EGXX03. With three of the industries recognized now on board, three more forward thinking TFA members followed suit. Walter Justice, Tim Koskovics and Sam Corolla.

Some of the Founding Eagle XX Members - L-R - Ron Brown, Kelly McGivern, Millard Land, Kenny Barnes, Tim Koskovics, Peggy Chapman, Chris Campbell

The first woman to join the group was Kelly McGivern. She was followed by, Rich Whittaker, Steve Dove, Peggy Chapman, Robert Hoel, Patrick Dunleavy, Charles Wilson, Patrick Altes, Jason Kummerfeldt, Jerry Farese and his partner Bob Stankovitch. Billy Whittenton, Walter Gauntt, Leslie Scharlin, Kenny Barnes, Andy Cowan, and Evan Wise.

In their first meeting, it was agreed that the primary goal of Eagle Group XX would be to advance their professionalism far beyond that of any other organization in the recovery industry and become recognized as innovative leaders, building on knowledge and full statutory compliance. Also agreed upon was the group selfless dedication to the success of the other members within the group. The members vowed to share information as well as life experiences based on the Latin motto, *"Dia Matheseos Dynamis"*, translated as, *"Through Knowledge Power"*. As of this writing, there are 78 members of this "20 Group."

Today, Eagle Group XX exhibits at major credit union and automobile finance conferences seeking out clients who understood the value of using a professional and were willing to pay a fair wage for their service. Through a proprietary 800 phone number they offered these clients a national "NO

CHARGE" referral service. The reputation of Eagle Group XX has since grown and developed a strong and loyal following of clients.

The Industry Fights Back

Fighting back against the rising tide of forwarding companies gobbling up and controlling huge swaths of the national repossession volume, the ARA fought back. Spearheading this project was Mike Plue, Dick Frame, Joe McOwen, Kevin Camping and Chris Dunleavy. Understanding that the forwarding model wasn't the problem as much as a third party managing it, they stole a page from Harvey Altes' late 1990's "Transnet" TFA based cooperative and established their own forwarding company. So, in 2011, the ARA founded "Relliance, Inc."

In their first six months, Relliance contracted several regional and nationally known large lenders including captive automobile finance companies, national credit unions, large regional and national banking entities, and finance companies. Early on, they found the clients major concern was in compliance; Equal Employment Policies, Privacy Policies, Compliance Tracking, Standardized Selection Processes, Audit Procedures, etc. As a consequence, Relliance became quite proficient in these fields. By 2012, Relliance had developed their first repossession assignment, which was successfully recovered as well as remarketed.

Slowly, but perhaps too slowly, assignment volume grew, and while the client reviews were favorable, the program was not catching on with the potential of the association agency network. Behind the scenes, in order to attempt to deepen the agency relationships, Relliance began to develop the securing of contracts for the discounted purchase of fuel, insurance, tires, and other services for the group. To add to their toolbox of lender services, they eventually partnered with a large national skip tracing firm as well. Unfortunately, client adoption was still sluggish and agency participation stagnant. All while they were working on this, something bigger was brewing at the association level.

The Wolves of Palm Beach

The champagne was flowing on a warm Boca Raton evening in the summer of 2010 as over a dozen agency owners and family attended a ritzy shareholder meeting for Florida based National Asset Recovery Corp. (NARC). NARC, founded in 2009, was a unique and new "roll-up" strategized repossession forwarding company that promised stock riches through an impending IPO. At its head as CEO, sat William G. Forhan, Chief Executive and Financial Officer and Bill Shrader as Chief Operations Officer. In the background was Jeffrey Sanger, a man with a prior arrest during two-year undercover penny stock sting operation named "Operation Bermuda Short."

Almost half-a-dozen reputable and respected persons in the repossession industry signed on as staff with at least one owner traded his company for over 600k shares, while others received undisclosed shares. These "employees" added credibility to a company with practically no experience in the repossession industry. COO, Bill Shrader was the one exception, while CEO Forhan's background came from a Ballroom Dance Fitness Company and a Casino Player club (shell companies). Senger was prohibited from involvement with the company or even being present in its operations, but that didn't keep him from having an office in the back of NARC's Palm Beach Gardens headquarters according to former employees.

According to NARC's SEC filings for the year 2010; "*On September 1, 2010, we purchased 400,000 common shares at a cost of $100,000 from Casino Players, Inc. ("CPI"), a publicly traded company that William G. Forhan, our former Chief Executive and Financial Officer, was and continues to be affiliated with. The common shares currently have no value, and we cannot predict whether the common shares will ever have any value. As a result, we have elected to fully impair the value of the CPI shares. We had no cash flows from investing activities for year ended December 31, 2010, or 2009. For the year ended December 31, 2010, net cash provided by financing activities was $732,145 and was comprised of net cash proceeds received from the sale of 3,020,360 shares on August 27, 2010, to fifteen (15) shareholders.*"

On December 6, 2010, NARC launched their Initial Public Offering (IPO) under the title "REPO" on the "pink sheets" (penny stocks.) In just over two weeks, Bill Shrader was fired allegedly due to disagreements with the board, and William Forhan was voted out from the CEO chair by the board of directors. In the meanwhile, Jeffrey Sanger was wheeling and dealing these worthless stocks out of the back office in secret.

On the morning of December 22, 2010, it all came crashing down. When NARC's employees arrived at their Burma Road, Palm Beach Gardens, Florida office to find the doors closed and locks changed. NARC's SEC filings indicate that it had never produced any income and that all its income was derived from Senger's sales. Senger would eventually be charged by the SEC and served several years in Federal custody before his release in November 2014.

From within and without, roll-up strategies were attempted with varying results. Unlike the others, whose intentions were legitimate, this was a clear attempt to garner public stock interest in an industry profiting on the Great Recession. This failed "pump and dump" scheme cost at least one agency owner their company and left many others holding thousands of shares of worthless penny stocks. Like a zombie, NARC's previously worthless stock (REPO in the pink sheets) showed signs of life with trading at $0.24 a share during June of 2021 only to again plummet to $0.05 a share in August.

The $400 Murder

At about 6 p.m. on March 2, 2011, a murder occurred that shook even the most seasoned of industry veterans. Twenty-five-year repossession industry veteran Wilfred Rivera, forty-eight, and his best friend and partner, Delbert Charles Power Jr., thirty-one of ATCO/Bennett Recoveries arrived at a

Saint Augustine, Florida residence to repossess a Ford Ranger. When they arrived, the borrower, fifty-one-year-old Jesse Ramirez was on the phone with a collector from the lending company. Coming out to meet them, Ramirez talked and joked with Rivera and Power, before returning inside to talk to the lender.

After about twenty minutes on the phone with the lending company collector, Ramirez was advised that to stop the repossession he had to come up with $400. Ramirez became angry and the collector did nothing to warn Rivera or Power of the danger at hand. The entire conversation was recorded.

Ramirez then emerged from his home with a gun and fired upon the men as they were preparing to leave. Rivera was killed on the spot and Power survived after being shot numerous times.

Rivera's death was taken hard by all that knew him but no one took it harder than his widow, Illena Rivera, whose written letter was read at Ramirez's trial.

"You took it upon yourself to murder an innocent man, cold-blooded. An excellent husband, father, grandfather, brother, family man, hard worker, and dear friend to many. God gives the life, and only he is the one who has authority to take it. But, instead, your coward non-manly actions decided to murder my husband, Mr. Rivera, an innocent, humble, dear man who was only doing a job, and also attempted to murder his partner. Your actions have caused much pain to many, and today — today is a 'great day.' For crimes deserve justice here on Earth. And, today, justice is being served to you."

Ramirez confessed and was sentenced to life in prison in exchange for the District Attorney waving the death penalty.

A Pillar Falls – Jack Barnes

On Sunday January 15, 2012, NFA leader and industry legend Jack Spencer Barnes died at the age of seventy-three in an ATV accident near his home in Wagoner County, Oklahoma. Jack was a self-dubbed "Jack of All Trades." A wrestler, political candidate, flight instructor, outdoorsman, marksman, diver, and photographer. Every Friday night at the Broken Arrow Elks Club, Jack sang karaoke, one of his favorite activities. During his repossession career, Jack served as President, Past-President and Executive Director of the NFA.

Jack Barnes, Bear Wrestler, Politician, Diver, Marksman, Writer and Past-President of the NFA

Despite his passing, Jack goes on to share his wisdom and experience through his three books, one of which, "The Repossession Process" is in its 11th print. The former wrestler, Jack, actually preferred hugs to headlocks, according to family members. "*He believed everyone needs at least 12 hugs a day to be healthy,*" his daughter Shelli Bates stated at the time of his death. "*He was known as a great hugger.*"

Barnes' was survived by his wife, Brenda Barnes, daughters, Shelli Bates, and Leslie Barnes, two sons, Robert Mynheir and Jeff Hilliard and nine grandchildren and two great-grandchildren. Jack left humungous shoes to fill in the NFA. Perhaps too big as time would prove.

Edward F. "Eddie" Dunleavy, Founder of TCAR and the Dunleavy Repossession Family – (photo courtesy of Chris Dunleavy)

A Vacancy in New York

On March 3, 2012, TCAR founder and World War II veteran, Edward "Eddie" Francis Dunleavy passed away peacefully in the presence of the people he loved most, his large Irish family. Aside from his decades in the repossession industry, Edward served as a past president of the Schenectady Lions Club, Retail Credit Association and The Oil Dealers Associations. Ed was well known for his social personality and enjoyed entertaining. He had a special place in his heart for Lake George and enjoyed summers at his camp on Cotton Point and cocktail cruises on his boat "Easy Rider."

Chris had already been running TCAR and working with his father since 1975. His nephew, Patrick joined TCAR in 2005. Like his father and grandfather before him, Patrick worked his way up the ladder the old-fashioned way by sweeping, doing admin work, and repossessing cars before rising to the company role of VP of Recovery operations in 2017. The Dunleavy family are one of the archetype multigenerational repossession agency owners that have been cornerstones of the industry.

Dirty Laundry – The Huffington Post Article

The repossession industry had been railing against the dangers of contingent assignments, forwarders and low repossession fees for years before it caught the attention of the mainstream press. On March 22, 2012, the Huffington Post published an article written by Dave Jamieson titled "Repos Gone Bad: Are Big lenders to Blame for Driveway Violence?" In his lengthy article, he spelled out a great number of the grievances of the time, grievances that, for the most, remain unchanged. Sharing the tales of Jimmy Tanks death in 2008 and of course the Michael Faron Brown killing of Bill Jacobs in 2009, he set the stage for the industry to share its dirty laundry.

Dave Jamieson did his homework. He worked briefly for a repossession company, read my articles in CUCollector.com and reached out to some of the industries vocal opponents of contingent repossession assignments. Quoted in the article was Mary Jane Hogan, President of the American Recovery Association, Joe Taylor, founder of the CARS compliance program for RISC, Debra Durham, owner of Midwest Adjusters, Ed Marcum of RSIG, Patrick Altes of the Time Finance Adjusters and myself. By then, I had already been very vocal on my concerns of the state of the industry and had ruffled a lot of feathers in the forwarding world.

Representing the forwarding industry side of the conversation was Renovo CEO and founder, Kevin Flynn. With Jamieson highlighting the Clements and Tanks deaths, in hindsight, I kind of feel now that Kevin Flynn was set up. Regardless, he really didn't help himself in the quotes that he made. Whether or not these were all in context with the questions actually asked is unknown.

When the reporter inquired about the Jacobs killing, Kevin Flynn stated that there was nothing that Renovo could have done to prevent the tragedy. He added that all of Renovo's agents were trained professionals, and that contingency payment systems had nothing to do with Jacob's death. Kevin also stated that it was a one in a million incident and when you do two million, you're bound to get two deaths and that if it were the pizza delivery business the danger would be greater still.

As a leading insurance carrier in the repossession industry, Ed Marcum stated that he had seen the numbers of violent incidents rise from 2 or 3 a month, ten years earlier up to 5 or 6 at that time. Ed directly attributed the injuries to the additional risks' agents were taking to get the cars adding that when there are agents in the field getting paid nothing if they don't pick up a car, they're going to take more risks. With the larger lenders all adopting the forwarding contingent model, Ed stated that the agency owners hate working for the forwarders and the low contingent fees but do so anyhow because they have to have some form of income and it was almost the only game in town.

Patrick Altes stated that the business model endangered consumers adding that when agents don't get paid when they don't pick up a car, it alleviates the lenders from providing accurate location information. Being all free for their failure to provide good information, he accused lenders and forwarders of simply pulling up credit reports and assigning accounts to half a dozen different agents.

Mary Jane Hogan of the ARA had stated that the lender's cost cutting push to the contingent forwarding model was lowering industry standards. She lamented on the change in how lenders were now treating agencies and that all they seemed to care about anymore was getting the lowest flat rate they could.

Reiterating, to some degree, Ed Marcum's statement, Joe Taylor of RISC summed the situation up pretty good in stating that the activity of repossessing is dangerous enough, but with the field agent knowing that if they don't pick up the car, they don't feed their family. As such, contingent assignments make repossession agents take greater risks than an intelligent person would otherwise take. Debra Durham of Midwest Adjusters simply stated that contingent repossession assignments make good people do bad things.

Me? I didn't get quoted much but stated that a repossession is when a recession and the finance world come into the front yard. My website, CUCollector.com was quoted and linked to a page I used to maintain of all the known repossession deaths. I soon after deleted the list after complaints that it was morose and that I was an "ambulance chaser." A complaint that I am likely to hear again after publishing this book.

Kevin Flynn further deflected allegations that Renovo was at fault for driving down repossession fees and abetting the spread of contingency. Flynn claimed that Renovo had simply created a standardized and professionalized national brand that lenders were looking for. He also said that Renovo itself was struggling with lenders who had come to expect more for less. Kevin claimed that eight of his ten biggest clients (lenders) had reduced the fees they would pay over the past two years and that it was the lenders who were at fault.

Kevin further added that the other new forwarding companies were adding to this problem in creating additional competition in the market space. Looking back, I have come to agree with Kevin on at least his last points. Kevin may have pioneered the roll-up agency and forwarding model, but the forwarding market was getting thick with KAR Global's PAR in the market as well as many others. While forwarding had been around since the dawn of the industry, the industry failed to capitalize on it and had come to pay the price, and the price was now contingent and paid with thin profit margins and many lost lives.

Frosty Passes

On Oct. 10, 2012, Forrest D. Frosty Thomas passed away at the ripe age of eighty-nine in his Cedar Hill, Texas home. Frosty was a proud World War II Army veteran and celebrated his forty-year membership in the ARA a year earlier. Frosty founded his first company, Frosty Thomas Adjusters in Lubbock, Texas which eventually became Interstate Adjusters. Without Frosty, there probably wouldn't hve been Jim Golden and ALSCO or the Time Finance Adjusters (TFA) which has been attributed to having been his idea.

Frosty Thomas

Renovo Changes Hands

Perhaps tired of fighting the repossession industry and all the calamity that had fallen on his company, on October 17, 2012, Renovo Services, LLC was purchased by Primeritus Financial Services of Nashville, TN. In concluding the sale to Primeritus, Kevin Flynn, former Chairman and CEO of Renovo Services stated, "*I'd like to thank the whole team of employees for all they have done to make Renovo Services an industry leader. I would also like to thank the Renovo Services customers for their business and their trust. I believe the combination with the team at Primeritus is a true win for Renovo employees and its customers.*"

Less than a year later, on August 16, 2013, at about 5 p.m., Flynn went for a recreational bike ride near his vacation home in Chikaming Township, Michigan, when he was struck and killed by a car. He was not well liked by many in the industry, and his funeral is not known to have attracted much respect from the repossession industry. Regardless, he and Renovo had made an impact on the repossession industry that lingers to this day. Looking back on Flynn, he was an outsider that interrupted an industry that does not like outsiders, regardless, he was an industry pioneer.

Last I Saw Lee

I first met Lee McDaniel of Eagle Adjusters in late 2010, shortly after I launched CUCollector.com. We hit it off right away and talked frequently until meeting face to face at the North American Repossessors Summit (NARS) in Dallas where I was scheduled to speak the following Spring. Together with one of his best friends and local competitor, Scott Patterson of Dedicated Recovery, they sat front and center and gave me a standing ovation before I even began my self-righteous and tiresome anti-forwarding industry rant. It was embarrassing, but affirmring and I will never forget it.

Lee McDaniel

Fast forward to late 2013 and Lee called me to ask if I was going to NARS the following spring. I'd skipped the last year and hadn't planned to go, but Lee really wanted me to join him. After he told me why, there was no way that I wasn't. Lee had been diagnosed with terminal cancer and had about a year left to live.

Lee was always a big ball of energy. He was still working in the field the day before his first chemotherapy appointment in February of 2013, when he was credited for spotting and reporting mass murderer Christopher Dorner. A feat that weighed heavy on his mind after Dorner went on to kill another. Even facing his own death, Lee was still thinking of others.

Thinner and bald from the chemotherapy, had I never met him before, I probably wouldn't have known just how sick he was. With his son Robert, Scott Patterson, Rocky Allen and others, we spent hours of that week chatting like there was nothing wrong. Something about Lee's high energy personality almost seemed strong enough to defy the doctor's diagnosis. I was wrong, and that was the last I saw him.

Lee didn't make it a year and passed away at the age of fifty, just a few months later on June 17, 2014. Lee left behind his four sons, four grandchildren and his wife Cindy. Cindy closed the office for four days and picked up the torch. Behind her, Lee's sons, Robert, Danny, and Cody all became adjusters.

The Atlanta 8

As soon as the original NAAFA split in the late 40's, many agencies had been members of two or more repossession associations at the same time. Leveraging these memberships for secured territories and marketing exposure made a lot of sense. That was until the internet and the flood of forwarding companies came in and relegated association directory books to the role of office shelf ornaments. Tired of the division of the industry and seeking the benefits of unity, Bob Stankovitch, Jerry Farese and Chris Dunleavy devised a plan titled "One Recovery Industry."

The Atlanta 8 – (photo by Chris Dunleavy)

Armed with their twenty-two-page PowerPoint presentation, they proposed a meeting of the heads of the ARA and NFA in Atlanta, Georgia in late January of 2013. Invited were, ARA President Mary Jane Hogan, Executive Director Les McCook, their NFA counterparts, Jerry Wilson and Harry Forrest and Chad Latvaaho. According to Bob and Chris, all but Harry and Chad knew exactly why they were meeting but sensing the urgency, they flew in anyhow. What followed was a nearly twelve-hour meeting with working meal breaks as they went over the detailed merger plan.

With the three men being members and executive board members at one time or another of both associations, they knew and experienced firsthand the redundancy created by this division. Having seen other merger efforts fizzle after being taken off table for legal analysis and paralysis by over-analysis, they played tag team and kept the attendees glued to their chairs as they pitched the benefits of uniting. At the forefront of the benefits of association unity, they highlighted the obvious cost reduction benefits gained through having only one directory to print and send, home office expenses, insurance, marketing and other expenses. In addition, both associations had co-op's, Relliance, the ARA's forwarding company and ARMS, the NFA's member provided centralized billing co-op and both had their own duplicative operating expenses.

It was suggested that in addition to the financial benefit of merging the co-ops, the member benefit could foster membership acceptance of these co-ops and help to better build the size and enthusiasm to these networks. Proposed was the opportunity that all members, of both associations, could join Relliance for $2,500 during the first ninety days. The merged co-op would be led by a board comprised of two members of each association to maintain association balance. These aspects of the proposition weren't difficult to achieve since only thirty-seven of the ARA's members weren't also members of the NFA.

The meeting concluded late in the evening with Bob, Chris and Jerry all having done their best. Member enthusiasm in the NFA could be best defined by the attendance of a mere twenty or so members at their 2012 conference in California. While financially sound under the financial management of Buzz Greenwood, membership numbers in the nation's second oldest repossession association were on the decline. While the ARA's member numbers were holding and conference attendance was still strong, they weren't growing and their finances were not adequate to support the industries needs for the future. This proposal would be brought up to the member base and board of directors in March.

And Then There Were Three

After both associations voted and approved the "Atlanta 8" merger proposal, on March 7, 2013, the American Recovery Association (ARA) and the elder National Finance Adjusters (NFA) merged. Their merger closed out the NFA's long history but enhanced the ARA's membership numbers and drove the industry one step closer to association unity. This merger occurred during a period in which the repossession industry had been in and out of numerous discussions of merger between themselves with

Jerry Wilson of the NFA and Mary Jane Hogan of the NFA – (photo by Chris Dunleavy)

numerous variations of mergers discussed between the TFA, AFA and ARA.

Jerry, Chris and Bob and the rest of the "Atlanta 8" had succeeded in what had been tried many times before and brought the fractured industry one step closer to unity.

A New NFA

Following the merger of the ARA and the NFA, Relliance repurposed and adopted the long-known name of "National Finance Adjusters" as their name and as planned merged the NFA's centralized billing program, ARMS into it. *"The name change has been designed to embrace the history of the former trade association and pave the way for a new more substantial recovery cooperative. Just as before, the goal of the cooperative is to secure business from national lenders and compete in the existing forwarding company space"*, said Darren Frame, Executive Director of the new NFA cooperative.

"The cooperative model calls for a central corporate presence to do the marketing and administrative functions required in the forwarding model, but with the ownership and profits flowing through to the member companies and contracting agents," said Frame.

The rebranded NFA

"The newest goal of the cooperative is to dramatically increase the number of member companies which will allow us to demonstrate a more significant national coverage, while still maintaining very high standards of performance and compliance of those agents involved.", said Chris Dunleavy of TCAR Recovery and Chairman of the new NFA Board of Directors.

The existing cooperative had thirty-five member-owner recovery companies, all ARA members. With the merger, the ARA had grown to 268 members and the need to grow the new branded NFA was urgent. So, in order to attract more of both the new and old ARA members to join, the cooperative made some changes. New agents coming onboard received the same full ownership status as existing companies, and recovery assignments were to be divided equally among members covering any particular area at the outset, a change from the original terms that founding ARA Relliance agency owners were probably not very happy about since assignment volume had yet to grow to anything substantial.

Over this year, business development had continued the be the major imperative. So, in September of 2013, the new Director of the National Finance Adjusters (NFA), Bob Stankovitch, President of the Peak Service Corp. from New Jersey, replaced former California agency owner Mike Plue with

John Houston as their new Director of Business Development. Unfortunately, Houston had no better luck than Plue. By 2015, the NFA's capitalization issues had become so dire that Bob Stankovitch had to move the accounting functions into his offices in New Jersey and Chris took the operational functions into his New York office.

By late 2016, and by no means due to a lack of effort, the new National Finance Adjusters (NFA) repossession cooperative had closed its doors. Chris and Bob remarked that its failure could be attributed to a lack of members embracing the model and a lack of lenders showing an interest. Despite this failure, the merger accomplished the establishment of the ARA's well accepted compliance program which is still in operation to this day. Two out of three ain't bad and Chris, Bob and Jerry pulled off a truly industry shaking event.

A Founder Falls

According to Frank Mauro's son, Frank met his wife, Rita O'Connor, at a dance at the Aragon Ballroom. On their second date, he took her to the racetrack where her horse was winning, and she stood up on a chair to cheer her horse. He looked up at her and said, "*I'm going to marry you.*" They married in 1951 and were wed for sixty-three years.

In his final months, he was mostly limited to a wheelchair, but was practicing his walking to surprise his wife. According to his son, "He privately told me and the caregiver he wanted to dance with her one more time."

On April 1, 2014, Frank Mauro Gesualdo passed away at Highland Park Hospital in his beloved Chicago at the age of ninety. An alleged co-founder of the NFA and one of the three most powerful men in the long history of the repossession industry, he left shoes too big to fill, big shiny wingtip shoes. Wealthy beyond the wildest imagination of the eighteen-year-old sailor clinging for his life to a life raft in World War II, Frank was a self-made man in the truest tradition of the American dream. He'd built an automotive dealership empire, travelled the world, and stood as the backbone of his businesses, family, and his cherished repossession industry.

Despite all of his wealth and power, Frank had lost much. His daughter Roxane in 2003, whom he wore a locket with her picture around his neck every day, best friend Art Lamoureux in 2000, and his beloved NFA that had merged with the ARA just the year before. Nothing he had acquired in his life was not a consequence of his life in the repossession industry. It was in his blood until the day he died.

The Godfather Passes On

Harvey "The Godfather" Altes

On March 9, 2015, industry legend Harvey C. Altes quietly passed away in Daytona Beach, Florida. Harvey was born on March 3, 1928. Harvey served in the U.S. Army during the occupation of Japan. There are countless colorful stories about his law enforcement career in Daytona going back decades.

In the 1960's, Harvey was an amateur Jai Alai player and also owned a company that made the baskets. Daughter Nicki tells of his 1980's polygraph business in which he used polygraph for interviewing employment transgressions as well as preemployment he also founded the National Association of Fraud Investigators, as well as the International Society of Aromatherapists, and this was decades before essential oils became popular!

Altes also founded a private investigation and auto recovery agency, Falcon International, which has operated for sixty years. His investigation clients included many area attorneys, banks, and businesses, as well as CBS Television's "48 Hours". He also owned and operated the Time Finance Adjusters, co-authored the book "Manhunt", and presented a series of seminars by the same name.

In a memorial to Harvey, it was written; *"Few people have impacted the repossession industry more than Harvey Altes. He was always thinking of innovative ways to further the success he enjoyed in this industry...whether it was through co-operative efforts like Bankservice or founding an early form of "forwarding company" (one that benefitted the TFA membership), Harvey was continually coming up with ideas. Both he and his wife (my mother) Joan Altes were fully committed to their TFA "family", and their greatest friends were others in the business. Contrary to his public persona, Harvey Altes was a kind, generous, thoughtful individual, who is and will be greatly missed."*

Like Angels

You never know what's on the other side of the door. It isn't always danger, sometimes it is humanity challenging you. It was early December of 2015 when Scott, an Adjuster for Ohio based Relentless Recovery, and repo trainee Lisa Wixon were making contact to demand a Nissan at a home in Garfield Heights, when their souls got ripped out. With tear-soaked eyes they listened to the tale of Diana Parks.

"I can't do this one, Dave," Scott said to his boss and co-owner of Relentless, Dave Ziebro. *"Do what you've got to do to me."* Scott was no rookie. He'd been pulling in about 70 cars a month for years and had never let a car go. But this was too much.

Diana Parks had gone through a lot that year. A single mother of ten-year-old daughter Ania, she had just learned in May that she has a pituitary tumor. She was having seizures, difficulty walking and a myriad of problems the doctors were still trying to diagnose. Too ill to work or study, she had to drop out of pharmacy school at Cleveland State University and gave up her part-time job in the pharmacy department at a local hospital.

Out of work, she fell behind on car payments as well as rent, electricity and other bills. *"Don't apologize, you're just doing your job,"* Parks said as Scott apologized profusely. But Park's grace only cemented his emotions and resolve.

Scott's boss Dave listened and intently, struck by his genuine and deep concern. *"Repossessers are money-motivated people and you can't take too much interest in personal situations,"* Dave later said. *"We've heard it all. We hear a lot of people who try to excuse themselves from their obligations. So to see a guy walk away from a repo and to hear his concern, I was kind of compelled by that."*

In the immaculate living room, Scott emptied his pockets and insisted Parks take every penny he had. Scott told Dave that he would give up half his paycheck until Park's car payments were up to date.

Both Zeibro and co-owner, Amy Bednar, refused take his money and insisted to help pay her delinquent car payments themselves. In addition, they offered next month's payments and sought to help with the rent as well.

Bednar says they couldn't ignore her. *"If you see someone in need, just go ahead and help them. You can't take the money with you when you go. Just go ahead and keep passing it on. Pay it forward. Everything you've seen here today, take it with you. Pay it forward,"* said Bednar.

Armed with Park's daughter Ania's Christmas gift list, Scott and Lisa brought it back to the office. There, it was divided among the rest of the staff." *Trampoline, fake blood, North Face jacket, balance board for gymnastics and cheerleading, Spongebob Squarepants Christmas gumball machine, Disney Fairies Tinkerbell bubble fan, cotton candy maker, hoverboard, I really want the trampoline."*

The people at Relentless Recovery stepped up. Parks couldn't believe it.

"For him to do what he did, All I could do was say 'Thank you, Lord.' They're like angels," she later said to a reporter in the Plains Dealer. "My daughter says, "*Mom, there are nice people. I told you it would work out.*' She's just ten. And she's right."

This is just another one of the many dangers of the repossession industry. Being confronted with your own humanity. While it makes the job harder, it is reaffirming to the core conviction that what you are doing is right. Being in the right is what makes the job easier.

Relentless Recovery made the papers with this one and made the industry proud.

Personal Property Fees and the CFPB

Used Syringes and Drugs. Commonly Found items in personal Property in repossessed vehicles

On October 1, 2016, in the final throes of President Obama's second term and just over a month before the election of President Donald Trump, the Consumer Financial Protection Bureau (CFPB) released their Fall 2016 Supervisory Highlights. In section 2.2.1, titled "Repossession fees and refusal to return property", they dealt the fee stagnant repossession industry a major blow. When addressing the issue of personal property removal laws and procedures from repossessions, their seven-paragraph summary, stated; *"State law typically requires auto loan servicers and repossession companies to maintain borrowers' property so that it may be returned upon request. Some companies charge borrowers for the cost of retaining the property."*

By this statement, they acknowledged the precedence of state law in the matter but continued to state; *"In one or more recent exams, Supervision found that companies were holding borrowers' personal belongings and refusing to return the property to borrowers until after the borrower paid a fee for storing the property. If borrowers did not pay the fee before the company was no longer obligated to hold on to the property under state law (often 30-45 days), the companies would dispose of the property instead of returning it to the borrower and add the fee to the borrowers' balance."*

Keep in mind, these examinations were conducted on a selected group of the nation's largest auto lenders subject to their jurisdiction and that no repossession agencies were examined, or consideration made for the labor, danger or time consumed in performing these legally required duties. Regardless, they continued to lay their judgement.

"CFPB examiners concluded that it was an unfair practice to detain or refuse to return personal property found in a repossessed vehicle until the consumer paid a fee or where the consumer requested return

of the property, regardless of what the consumer agreed to in the contract. Even when the consumer agreements and state law may have supported the lawfulness of charging the fee, examiners concluded there were no circumstances in which it was lawful to refuse to return property until after the fee was paid, instead of simply adding the fee to the borrower's balance as companies do with other repossession fees. Examiners observed circumstances in which this tactic of leveraging personal situations for collection purposes was extreme, including retention of tools essential to the consumer's livelihood and retention of personal possessions of negligible market value but of substantial emotional attachment or practical importance for the consumer.

Examiners also found that in some instances, one or more companies were engaging in the unfair practice of charging a borrower for storing personal property found in a repossessed vehicle when the consumer agreement disclosed that the property would be stored, but not that the borrower would need to pay for the storage. In these instances, based on the consumer contracts, it was unfair to charge these undisclosed fees at all.

In response to examiners' findings, one or more companies informed Supervision that it ceased charging borrowers to store personal property found in repossessed vehicles. In Supervision's upcoming auto loan servicing exams, examiners will be looking closely at how companies engage in repossession activities, including whether property is being improperly withheld from consumers, what fees are charged, how they are charged, and the context of how consumers are being treated to determine whether the practices were lawful."

While acknowledging that a required duty was being performed, they refused to acknowledge the state laws already in place governing the process. On October 31st, they stated in a CFPB press release; "*It is an illegal and unfair practice to refuse to return a consumer's personal property until a fee is paid.*"

And just like that, this politically appointed bureau without congressional oversight created a law that the lending and forwarding community bowed down to without question for fear of stiff regulatory fines numbering in the millions. If one reads carefully, the CFPB did not say that the repossession agency was not due these fees. They merely said that these fees should not be forced upon the consumer contingent to the release of property and should be consolidated into the borrower's aggregate balance without interest as they would a repossession fee. The forwarders and lenders were quick to recognize this as an expense to them and more than eagerly accepted this as gospel refusing to pay anything at all.

A Common Volume of Personal Property That Must be Inventoried,
Removed and Stored, For NO Fees as-per the CFPB

Immediately, forwarders and the major lenders mandated to the repossession industry that they were not to charge personal property removal and storage fees, period. As alluded to earlier in this history, since the beginning, this dirty and sometimes dangerous process was always one of the worst parts of the entire repossession process. But as lenders began leveraging forwarding companies against each other for the lowest fees, repossession agencies, already suffering stagnant repossession fees, lost vehicle storage fees, transport fees and every imaginable fee under the sun. The repossession industries lack of unity or even a proper trade organization had made them helpless against one-sided contracts and unreasonable terms of business.

Thanksgiving

On a cold Illinois November morning in 2016, Bill Ford, co-owner of Illini Recovery Inc., arrived at the home of Stanford and Patty Kipping to repossess their 98' Buick. In a moment of softness, Bill went to the door to advise the retired couple in their seventies and eighties of what was happening and offered them time to remove their personal property. Struck by their humility and situation, Bill called the lender on the Kipping's behalf hoping to work out a deal with the bank. Unable to get the lender to provide any leniency, Bill carried on with his duty and repossessed the car.

This did not sit well with Ford and he set up a "GoFundMe" page soliciting others in the repossession industry to help. In one night, he raised $3,500. On Kipping's behalf, Ford paid off the lender, fixed the cars headlights, topped off the gas tank, radiator, and oil. Armed with a turkey and the remaining

$1,000, he and a friend went back to the Kipping's home in time to provide them a Thanksgiving to remember.

This incident made national news, but incidents like these are far more frequent than most could imagine. Traditionally, many, if not most interactions between recovery agents and borrowers are very polite and dealt with by the agents using the ages old "Golden Rule."

In recent years, most major lenders have prohibited recovery agents from making contact in order avoid potential litigious incidents. From a legal standpoint, this appears reasonable, but from a human standpoint, it can dehumanize the repossession experience and hinder opportunities to help people. – CURepossession.com – November 21, 2016

There are hundreds, if not thousands of untold stories like this through the years that the industry keeps to itself. This is an industry of ex-school teachers, police, little league coaches and despite the hard-boiled image, they are only human, just like the person on the other side of the door.

Hurricane Harvey

They had just moved into their Kingwood, Texas dream house in May and their last picture was hung in July of 2017. By August 25th, Hurricane Harvey had hit land and was coming right their way. All

through the night, Corey Cox kept watch on the rain swollen French drains until they'd backed up to street level. He knew it was now or never and woke Bryanna and their son Bentley to tell them the bad news, it was time to leave.

With only time to grab their pets and their most necessary items, they piled into two repo trucks and fled for safety. Fighting their way across town, Corey cleared debris and drifting cars from the flooding roadways with the truck's wheel lift until they found themselves confronted by a door handle deep swollen and surging stream. Driving his larger truck into the rushing waters, Corey created a breakwater allowing Bryanna and Bentley in the smaller truck to cross to safety. After three and a half hours, they found shelter and safety with friends

Debris scattered in front of the Cox home beneath a resilient American flag after Hurricane Harvey – (photo provided by Corey Cox)

northwest of Houston, just in time to see their own neighborhood on TV, flooded under eight feet of water.

They had lost everything they owned and worked so hard for. "What now?" they contemplated as they waited the storm out. As soon as internet and phone access were restored, they discovered "what now." The repossession industry was behind them.

Scott Patterson's donated SUV and supplies
– (photo provided by Corey Cox)

Help was on its way before the water had even receded. Scott Patterson of "Dedicated Recovery" in Ontario, California, had loaded up a truck and a donated 98' GMC SUV with several generators. Cindy McDaniel of Eagle Adjusters, and some other Southern California agencies had donated other supplies which Scott packed into the SUV and truck. Within two days, he was on the way.

Not far behind, Robert Freeman of "Vanished Repossession Agency" had left Santa Rosa, CA on August 27th. With a truck and trailer load of camping gear, tents, air mattresses, blankets, and clothes, he was soon in Houston as well. From the north came Ryan Miller of Northwest Repossession of Rolling Meadows, Illinois, Chad Hill of KC Towing from Janesville, Wisconsin. These were just a few of the dozens of other repossession company personnel that came from all over the country to help in any way that they could.

Finally allowed back into their home, Corey and Bryanna's worst fears were realized, they had indeed lost everything. But as they began to sort through and clear the sewage tainted debris, they found they were not alone. The team from Plate Locate, Bryan Russell from GM, and over sixty repossession industry people had showed up to help. From this fractured and often conflict-ridden industry they discovered a unity they had never known existed.

With donations from the AFA, RABF and gift cards for their son Bentley to replace lost toys sent by others, they had never felt more part of something bigger than themselves. Bryanna later said; "*I was blown away. I don't think we would*

Corey and Bryanna Cox –
(photo provided by Corey Cox)

have gotten through it without the love and support of the repossession industry. I knew right then that I could never leave the repossession business."

Fortunate for them, unlike several other local repossession companies, their business was spared any major damage, but their home was a total loss. Bryanna went back to the office and Corey back to field as they rebuilt. The next year, Bryanna doubled down and bought local competitor Paradigm Recovery in 2018, just before Hurricane Imelda came to town. Never forgetting all that the repossession industry had done for them, Bryanna and Corey went online and raised over $3,000 which, with their own contributions, they used to provide care packages and deliver fresh hot meals to their neighbors in the weeks that followed.

As their disaster-stricken neighbors were putting their lives back together, Corey and Bryanna Cox's home repairs were finished, and they moved back into the dream home. Corey returned to the oil fields of Nigeria where he was lucky enough to have survived a helicopter accident. That was enough drama for Bryanna and his overseas travels came to an end. Preferring to choose their own type of drama, Corey went back into the repo business, but like for all in the industry, a new kind of disaster was just around the corner.

A Golden Goodbye

Jim Golden was born on June 27, 1937, in Oklahoma, like many of the industries pioneers. He was eighty years old on December 3, 2017, when he passed away in Odessa, TX. An alleged 50's guitarist that passed on working with a young Ray Orbison, Jim left music and crossed paths with Frosty Thomas. What followed was a very long and successful career in the repossession industry.

Jim founded American Lenders Service Company and was a brilliant marketer that successful launched a franchise type operation in the industry and made a lot of waves.

Another Roll-up

Consolidation and mergers continued throughout this decade and in November of 2018, the largest combined repossession agency, forwarding skip and transport in the nation was created. At its head was former Ally Financial executives, Lee McCarty at CEO and Eric Gerdes, as President and COO. Accompanied by former PAR CEO, Jerry Kroshus in a subordinate company while his noncompetition contract was in place, and with the investment help of the Delaware Street Capital Group, Location Services was born.

Its repossession company was created through the acquisition of some of the industries most respected company owners. Chad Latvaaho's Repo Inc., covering the midwest, California's Michael

Eusubio of Digital Dog Recovery and Chuck Palazolo of CAR Recovery and Florida's Ron Keys of ARS, were some of the early acquisitions. Location Services created the largest national network of repossession companies operating under a single corporate ownership in the history of the industry. Over the next three years, Location Services grew and continued acquiring additional agencies stretching from coast to coast and border to border.

L-R - ARA President, David Kennedy with
Nicki-Merthe-Altes and Patrick Altes

For the field agents, this company offered the promise of stability, structure and something that most companies were being challenged to provide, paid time off and benefits. For some of the previous owners, this was all bitter sweet. They had all been paid handsomely for their companies and while Location Services had treated them all reasonably well, after all of their years building up their companies, losing control of their employees and companies was hard.

And Then There Were Two

The passing away of Harvey Altes paved the way for the most pivotal of association mergers in its history. Desiring to improve industry unity, his children, Patrick Altes and Nicki Merthe-Altes, released control of the TFA. On October 2, 2018, the Time Finance Adjusters (TFA) merged into The American Recovery Association (ARA). This was only the second association merger in the industries history. Now, only the youngest association, the ARA and the oldest, the AFA, were remaining.

Millard Steps Away

On December 1st, 2018, Adjusters Inc. of Houston, Texas closed its doors after seventy-two years in operation. It's owner, since 1973, the humblest of industry legends, Millard Land, chose to close his office to spend time with his lovely wife Cathey travelling and spending quality time visiting his friends. Millard was a co-author of, the industry skip-tracing bible, "Manhunt" with fellow legends and old friends Harvey Altes and Ron Brown.

A Repossession Industry
Legend and Great Friend at a
Retirement Ceremony, Millard

Millard's contributions to the industry were perhaps the most understated of all its legends. His departure from the industry left not only a huge vacancy but signaled a changing of the guard to an industry already too long on defense by this point. The very first, and most valuable, of interviews made in the creation of this book came from this man who wished his name not appear in. A wish that I obviously refused to grant.

A Family Roll-Up

It had been almost seven years since the passing of patriarch Edward Dunleavy when TCAR was acquired by Location Services in August of 2019. TCAR became a subsidiary of Location Services with Chris serving as a Regional Vice President role until his retirement in May of 2021. His nephew and Edward's grandson Patrick became a Director of Client Relations. With the roll-up acquisition of TCAR came the end of a sixty-year family business.

The Deadliest Decade

Prior to the internet and social media, Murders and injuries in the repossession industry had always been something that carried by phone or was stumbled upon in some local newspaper buried in page 7 or deeper, if covered at all. Tommy Deen Morris's murder in 94' was the first repossession murder in the industries long history that made the national news. With the internet came wider access to these tragedies and a greater understanding of their frequency.

For the families of the fallen, there is rarely insurance of any kind and the victims, usually young and married with young children, leave next to nothing behind for their loved ones. Funeral expenses continue to be a charity operation run throughout social media to alleviate the strain of these families. Beyond that, there are years of mourning as they struggle to put their shattered lives back together.

In my eleven years of reporting on the repossession industry, I can attest to the fact that at least ten repossession agents were murdered during this decade and dozens more left with long term disabilities and injuries. This is nothing new, this is a fact of the industry that gets downplayed by all and swept under the rug to keep the trucks on the road and feed the families of the living. Had they been soldiers, cops, or firemen, they'd have received parades instead of tow truck processions on their way to modest graves or post cremation ceremonies. But this is the way it is, was, and probably always will be.

I had considered writing out each of these incidents, but for the survivors, I feared these deaths were still too fresh. In honor of these men, their families, coworkers and friends, I at very least am compelled to immortalize them to the industry here. According to my reporting on this decade, below are the known names of the men who were killed on duty.

Allen Rose - February 23, 2011 - Colorado Springs, CO - J & J Towing – Murder

Todd Showell - November 20, 2012 – SC - Silverhawk Towing and Recovery - Murder

Scott Robins - August 6, 2012 - Marble Hill, MO – HJR Towing and Recovery - Murder

Shawn Brewster - January 5, 2013 - Richton Park, IL – Accident

Brendon Keith Wright - April 1, 2014 – Rice, WA – Police Killing

Junior Jordan Montero - June 6, 2014 - Marshall, VA - Murder

Steve Lawson - July 27, 2014 – Los Angeles, CA – Murder

Jeffrey David Lowe - June 11, 2015 – Columbus County, NC – Top Notch Recovery – Murder

Brandon Russell - October 1. 2015 – Odessa, TX - West Texas Auto Recovery – Murder

Johnny Lee Blanton and Charles Edward Powell Jr. - 16 May 2017 - Associates Asset Recovery – Accident

Elwood Allan Humphries - 10 January 2018 - Petersburg, VA - River City Recovery

Curtis Martin - Sugarland, TX – 6 July 2018 – Performance Collision - Murder

Zach Johnson - 3 December 2019 - Dallas, TX - Texas Auto Towing Service – Murder

The 20-teens were a dramatic decade for the repossession industry, but nothing could prepare any of them for what was to come.

Photo by Edwin Hooper on Unsplash.com

CHAPTER 12 – THE 2020'S – THE YEAR THE TRUCKS STOOD STILL

Former television reality show star and multi-millionaire Donald J. Trump had been the President of the United States for three years. America was now populated by 331 million people, almost three times the nations size in 1920. The unemployment rate was a record low 3.9 percent, the median household income was $68,700 and 17.5 million passenger cars and trucks were sold in the prior year. America was enjoying some of its most prosperous years in its history, but all of this was about to come to a screeching halt.

Wuhan

Pandemic struck after the release of a deadly virus originating from Wuhan, China first detected in early January of 2020. With the "Wuhan Flu", as it was earlier known, making its way to America, President Trump declared a public health emergency under the Public Health Services Act on January 31, 2020. This shut down travel to and

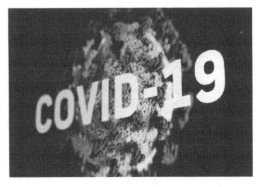

Photo by Martin Sanchez on Unsplash.com

from China but failed to contain the virus. On March 13th, he invoked two national emergency health declarations under the Stafford Act and the National Emergencies Act.

Within days, taking CDC guidance, state Governors began shutting down schools and non-essential businesses hoping to curtail the virus's growth. By then there were 2,700 cases and 5 deaths, but this was just the beginning.

The Longest Year – The Lockdowns

Lenders, sympathetic to the public wellbeing and at the urging of financial regulators, began offering multi-month loan deferments and placing repossessions on hold. Over the coming weeks, Governors were issuing moratoriums on all repossession, collections, and foreclosure activity. Repossession agencies in the affected states struggled to stay open. Only allowed to recover voluntary repossessions and impounds, many closed.

With record numbers of loans deferred and repossession assignments cut to next to nothing, even agencies in states not under moratorium suffered. Staff reductions occurred everywhere and like the public, many repossession agencies were forced to request loan deferments from their lenders. On March 27th, Congress and the White House approved the CARES Act. This provided Federal subsidies under the Paycheck Protection Program offering up to eight weeks of funds to cover payroll expenses, which was hardly enough for most.

In the weeks that followed, Federal legislation became proposed to the public even further protections. Senate Bill 3565 proposed a repossession and foreclosure moratorium for the entire length of the emergency, plus an additional 120 days. Fortunately for the repossession industry, this partisan bill, sponsored by democratic Ohio Senator Sherrod Brown, never came to vote under the Republican controlled Senate.

Another Pioneer Passes

On the 28th of April of 2020, industry legend and early AFA member, Al Michel passed away at the age of ninety-six years of age. Al was preceded in death by his wife Dorothy who passed at the age of ninety and was survived by his son John, daughter Diane Plumley and eight grandchildren.

After Al's passing, his son John posted on CURepossession.com's social media page, "*As Al's son I have been in and around the recovery industry now from my entire life. My father loved this industry. I have come to love this industry. I have served it now for over 25 years designing repo websites, hosting email accounts, and preparing marketing materials. I have found the people in this industry to be some of the most loving, generous, and caring people I have ever known.*"

"I would especially like to thank George Badeen on behalf of my family for his generous contribution to the Recovery Agents Benefit Fund. My father donated to the RABF when he was alive, following his retirement. He believed in it and wished that it would've existed during his time as he lost a couple of recovery agents. I will miss him and will continue to honor his memory."

George Badeen posted, *"Al was my mentor and my surrogate father. I learned the recovery and auction business from Al while working with him for many years. He put me on the path to take ownership when he retired. Al served as an executive member of Allied Finance Adjusters many years ago. He helped shape me into the leader I am today. Midwest Recovery is donating $1000.00 in his memory to the Recovery Agents Benefit Fund (RABF). He was a great man and will truly be missed. He will always be in my thoughts. May his memory be eternal.*

The Darkest of Days

Hundreds of thousands of Americans and millions around the world died from the COVID-19 virus, as it became more political correctly known. The repossession industry was not spared its share of cases and likewise deaths. Among the known deaths were;

Billy Ray Orr, the owner operator of Sundown Tow and Recovery from San Antonio, Texas.

Steven Scott, a twenty-year old Field Adjuster for Auto Recovery Bureau of Houston, Texas.

Jose Benjamin Lopez, a forty-two-year-old Recovery Agent for Done Right Recovery" in Lansing, Ilinois.

Gino Posinelli, a sixty-five years old and owner of G & R Recovery in Pennsylvania. Gino was a member of the Allied Finance Adjusters and, I am proud to say was a friend of mine.

Early in the pandemic, many agency owners and agents were "deniers" of the virus, believing the virus to be overhyped and not as dangerous as the hysterical media and politicians claimed. As such, when Covid did hit them, they kept news of it silent for fear of their businesses being closed by health officials and losing what little income was still available through voluntary repossessions and impounds. Cases of Covid made their way through countless agencies infecting larger numbers than will ever be admitted to or recorded.

A New Alliance

With a deluge of new proposed legislation to stop all repossession activity for the foreseeable future at the federal, state, and municipal levels, the leaders of the industry convened. The initial webinar meeting involved the heads of the ARA, AFA, RSIG as well as all the state associations. The idea of employing a lobbyist to represent the repossession industry in Washington DC became the focal point of discussion and by the end of the meeting, it was clear that there were two camps of thought. Hire a lobbyist or let the larger and better funded related industries, like the credit unions, banks and the ACA, whose lobbyists were already well entrenched, do the job.

True to form, the repossession industry remained divided on the issue. Not wasting any time, the ARA, aided by Michael Peplinski of Harding Brooks Insurance and a cast of many, launched a fundraiser. From this, "RepoAlliance" was born on May 15, 2020. This coalition was comprised of the ARA, the California Association of Licensed Repossessors (CALR), Texas Accredited Repossession Professionals (Texas ARP) and Harding Brooks Insurance. Within days they had raised $40k of a needed $120k for the full-time employment of an experienced DC lobbyist.

It is unknown just exactly how effective the results of this lobbyist were or are. What is strange to consider, is that the industry had never even seriously considered such an endeavor. Either way, the repossession industry was far from out of the woods with legal attempts to kill it. While not 100 percent united, an alliance to fight was formed and, after a hundred years of existence, the industry finally had a voice at the table in Washington.

More Bills, More Threats

Next up to kill the repossession industry was HR 7301, known as the Emergency Housing Protections and Relief Act of 2020. Introduced by California Congresswoman Maxine Waters to the Democratic controlled Congress on June 24th, it was passed on June 29th. This bill included a six-month moratorium on all repossession and foreclosure activities beyond the period of the passage of the bill. Again, the Republican controlled senate, refused to bring the bill to vote and for the time being, there was no Federal intervention to self-help repossessions.

Where the Federal government failed, some states stepped in. Many Governors, using emergency declaration powers, enacted various repossession moratoriums. These moratoriums, further exasperated by the record numbers of auto loan modifications, affected an estimated 7 percent of all auto loans. This drought of assignments crushed many already struggling repossession agencies and made many more wonder if they would make it through the summer. No actual aggregated national or state data exists to illustrate the impact of these moratoriums, but the numbers of repossession agencies closing spoke volumes.

Federal PPP loans provided short term relief to keep some companies in business. But for an industry already suffering from rising operational expenses and stagnant and reducing fees, they were "band aid on bullet-hole" solutions. While some repossession activity was beginning to emerge in the following summer, by September of this year, an estimated 10 percent of the entire repossession industry was gone. Most had had switched their operations to the more stable industry of towing or simply closed their doors.

Even larger entities, such as Location Services, LLC, which had flourished in the previous decade, now found the massive expenses of running a company of this scale unsustainable. Huge waves of layoffs came immediately as executive staff scrambled for additional capital investment to keep their skeleton crews afloat. Fleets of new tow trucks purchased before the pandemic sat idle, as well as leased office spaces, unused and vacant. The repossession forwarding industry was likewise unspared of the impact of the pandemic.

Another Kick in the Crotch

On October 13, 2020, the CFPB, relatively quiet under the Trump administration, stomped its jackboot on the throat of the repossession industries personal property arguments with a $4 million civil money penalty agreed to with Nissan Motors. In addition, Nissan agreed to a consent order stating requiring, among other remedies, that Nissan was "*to prohibit its repossession agents from charging personal property fees to consumers directly and from demanding fees as a condition of returning personal property.*"

Never in My Life

Lee McDaniel's old Norco office at Eagle Adjusters had sat vacant and untouched since his death in 2014. Like her home office, it was draped in Cleveland Indians and Browns jerseys and memorabilia. Finally having to clear it, Cindy found a bottle of Lipton Sweetened Iced Tea in one of the cabinets. Lee used to drink it so compulsively that the grocery store manager made special orders to keep Cindy and Lee from emptying the store shelves.

"*Never in my life did I think that I would end up running a repossession company.*" said Cindy as she described their lives together. It just became a part of her. Like so many before her, it got under her skin and her sons alike.

Cody was in the Marines when Lee passed away. After leaving the service, he carried on in his father's footsteps, but after some conflicts at Eagle, ended up working for Lee's best friend Scott Patterson. It was during his employment there that on August 30, 2016, he was shot in the abdomen, damaging his liver, colon, and large intestine. And with that same stubborn drive and conviction, he was back in the field a short while after being released from the hospital.

Cody eventually left the business and ended up with a successful career as, wait for it, an insurance adjuster, full circle. Robert kept up his work with Cindy at Eagle Adjusters until the pandemic struck. Low repossession volume coupled with mostly low paying client fees had already made things hard enough, but the lender-imposed repossession moratoriums, they were running on empty. Even after the moratoriums ended, the low assignment volumes coupled with low fees and rising expenses had become more than the family-owned company could endure.

Lee, Cindy and The McDaniel Clan

In January of 2021, Cindy McDaniel closed Eagle Adjusters doors. And with it, a business that Lee had hoped to pass on to his sons. Talking with Cindy about the industry and state of things, her fire was still there. She hadn't left the repossession industry, it left her.

A Long Year Comes to an End

By January of 2021, President Trump had lost the last election and the pandemic had infected 20 million Americans and killed 346 thousand. Globally, over 20 million were infected and 1.8 million killed and this was only the second peak. Fortunately, under President Trump's "Operation Warp Speed", a vaccine was developed and rolled out just before the end of this month. Unfortunately, 2021 wasn't done with the virus or the repossession industry and asked 2020 to "hold my beer."

All through the 2020 election, Democratic party candidates, pandering to fringe element socialist idealists, had turned on capitalism. Repossession moratoriums, mostly gone by 2021, were mere steppingstones to what was to come next.

A Sabotagued Roll-Up

In the midst of this disaster, a group of west coast repossession agencies banded together to create a unique company. Camping Companies, Paramount Recovery Service, Accurate Adjustments, Able Auto Adjusters, Advanced Services of Redding, California, and Tri-State Recovery of Arizona merged and consolidated into form ART Asset Adjusters as of January 1, 2021. As illustrated repeatedly in this book, unity in the repossession industry is hard to come by. By April 2nd of the same year, this company was already divided and millions in debt when they filed a state motion for receivership citing the assertion that;

"*Because of the ongoing internal strife and lack of trust among ART's owners, ART is unlikely to survive without intervention.*" The result of this receivership cost most of these agency owners their businesses and all the assets that they had spent years growing. Long before this announcement, one owner allegedly had the audacity to brag that he was planning to buy up all the assets for pennies on the dollar in the receivership. This same owner was accused of hindering and obstructing the company's executive leadership.

Between a worldwide pandemic, a floundering economy and repo shy lenders, 2020 may have been the worst year the repossession industry had ever faced. 2021 was only slightly better.

Auld Lang Syne

As if the low fee forwarder dominated repossession volumes hadn't done enough damage to the industry before the pandemic, the repossession moratoriums had them on their last legs. By the time California had lifted it's second state and county mandated lockdowns in late 2020, the repossession volume was so low that the numbers no longer added up. My old friends from NARB saw the signs and called it quits.

Marty Fisk, who we all had the pleasure of working with at NARB was still working with Jimmy Hunt at "New Era Recovery" in Martinez when he died in November of 2020 of a heart attack. Jimmy had lost his sister and co-founder Mary of cancer just a few years earlier and by the beginning of 2021 was done with the business and called it quits on "New Era Recovery", taking a job leasing cars. In January of 2021, our old friend Warner Silber sold "Golden State Recovery" in Santa Maria and retired to his mountain home in Ben Lomond, California.

As of the time of this writing, Bud Krohn is ninety-five years old and still living in Concord, California. His wife, Janice "Repo Rita" died in a car accident many years earlier. Ken Krohn is retired and enjoys weekend Harley rides with his wife. Warner, Ken and Bud still get together every month for dinner and Warner and I used to get together for football games before the pandemic.

Yet Another Debt Collector Threat

H.R. 2541, also known as "The Comprehensive Debt Collection Improvement Act", was littered with enhancements to the Fair Debt Collections Practices Act (FDCPA.) Of dire concern to the repossession industry was an attempt to impose the restrictions of the FDCPA on it. Title VIII was a two-sentence section that intended to strip away the protection of this definition, already unanimously agreed to by the Supreme Court in the 2019 case of Obduskey v. McCarthy and Holthus LLP. This bill had already passed vote successfully in the House by an almost fully partisan vote at the time of this writing.

Fortunately, for the auto and repossession industries, this bill languished in committee and went nowhere.

Not Even the Strong Can Survive

On August 30th of 2021, start-studded and massively financed rollup company, Location Services, threw in the towel on its direct assignment repossession operations. Despite massive capital injections to stay afloat, the lack of profitability at the fee level coupled with drastic reductions in repossession volume proved unsustainable. Along with its closures came hundreds of layoffs and a refocus on the more profitable elements of their business such as repossession forwarding.

On a more positive note, Brad Webb repurchased Premier Adjusters in Texas and third generation Dunleavy, Patrick saw the same opportunity and took it.

In late October of 2021, Patrick Dunleavy relaunched the family business with a new name, but the same family dedication to hard work and the core principles instilled by the Patriarch of the family, Ed Dunleavy; professionalism, ethics, and quality customer service. Fittingly named, the Dunleavy legacy carries on with Patrick's "Legacy Recovery & Remarketing Services LLC" operating out of Burnt Hills, New York.

Senseless

On June 14th, 2021, in Oakland, California, forty-three-year-old repo agent Tim Nielsen of Auburn was found dead inside his tow truck. His truck was found running and crashed into an East Oakland building at 4:13 a.m. where police discovered that he had died from a gunshot wound. Nielsen, an employee of Any Capital Recovery was pronounced dead at the scene by paramedics, but Alameda County Sheriff's Office coroner's staff who examined the man's body later discovered he had been shot.

Police said it appears that Nielsen was driving westbound along East 12th Street when something caused him to leave the roadway and crash into the building. Investigators shared few preliminary details but did say they were not sure if that was where the shooting occurred or if it happened at another location. Nielsen was not in the process of a repossession and there was no known contact with a debtor or anyone else. According to company owner Lerron Payne, records indicated that Nielsen was in the process of providing an update during the shooting.

"This is a man that I can say gave unconditional love to everyone and all he ever wanted to do was help people. That was his dream, his purpose in life," said Jennifer Huff-Wensmann, the victim's girlfriend. Nielsen and Huff-Wensmann shared four children. Arrests in Tim's murder were made in October of 2021. The suspects were both twenty-years old and their motive was believed to be robbery.

Tim's murder occurred in the middle of the city of Oakland's crime and murder surge with Tim being the fifty-seventh victim. His death is just the most recent of the countless deaths that have occurred over the long century of this industry. The vast majority of which have gone with little notice to the lending world and the general public.

Like all that have fallen before him, his name and memory will too soon be forgotten by all except those that knew and loved him. Unknown and forgotten to a thankless nation whose economy and easy access to credit is maintained through the brave labors of a maligned industry.

THE END

Epilogue - The Future Of The Repossession Industry

As bleak as the future may appear for the repossession industry, one must remember all this industry has gone through in its first hundred years. Legal action and anti-self-help repossession legislation existed almost from the very start. The fledgling repossession industry survived the Great Depression and World War II. It should also be noted that the first auto loans, that spawned the repossession industry, began at the tail end of the "Spanish Flu" pandemic in 1920 and just over a year after the end of the first World War.

Its survival in the face of adversity over the century can be attributed to the masses of unnamed men and women, who through these hundred years have spent their lives in a profession under fire, both literally and figuratively. Leaders like Harvey Altes, Frank Mauro and Ray and Lorna Lou Barnes are long gone, and while their leadership is dearly missed, new leaders have and will step up. Who can wear shoes that big? Perhaps, someone I wrote about, perhaps someone who hasn't even entered the industry, time will tell.

Over the years there have been numerous attempts to legislate away self-help repossession and fortunately, they have all failed. There is a unique symbiotic interdependency that has developed between it and the American economy. Without self-help repossession, lenders lose money and access to auto loans tightens and dries up. With tight lending, auto sales slow to a crawl and auto manufacturing withers and with that, millions of jobs and the economy suffers.

Of all these functions in the automotive industrial cycle, the repossession industry is without question the most overlooked and underappreciated. Nowhere in the world is credit as easy to acquire and that is mostly because of self-help repossession. The self-help repossession process, and the people who perform it, are uniquely American.

The repossession industry as it was, is long gone. Despite the marvels of technology and the positive evolution that has occurred that should have improved professionalism and sustainability, the industry is on the ropes. This has nothing to do with hard work or character, this is a simple matter of dollars and cents and unity. Dollars and cents squandered away in competition with one another for assignment volume and a lack of unity to stand up to unreasonable demands.

As illustrated repeatedly, a repossession in 2021 costs no more or less than it did in 1921 or at any point in between and that would be fine if the requirements of the job were the same. In 1921 all that was needed to do the job was a car, a phone, a piece of wire, a chain for towing and an attitude. Fast forward to 2021 and the requirements have changed to adapt to emerging technologies and legal compliance requirements. Wheel lift tow trucks, laptops with field access to repossession management programs, LPR cameras and of course, insurance and compliance training expenses are sucking are it dry while fees remain stagnant.

Take into consideration that repossession fees of old were only for the cost of the recovery. In addition, the agencies earned ancillary income through storage fees, locksmith fees, personal property removal and storage fees, redemption fees and closing fees when the lender decided to send it to a skip-tracer to locate the "chattel." You can easily see the earnings were actually far greater than the average $350. For agencies working for the nation's largest lenders who control up to 80 percent of all repossession assignment volume, these fees do not exist.

In the absence of realistic fee structures, the industry will die. These fee conditions are unsustainable and create dangerous work conditions. Conditions that deprive the agencies the ability to provide for most, even the most basic medical or dental insurance, let alone life insurance. Compound that with contingent, commission only conditions and with rising minimum wages, the average McDonalds worker will be making more than a field agent before long and no one will be willing to do the job.

This is not the same job it was in 1921 or at any point well into the 2000's when lenders knew their agent owners and adjusters. It has become mostly a distant relationship managed by third party forwarding companies in constant competition with other forwarding companies. Much of this competition is driven more on cost reductions than on actual results or loss reductions, which is why these same lenders now consider a 40% recovery rate good, when the direct assignment model of old was closer to 70%. It's not so much about recovering the collateral to save the bank money anymore as it is saving money to appeal to the bottom line of every lender, the budget.

In banking, the dollar drives all. When the opportunity to save money by outsourcing repossession management to the forwarding companies came along, they eagerly jumped onboard. Seeing the opportunity to save even more money, the lenders demanded the forwarding industry waive fee after fee, which they did to keep up with their forwarder competition, they had no choice. This precedence has carried on until now there is essentially nothing left to waive.

These banks and most captive auto lenders have saved tens of millions of dollars a year and have been laughing so hard they're probably wetting themselves. In the meanwhile, agency after agency have closed or are close to it. These are family businesses whose blood, sweat, tears and lives were founded on serving the banks and lending industry, the very same ones squeezing the life out of them. But in all fairness, the banks can't help themselves, it's just what they do.

There is some dialogue from chapter 5 of John Steinbeck's 1939 book "Grapes of Wrath" that sums it all up very well to me.

'We're sorry. It's not us. It's the monster. The bank isn't like a man."

"Yes, but the bank is only made of men."

"No, you're wrong there—quite wrong there. The bank is something else than men. It happens that every man in a bank hates what the bank does, and yet the bank does it. The bank is something more than men, I tell you. It's the monster. Men made it, but they can't control it."

This dialogue in the book took place between the men foreclosing on the farm and the tenants. Here we are eighty-five years later, and I find it a sad irony that Steinbeck's scene and dialogue now fits the state of the repossession industry. I suppose the unquenchable and infinite appetite of the "monster" turns on everyone eventually. And over the past decade, it's been sucking them dry.

I am sure that somehow the industry will survive, but the era of the family-owned repossession agency is struggling and on its last leg. Is that good or bad, history will judge, but the industry and America will be the lessor in their absence. It is what it is, and what happened, happened, but what happens next is entirely up to those in it now and it is up to them to write their own futures.

Afterword

It all started with a text in early April of 2020 from friends and repo agency owners Corey and Bryanna Cox of Paradigm Recovery and Asset Resolutions of Houston, Texas. The pandemic was just ramping up and here in California we were in our first extended lockdown when I received the message "*You should write a book on the history of the repo industry.*" "*Okay.*" I replied with a big thumbs up emoji and the seed was planted.

The pandemic was just ramping up and the repo industry was, for all intents and purposes, dead in the water and there was much concern about the industries survival. Lender and state level moratoriums on repossession activity were in place for most of the nation and the future of the already struggling repo industry was in doubt. I realized that if I didn't write the story then, it may never happen and a hundred years of an industries history could have been lost in time.

I thought this would be a quick project. Boy was I wrong. Cruising the internet, it was all bits and pieces with no linear connective narrative. Asking around the industry, someone suggested I speak with the one and only, Millard Land.

Taking one of my sanity walks from the shelter-in-place restrictions, Millard called me back. What transpired was an hour and a half serving of the stories of people and incidents I had never heard of which I was jotting down on a small notebook while walking. By the time I walked back inside my home, I switched to the yellow legal pad and ended up with about ten pages of chicken scratch. Managing to decipher my own illegible scribbling, I transposed them onto my PC and soon after had the backbone of the history.

I reached out to many people for help and the second to come forward was Chuck Cowherd of the Allied Finance Adjusters (AFA) and California Association of Licensed Repossessors (CALR.) Unsure of what I was looking for, Chuck sent me over a huge number of photos from the AFA Directories going back into the late 40's. It was like a treasure chest from the past that linked together the names of the people Millard had told me about with the faces and from their era.

By the summer of 2020, I had written the book's first draft, which was, as expected of all first drafts, crap. So, I put it back on the shelf and jumped into another project, which took almost a year as financial necessity had forced me into an office job slowing its completion until in May of 2021.

Jumping back into the repo history book, I reached out to Kevin McGivern, a founder of the modern ARA, another excellent source in the book and one of the nicest people you would ever meet in the industry. Huey Mayronne, Kevin's co-founder of the ARA was also a great help in the process as was Kevin's daughter, Kelly McGivern. Next up was Ron Brown, who I had been in contact with every few months anyhow, just because he's such a great guy. There was no way I was writing this book without bringing him into it.

Steven Summs and the Summs family, Chris, Patrick and the Dunleavys, Cindy McDaniel, Corey and Bryanna Cox, Mark Lacek, and I could go on and on. I honestly could have made this book four-hundred pages if I wanted to, but I thought that would be too much. There are just too many people and stories to include. So much that I'm afraid it might drag down the reading experience for anyone not in the business as well as those in it.

Of course, I have to give massive appreciation to George Badeen and the Allied Finance Adjusters for their contribution of so many of the AFA images in the book. George specifically for providing us some background on himself, which he can be somehwhat reluctant to share. Likewise, I am grateful to Les McCook and the American Recovery Association for their permission to print so many of the ARA, TFA and NFA images as well as Les's contribution of his early years in the repossession industry.

I hadn't talked to my old boss, Bud Krohn since the "Railway Rollup" went bust. My old friend Werner gave me his number for Kevin McGivern, who had told me he had a great conversation with him, so I called him. Now ninety-five-years old, Bud had just awoken from a nap and was having trouble breathing. I had hoped to speak more, but I didn't want to push him and let it go, I was just glad to hear his voice and that was enough.

While I did mention a few repossession forwarding companies, lenders and forwarders, I tried to shy away from them unless they also ran their own trucks. Many of these people and companies are old friends and supporters of me and my writing, for which I am very grateful. While they are all important parts of the industry and its development, this is a book about the repossession industry and not the lenders, forwarders, or vendors. With all due respect I offer my sincerest apologies to anyone who may feel slighted by their omission.

I made a lot of mention of fatalities and injuries and that may seem a little heavy to some, but these are part of the realities of the business. To omit them all would be an obfuscation of truth and honestly, I could have added a lot more, but many of these were still fresh and out of respect for the families and coworkers of these men, I chose not to sctach at wounds that are still struggling to heal.

So much has changed since I first climbed behind the wheel of a repo truck. The "good old days" weren't really always that great anyhow. Regardless, as frustrating, conflict-ridden and sometime dangerous as the repossession industry can be, it got into my blood and like so many others before and after me, damned if I can truly get it out.

I sometimes feel a little disingenuous writing about an industry that I'm no longer in, but like many, it's in my blood. Twenty years in lending and collections, from manager to VP, up and down the ladder, it just doesn't go away even though the adrenaline rush is nothing more than a faded memory. From $75 the hard way to now, a large part of everything I am, everything I have and everything I care about, I owe to those cold nights as an Adjuster creeping around in the dark. I was a Repo Man, and as despised, dismissed and scorned as it might be, I am still oddly proud that I was one.

Thank you all and God Bless you!

About the Author

Kevin W. Armstrong, a native of the San Francisco Bay Area in Northern California, has been writing and following the repossession industry through his websites CUCollector.com and CURepossession.com since 2010. His connection to the industry began in 1990 when he worked as a field adjuster for three years before becoming an agency office manager. He has spent twenty years in the banking and credit union sectors as a vice president of collections and director of consumer lending.

Printed in the United States
by Baker & Taylor Publisher Services